PROUST

Odilon Redon, *Silence*. **Oil on gesso on paper,** $21\frac{1}{4} \times 21\frac{1}{2}$ **in., ca. 1911.** (*Courtesy of The Museum of Modern Art, New York. Lillie P. Bliss Collection.*)

PROUST
The Creative Silence

Angelo Caranfa

Lewisburg
Bucknell University Press
London and Toronto: Associated University Presses

Associated University Presses
440 Forsgate Drive
Cranbury, NJ 08512

Associated University Presses
25 Sicilian Avenue
London WC1A 2QH, England

Associated University Presses
P.O. Box 488, Port Credit
Mississauga, Ontario
Canada L5G 4M2

The paper used in this publication meets the requirements
of the American National Standard for Permanence of Paper
for Printed Library Materials Z39.48-1984.

Library of Congress Cataloging-in-Publication Data

Caranfa, Angelo.
   Proust: the creative silence/Angelo Caranfa.
      p.   cm.
   Bibliography: p.
   Includes index.
   ISBN 0-8387-5165-2 (alk. paper)
   1. Proust, Marcel, 1871–1922.   A la recherche du temps perdu.
2. Proust, Marcel, 1871–1922—Philosophy.   3. Creation (Literary,
artistic, etc.)   4. Silence in literature.   I. Title.
PQ2631.R63A7739   1990
843'.912—dc20   88-43408
                                                                      CIP

PRINTED IN THE UNITED STATES OF AMERICA

Per i miei genitori
Pour la reine de mai et ses parents
For Erminda

"Et voyez-vous, mon enfant, il vient dans la vie une heure, dont vous êtes bien loin encore, où les yeux las ne tolèrent plus qu'une lumière, celle qu'une belle nuit comme celle-ci prépare et distille avec l'obscurité, où les oreilles ne peuvent plus écouter de musique que celle que joue le clair de lune sur la flûte du silence." (*R*, 127)

"And see you this, my boy, there comes in all our lives a time, towards which you still have far to go, when the weary eyes can endure but one kind of light, the light which a fine evening like this prepares for us in the stillroom of darkness, when the ears can listen to no more music save what the moonlight breathes through the flute of silence."

Ah, ne troublez pas le silence, et laissez-moi faire attention à ce parfum, je le sais, qui va revenir! (*CGO*, 180)

Ah, do not disturb the silence, let me wait for this perfume which, I know, will come again!

Contents

Preface

The topic of this study is the notion of silence in Marcel Proust's *A la recherche du temps perdu*. By this approach I hope to gain access to Proust's themes of the self, reality, form, speech, perception, mystery, love, beauty, and artistic expression as well as to illuminate his centrality in the overall scheme of twentieth-century French thought. As a moving example of a creative individual who expresses the philosophy of pure phenomenalism, that is, subjective idealism, Proust has created a work that offers an ideal point of departure for examining how French thought oscillates between subjective and objective realities. To accomplish this, I have chosen the works of such figures as Maurice Merleau-Ponty, Paul Claudel, Georges Braque, and Gabriel Marcel, as well as Augustine and Bonaventure. Merleau-Ponty has been selected because of his phenomenology of perception as an encounter with the world; Paul Claudel because his musical esthetics leads to an experience of delight that is at once sensual and spiritual; Georges Braque because he declares that the artist strives to express the beautiful by means of forms and colors; Gabriel Marcel because of his phenomenological ontology of the mystery of existence; Augustine because he bases the notion of time in the memory and in a transcendent Being; Bonaventure because he provides us with an esthetic measure by which Giotto's artistic intentionality can be compared against Proust's interpretation. Thus, each figure not only expresses the subjective and objective aspects of artistic creativity, but also serves as a mirror for the other and for the entire work, so that the esthetic structure of Proust's creative silence is seen within twentieth-century French thought and a larger historical context.

Because my study is suggestive rather than exhaustive in scope, it limits itself to volume 1 of *A la recherche du temps perdu*. Although this approach is not without risks, Proust himself provides some justification for it when in *Le temps retrouvé* he talks about recapturing what is primordial but forgotten in the human person. In volume 1, Proust explains human existence from the perspective of its most primordial level—dreams. From this level he is able to penetrate the meaning of existence and finally arrive at art as his means of securing love and beauty. Confronted with the love and the beauty that perish, Proust flees into silence he creates rather than discovers it outside him in the phenomenal world. Hence, by concentrating on volume 1 of *A la recherche du temps perdu* I hope to provide some insight into Proust's other two volumes, which carry the themes of volume 1 to a deeper level.

While focusing on a series of individual texts from one work may have certain limitations, such an approach is helpful in organizing my themes in a clear, logical, and simple manner. Similarly, I have limited references to supporting evidence that is to be found in selected works of each author discussed here. The use of specific texts avoids the proliferation of footnotes, making my study readable to the general audience. The use of such texts has forced me to make judicious choices from a work that is representative of the author's *opera*, with a view to rendering my overall analysis more accurate and easier to follow. I have avoided secondary sources for the same reasons and I felt that secondary material did not supplement the exposition of my argument substantially. On the contrary, I feared that the development of my argument might be rendered obscure with a plethora of citations that did not make this study more conclusive or more convincing. I have included an extended bibliography of secondary sources on the authors discussed as a help to serious scholars who desire to explore further the manifold aspects of the authors whose views I have analyzed.

This study was facilitated by the help of Gregg De Young and Constance Gosselin Schick. De Young, who for an entire year worked patiently with me in defining the problem and in editing the first draft, gave clarity and logic to the work. Schick, who also edited and refined the manuscript, gave it harmony and unity through her knowledge of French poetic, literary, and visual currents. Her many questions became a source of strength, since they made me see problems concerning literary and artistic interpretation that I had not seen before; her power of interpretation rescued me from my inadequacy at expressing the silent world of painting in Braque and Giotto. The patience, the love, and the labor of my parents and sister nurtured this work. To them, to Schick, and to De Young, I remain forever grateful.

I am equally grateful to Bucknell University Press and its readers for their many helpful suggestions, as I am to Lauren Lepow and Paula Wissing of Associated University Presses for taking my work to heart.

Note on the Translations

Throughout the text, English translations for all quotations in French have been provided in the form of endnotes. I have made use of published translations where these were available. I myself have provided translations for the following works by Paul Claudel: *Présence et prophétie*, *Cinq grandes odes*, and *Partage de midi*.

Excerpts from the following works are reprinted by permission of Editions Gallimard: *A la recherche du temps perdu*, by Marcel Proust (*Remembrance of Things Past*, trans. by C. K. Scott Moncrieff and T. Kilmartin and reprinted by permission of Random House, 1981); *Phénoménologie de la perception*, by Maurice Merleau-Ponty (*The Phenomenology of Perception*, trans. by C. Smith and reprinted by permission of Routledge and Kegan Paul and the Humanities Press International, 1962); *Présence et prophétie*, by Paul Claudel; *Cinq grandes odes*, by Paul Claudel; *Partage de midi*, by Paul Claudel. Excerpts from *Le mystère de l'être*, by Gabriel Marcel, are reprinted by permission of Editions Aubier (*The Mystery of Being*, trans. by R. Hague and reprinted by permission of Collins Publishers, 1960). Excerpts from *Illustrated Notebooks, 1917–1955*, by G. Braque, trans. by S. Appelbaum are reprinted by permission of Editions Maeght and ARS N.Y. / ADAGP, 1971. Excerpts from *The Soul's Journey into God*, by Bonaventure, trans. by E. Cousins and reprinted by permission of the Paulist Press and the Society for Promoting Christian Knowledge, 1978. Excerpts from *The Confessions*, by Augustine, trans. by R. Warner and reprinted by permission of the New American Library, 1963. Excerpts from *Cubism*, by Roger Fry, are reprinted by permission of Thames and Hudson, 1966. "Augustine and Proust on Time," by Angelo Caranfa, is reprinted by permission of Pergamon Press, 1986.

References

References to the works are placed in parentheses next to the text and are abbreviated as follows:

C   Augustine, *The Confessions*. Translated by R. Warner. New York: New American Library, 1963.

CGO   Claudel, *Cinq grandes odes*. Paris: Gallimard, 1957.

CU   Fry, *Cubism*. New York: Thames and Hudson, 1966.

IN   Braque, *Illustrated Notebooks, 1917–1955*. Translated by S. Appelbaum. New York: Dover, 1971.

M   Marcel, *Le mystère de l'être*. 2 parts. Paris: Aubier, 1951.

P   Merleau-Ponty, *Phénoménologie de la perception*. Paris: Gallimard, 1945.

PM   Claudel, first version of *Partage de midi*. In *Théâtre*, vol. 1. Paris: Gallimard, 1956.

PP   Claudel, *Présence et prophétie*. Fribourg, Switzerland: Librairie de l'Université Fribourg, 1942.

R   Proust, *A la recherche du temps perdu*. Vol. 1. Paris: Gallimard, 1954.

S   Bonaventure, *The Soul's Journey into God*. Translated by E. Cousins. New York: Paulist Press, 1978.

PROUST

Introduction

Although there is a great deal of secondary literature devoted to Marcel Proust (1871–1922), much of this writing considers him primarily from a stylistic and psychological orientation. Such an approach to Proust's monumental *A la recherche du temps perdu* carries certain inherent limitations, of which many literary critics seem unaware. These same critics are fond of talking about Proust's novel as a work of art, his religion of art, and his relationship with Dante, Plato, and other philosophers. However, they do not penetrate to the philosophical, religious, and esthetic meaning of Proust's concept of the self and the nature of the world where the self lives that is the central theme of his novel. Also, they fail to locate the problem of the self as it emerges in Proust's work within a larger historical tradition. Awareness of this issue arose during the fourteenth- and fifteenth-century Italian Renaissance, received further impetus by the philosophy of Rousseau and Voltarie, and seems to have blossomed as the dominant theme of twentieth-century French culture, particularly in its arts and letters.

I would like to suggest in this study that Proust's notion of the self is the summit of what he himself calls "l'idéalisme subjectif" or "le phénoménisme pur." What Proust reveals in his analysis of the self is his understanding of its subjective nature. This subjectivity is the central thread in twentieth-century French cultural consciousness, both literary and artistic, whose antecedents go as far back as the humanistic tradition of Boccaccio and Petrarch: the idea of an inner self that exists separate from everything outside that self. This subjective self perceives itself, thinks itself, and imagines itself as a "sol mental"—to use Proust's own word—of self-created memories for which even its own existence is meaningless and dark. This subjective self is alienated even from itself—it is a strange world that the artist creates from remembered artistic forms. Still, it is imperative that the self discover an outside realm, a stable image, a permanent source, an objective form; for without this external reality there is nothing.

My inquiry attempts to overcome the limitations of the traditional scholarship by means of a philosophical and theological study of Proust's view of the self and by a comparison of his view with those of certain thinkers. These thinkers present specific alternative approaches and theories, and

although they differ intellectually from each other and from Proust, they
can serve as foils to reveal Proust's central vision. Each of them has taken a
literary approach to philosophical and religious questions, thereby making
clear the conflict about and continuity of the meaning of the self through
the history of Western thought. It is the unity of this philosophical analysis
with a comparative approach to literature that makes this study original.
Yet, since this study is intended to be suggestive rather than exhaustive,
my discussion will be limited to books 1 to 3 of *A la recherche du temps
perdu*, which provide a representative introduction to Proust's ideas.

Proust's entire novel asks philosophical questions about literary discourse and the meaning of speech, and my first chapter discusses this theme,
laying the groundwork upon which the remainder of my study will be built.
Chapter 1 addresses the written word and its use as creative metaphor.
Proust and other literary artists use metaphors to raise questions related to
the nature of the universe, the nature of physical existence, esthetic experience, and the meaning of the self, questions a philosopher also asks.
Through speech, great writers give form and expression to thought itself;
the word is spoken to designate what Proust calls the "milieu vital," where
the word is an image, and the image speaks "comme la parole."

The creative artist's use of metaphor to perceive reality leads in chapter
2 to a discussion of Merleau-Ponty's view of perception. This perception
emphasizes the "milieu d'existence," which opens toward the invisible, the
transcendent that is neither pure thought nor pure phenomenon, but it uses
phenomena to grasp the "couche primordiale où naissent les idées comme
les choses" (*P*, 254). Proust, on the other hand, rests his notion of perception on the "zone d'évaporation" (*R*, 84) that always veils material reality,
making it impossible for the self to make contact with the "réserve" or
"grand réservoir" of things. (Throughout this book, I use the English
"reserve" as a translation of Proust's "réserve" by which he means the
essence, the form of things.) As a result, the self seeks ecstatic rapture
in "parties immatérielles" that it has created through music, art, and
metaphor and has projected onto the "zone d'évaporation." Thus, in chapter 3, I consider the role of music in the spiritualization of the self by juxta-
posing Proust with Paul Claudel. Vinteuil's little musical phrase in *A la
recherche du temps perdu* is a means for Proust to create his own reality, his
own symphony from his memory, a reality that has no connection with the
phenomenal world. This world seems more beautiful and more lovely than
any existing sonata; yet it inevitably degenerates into total silence, into the
"grande nuit impénétrée et décourageante de notre âme" (*R*, 350).
Claudel, in contrast, uses music as a ladder by which the soul can ascend to
discover perfect rapture in the song of praise to God, "dans la sonorité
divine." However, the self does this without reaching perfect identity with
the Godhead, without immersing itself totally in the absolute. In chapter 4,

I consider the visual arts as a way to grasp the unique essence, the form, the idea, that infuses reality. Proust says that Elstir's paintings reveal a total metamorphosis of phenomenal forms within the artist's creative memory, whereby Elstir empties reality of its "médiocre contenu" and replaces it with his own creative spirit; Elstir's paintings "sont avant tout des Elstir" (*R*, 851). Georges Braque, on the other hand, although he also attempts to transform reality into mere form and colors, still recognizes the intractability of the phenomenal world, since colors must always be the support of forms, so that for him artistic creation is always limited. According to Braque, "Ce n'est pas assez de faire voir ce qu'on peint. Il faut encore le faire toucher" (*IN*, 4). The logical conclusion to Proust's vision of artistic creation leads to the idea of the artist as the only one who can perceive the mystery in phenomenal forms. In order to perceive the mystery, however, artists must totally purge forms of their "médiocre contenu" and replace them with "parties immatérielles" of their own creation by which they become incarnate in their work. Through this incarnation, the artist becomes the divine artist. In contrast to this view, Gabriel Marcel, in chapter 5, explains that the mystery of Being proceeds from the "milieu intelligible" and becomes accessible through faith. For Marcel, the mystery is not created but is encountered as the human person confronts the other in the wholly Other, in the absolute Thou.

The philosophy of *A la recherche du temps perdu* reinterprets even history from the point of view of "le phénoménisme pur," "l'idéalisme subjectif." Although this philosophy tries to root human beings in time, it also removes them from their historical milieu, from their phenomenal ground, from their subjective structure. The loss of historical roots is considered in chapters 6, 7, and 8. In chapter 6, Proust considers the artistic form of the Renaissance and removes it from its historical content. Proust found Renaissance paintings appealing and referred to them often. Yet they only appealed to him in their function as symbols, not for the content that Renaissance artists had intended these symbols to convey. For Proust, Renaissance paintings are not images but are recreated as personal icons. Just as religious icons had no direct connection with phenomena, these new personal icons of Proust also have no roots in historical phenomena, since they represent only the creative rearranging of his memories. Chapter 7 treats this idea by regarding the frescoes in the Arena Chapel of Padua as a representation of Bonaventure's esthetics, a meditative poem on the mysteries of the Incarnation, Death, and Resurrection of Christ, in comparison with Proust's reinterpretation of these frescoes in the light of his "phénoménisme pur." For Proust there is nothing but pure memory, "le profond sommeil," within which artistic forms develop and come to fruition. This development is what Proust sees as the true meaning of time. In chapter 8 we see that he agrees with Augustine, who also saw time as something that

exists within the memories of human beings, not as some mechanical progression measured by the motions of a clock. However, unlike Augustine,
who roots time in the eternity of God, Proust is left with only his mind and
its inability to externalize its temporal perception.

I have addressed these themes because Proust himself does so: in a way,
he is the eye that oversees this work. To contrast with Proust, I have
selected French creative figures of the twentieth-century in order to
emphasize the French cultural phenomenon of subjectivity. I have included both Bonaventure and Augustine because they show how Proust
empties history of its content and because Proust himself uses the same
themes and images to create a different angle of vision from the "milieu
vital" within his memory.

Because the vision conveyed in *A la recherche du temps perdu* has no
ground outside the self and its memories, the self seeks temporary pleasure
or bliss in the privileged moments wherein it separates itself completely
from the phenomenal world. The fleeting nature of this redemption inevitably reduces the self to tears and despair, for it sees itself as a mere shadow. Then the human self will hear the silence. But it is a silence that
speaks of darkness and of creative subjectivity rather than the beauty of
creation and its source. In this silence, the creative act itself is as beautiful
and meaningless as external fleeting beauties.

1
A la recherche du temps perdu as Creative Word

Dans une langue que nous savons, nous avons substitué à l'opa-
cité des sons la transparence des idées. (*R*, 583)[1]

A central question regarding the artistic symbolization in Marcel Proust's
A la recherche du temps perdu is the relationship between its metaphoric
expressions and the phenomenal world to which these metaphors refer.
Stated differently, the question becomes: what is the relationship between
artistic creation and philosophic discourse? Artistic forms derive their power and significance from multiple levels of meaning and layers of symbols
within which artists embed their vision of reality. Philosophic discourse, on
the other hand, derives its power from the philosopher's ability to isolate
ideas and to express them clearly through language. As a metaphoric expression of Proust's vision of reality, the novel is indeed a work of art. At
the same time, it embodies a philosophic inquiry into the nature of language. Whether philosophical or metaphorical, therefore, language is the
expression of thought. Proust says:

Il en est ainsi pour tous les grands écrivains, la beauté de leurs phrases
est imprévisible, comme est celle d'une femme qu'on ne connaît pas encore; elle est création puisqu'elle s'applique à un objet extérieur auquel
ils pensent . . . et qu'ils n'ont pas encore exprimé. (*R*, 551)[2]

The beauty of the written word is "imprévisible" because for every given
thought there is no formulable essence, no permanent speech, no objective
idea for expressing reality; speech must be creative because it must be
changeable and flexible, always defining and redefining external objects.
According to Proust, literary discourse is related to the phenomenal world
as beauty is to an object that has never been seen and, ultimately, to an
imaginary reality. Here, the *being* of the "phrases imprévisibles" of great
writers is invoked in the creative aspect of thought in order to give expression to that which cannot be perceived, that of which thought is the ideal

norm, the form, the truth of what constitutes speech. Great writers, then, must make speech "imprévisible" so that truth itself or the beautiful becomes an expression of thought, a creation of the writer's own imagination. Hence, when reality is reduced to thought and literary discourse reduced to "phrases imprévisibles," speech becomes a work of art, a created form, a complex of images.

> Au fond, les anciennes formes de langage avaient été autrefois. . . des images difficiles à suivre, quand l'auditeur ne connaissait pas encore l'univers qu'elles peignaient. Mais depuis longtemps on se figure que c'était l'univers réel, on se repose sur lui. (R, 552)[3]

In speech, therefore, the human person as speaker and listener confronts the real universe, and great writers express the universe through images. Speech, then, is related to images, and it is justified by a universe that exists. Thus what great writers articulate through their speech is the beauty of the "milieu vital" that they themselves have thought (imagined) and wish to translate into words in order to reveal it to those who have not yet become cognizant of its rational meaning. Great writers, according to Proust, are "des dieux régnant chacun dans un royaume qui n'est qu'à lui" (R, 549), and as gods they give form, through speech, to the universe. Words are spoken in order to externalize images, to give expression to thought itself; words are spoken to designate a world beyond discourse where words are images, and images speak as words. Speaking of the writer Bergotte, Proust's narrator insists:

> Dans certains passages de la conversation. . . j'ai été long à découvrir une exacte correspondance avec les parties de ses livres où sa forme devenait si poétique et musicale. Alors il voyait dans ce qu'il disait une beauté plastique indépendante de la signification des phrases et, comme la parole humaine est en rapport avec l'âme, mais sans l'exprimer comme fait le style, Bergotte avait l'air de parler presque à contresens, psalmodiant certains mots et, s'il poursuivait au-dessous d'eux une seule image, les filant sans intervalle comme un même son, avec une fatigante monotonie. (R, 550)[4]

The specifically artistic dimension of literary discourse is, therefore, to take possession of that vital image which thought itself has created and verbalize it by means of speech forms that show "la suite des images et l'harmonie," communicating reality in its "milieu vital," in its plastic beauty, independent of what words may actually mean. Yet beyond the plastic beauty of words, beyond speech forms as poetical and musical discourse, it is "quelque élément précieux et vrai" (R, 550) that great writers express, thereby enlarging their kingdom, thought itself, even if it appears that they speak nonsense. Even in their apparent nonsense, great writers still establish images to express the universe, and within these images listeners can move from an instinctively accepted reality to a conceptually understood world in which they ultimately grasp the relationship between words and the ideas they express.

> Aussi. . . c'était parce que Bergotte appliquait cette pensée avec préci-sion à la réalité qui lui plaisait que son langage avait quelque chose de positif, de trop nourissant. . . . Enfin la qualité toujours rare et neuve de ce qu'il écrivait se traduisait dans sa conversation par une façon si subtile d'aborder une question, en négligeant tous ses aspects déjà connus, qu'il avait l'air de la prendre par un petit côté, d'être dans le faux, de faire du paradoxe, et qu'ainsi ses idées semblaient le plus souvent confuses, cha-cun appelant idées claires celles qui sont au même degré de confusion que les siennes propres. (*R*, 551–52)[5]

Metaphoric and Habitual Discourse

Bergotte's precise use of thought to express reality through the clear use of language is of great philosophical importance. Insofar as literary dis-course is philosophical, it must explicitly consider the question of truth (precision) or falsity about the meaning of words in their intelligible form. In fact, in order for Bergotte to apply thought with precision, his ideas must be verifiable in the actual world of the here and now, in the world of phenomena, and not in the fictitious world of literary discourse. Whereas on the one hand literary discourse imagines a universe—object, historical event, or person—on the other hand philosophical discourse begins with the world—with events and human beings in their concrete existence. Whereas literary discourse is an imaginative construct of reality, philo-sophical discourse assigns itself the task of uncovering, penetrating, and determining the truth and the falsity of images so that everyone may en-gage in a clear dialogue. And great writers concern themselves with giving voice to the visible reality of images—ideas, or thought itself.

> D'ailleurs toute nouveauté ayant pour condition l'élimination préalable du poncif auquel nous étions habitués et qui nous semblait la réalité même, toute conversation neuve. . . paraîtra toujours alambiquée et fatigante. Elle repose sur des figures auxquelles nous ne sommes pas accoutumés, le causeur nous paraît ne parler que par métaphores, ce qui lasse et donne l'impression d'un manque de vérité. (*R*, 552)[6]

This "conversation neuve," which employs figures of speech, cannot be separated from the ideas, the images of things. Bergotte, the great writer, can only use reality, or phenomena, to expose the images, and he expresses them with metaphors because they give that unforeseeable quality, that plastic element to his words, which thereby allows him to preserve images in their "milieu vital" and at the same time create new forms of discourse by which he soars above the stereotyped ideas of reality in which habitual or ordinary language is confined. Therefore, the word emerging from the thought of the great writer is at first confusing and exhausting to listeners because the latter are closed off to themselves in the familiar usage of words; they fail to see the image behind the words, the same images that constitute the writer's self-awareness and this "conversation neuve" of literary discourse verbalizes. Thus, to the extent that reality itself cannot be expressed except in metaphors (which are themselves real), even philosophic language must assume the same speech forms as literary discourse.

> Et il est vrai qu'il y avait dans le style de Bergotte une sorte d'harmonie pareille à celle pour laquelle les anciens donnaient à certains de leurs orateurs des louanges dont nous concevons difficilement la nature, habitués que nous sommes à nos langues modernes où on ne cherche pas ce genre d'effets. (R, 556)[7]

In Bergotte's style, as in the language of the ancients, each word of the sentence is precise and clear in its meaning, poetical in its form and musical in its sounds, rich in its depth of imagery, and original in thought. All of the artist's words in the sentence form a rhythm, a continuous note, a lingering tone, "une sorte d'harmonie" of something divine not "séparable de sa personnalité la plus intime," creative of new speech forms delightful and plastic in their beauty, truthful in their reality, sonorous in their expression, yet simple in style. Bergotte weaves his intimate self into a tapestry of words using images of his own perception; thought gives unity to his speech forms: "C'est cela qui portera témoignage sur sa nature" (R, 553). Thus he is related to images in a most intimate way through his creating of new speech forms, so that he achieves a poetic understanding of things that is portrayed as a divine illumination of reality. It is because of this intimate contact with images that his words do not become devoid of meaning; rather, they become defined and clarified within their function in discourse.

> C'était surtout un homme [Bergotte] qui au fond n'aimait vraiment que certaines images et . . . que les composer et les peindre sous les mots. . . . Et s'il avait eu à se défendre devant un tribunal, malgré lui il aurait choisi ses paroles, non selon l'effet qu'elles pouvaient produire sur le juge, mais en vue d'images que le juge n'aurait certainement pas aperçues. (R, 559–60)[8]

The images, which the ordinary eye does not see and ordinary discourse does not express (but with which Bergotte wants us to converse), would remain imperceptible and unspoken if they could not be seen in terms of the objective manifestation of thought that conditions them. Unlike the judge, the great writer Bergotte is in communion with images, for he is one with the image, word, idea or thought, which both hides and reveals reality. His words are like mirrors where the phenomenal and the imaginary worlds intersect, and yet the words that reflect and reveal the imaginary world are still part of the phenomenal world. However, these poetic words are more intelligible, more precise, clearer than the words that reveal the phenomenal world, since the former are the very expression of the "milieu vital" from which words emerge.

> . . . les paroles qu'il [Bergotte] prononçait en ce moment étaient fort claires pour moi et me donnaient une nouvelle raison de m'intéresser au jeu de la Berma. Je tâchais de la revoir dans mon souvenir. . . . Mais pour que ces pensées pussent m'embellir le geste de la Berma, il aurait fallu que Bergotte me les eût fournies avant la représentation. Alors pendant que cette attitude de l'actrice existait effectivement devant moi, à ce moment où la chose qui a lieu a encore la plénitude de la réalité, j'aurais pu essayer d'en extraire l'idée de sculpture archaïque. Mais de la Berma dans cette scène, ce que je gardais c'était un souvenir qui n'était plus modifiable, mince comme une image dépourvue de ces dessous profonds du présent qui se laissent creuser et d'où l'on peut tirer véridiquement quelque chose de nouveau, une image à laquelle on ne peut imposer rétroactivement une interprétation qui ne serait plus susceptible de vérification, de sanction objective. (*R*, 560–61)[9]

For Proust, thus, whether habitually or figuratively spoken, words are ultimately thoughts the mind has either inherited ("il aurait fallu que Bergotte me les eût fournies avant la représentation") or created as images. This means that through spoken words one comes to understand one's own thoughts in the speech forms of others, which exist "effectivement devant moi [nous]." But that which exists concretely before us, that which we understand, is embedded in a context of archaic images that constitute the content of words and we try to extract as ideas. In this way, a great writer's words, which we have inherited, are on an equal footing with our own thoughts and partly condition our new image: "Quelque chose de nouveau" impressed on our mind and at the same time verified by a "sanction objective." In other words, here Bergotte's idea reveals itself in a language that Proust himself knows and that is inseparable from his intimate personality, since the idea stands in a most intimate union with the new image that he himself beholds. This new image, however, is inseparable from the memory and so transcends the time and space in which it exists. In the memory, words either point to thought itself (inherited images) and find conceptual meaning in the self alone or extract from the present (as in the discovery of something new) new images that depend on the knower for their expression and verification. The words that point to thought are clearly understood by the self alone and do not need verification, since they find an objective measure in the archaic images inseparable from the self's intimate personality. Those words that derive from memory, on the other hand, are the images that express the self's creative power and artistic genius—provided that they are perceived as having a standard of truth, a verifiable point of reference in the idea of things. And the words that make visible "une image à laquelle on ne peut imposer rétroactivement une interprétation" are not susceptible to modification and therefore are verifiable only by the self's own memory, thoughts, and speech forms. Conceived this way, a word is a remembrance of things past on which a stream of images flows from the self's own thoughts, articulating the idea, the form of things. Through words, then, ideas come stream back, one image after another, unfolding reality, which is infinitely more rich and more profound yet narrower than thought itself or the mind. Words transform the external world into images in memory, and memory creates words that involve no "régression du dehors vers le dedans" (R, 579), since the self converses with itself and not the phenomenal world.

> Seul, je continuais à fabriquer les propos qui eussent été capables de plaire aux Swann et . . . je me posais à moi-même des questions fictives choisies de telle façon que mes traits brillants ne leur servissent que d'heureuse repartie. Silencieux, cet exercice était pourtant une conversation et non une méditation, ma solitude, une vie de salon mentale où c'était non ma propre personne, mais des interlocuteurs imaginaires qui gouvernaient mes paroles. . . . (R, 579)[10]

This brings us to the heart of the question: exactly what is the relationship between A la recherche du temps perdu as work of art, as speech form, and reality? An adequate response requires considering the novel as philosophical discourse. One must examine whether fictitious questions, imaginary characters, and words may be said to refer explicitly to objects, events, places, ideas, and persons outside the mental exercise—the imagination and memory—of the writer. Proust's answer is yes, at least prephilosophically speaking, that is, in terms predating the rational language of philosophical discourse when "interlocuteurs imaginaires" did indeed exist in mythical traditions, in the archaic images of ancient epics, plays, and art. At that time, one could not verify the truth or falsity of one's questions unless one appealed to the past, unless one acquired the language of "ce vieillard infiniment sage [Bergotte] et presque divin" (R,

410), the words of "cet homme de génie, ce sage [Elstir], ce solitaire, ce philosophe à la conversation magnifique" (*R*, 863), or the speech forms of "ce frère [Vinteuil] inconnu et sublime" (*R*, 348). In short, in order to participate in this prerational discourse, one's language would have to become as creative, flexible, clear, and precise as the world's "premiers physiciens" (*R*, 586) who were at a loss face to face with the phenomena of nature because their speech forms had not yet developed into a science establishing a connection between one phenomenon and another and to whose minds the world simply existed as an image, a memory, a thought, a word, an idea in the mind's eye or inner self, "le moi intérieur."

La philosophie parle souvent d'actes libres et d'actes nécessaires. Peut-être n'en est-il pas de plus complètement subi par nous que celui qui. . .une fois notre pensée au repos, remonter ainsi un souvenir jusque-là nivelé avec les autres par la force oppressive de la distraction, et le fait s'élancer parce qu'à notre insu il contenait plus que les autres un charme dont nous ne nous apercevons que vingt-quatre heures après. Et peut-être n'y a-t-il pas non plus d'acte aussi libre, car il est encore dépourvu de l'habitude, de cette sorte de manie mentale qui. . .favorise la renaissance exclusive de l'image d'une certaine personne. (*R*, 822–23)[11]

From Proust's "interlocuteurs imaginaires," the notion that the phenomena of nature fade away when we begin to speak "d'actes libres et d'actes nécessaires," is intelligible because for these interlocutors reality is communicable through conversation conducted in silence, through memory that links the world of habit and the world of archaic images and cannot be embodied in a conceptual language of metaphysical discourse; for memory is the outward projection of the past (archaic images) and the means by which the hidden and the impenetrable reserve (essence, form) is made visible and transparent. It is the tool by which lost images of places, objects, and people we have known are recaptured. The universal human memory of course contains more charm and is more vast than that of the great writer, whose memory, in turn, is more general than that of the ordinary person; but there is a common illumination in all memories.

Nous nous imaginons toujours, quand nous parlons, que ce sont nos oreilles, notre esprit qui écoutent. . . . La vérité qu'on met dans les mots ne se fraye pas son chemin directement, n'est pas douée d'une évidence irrésistible. Il faut qu'assez de temps passe pour qu'une vérité de même ordre ait pu se former en eux. (*R*, 612)[12]

When Proust's "interlocuteurs imaginaires" attain to this wisdom they will have knowledge of the phenomena of nature, the real universe, or ultimate ideas such as truth and falsity, past and present, birth and death, being and nonbeing, beauty and ugliness, mutability and finality, regret and joy. This is so because it would become clear to them that what they know is not the stars, sky, atmosphere, earth, objects, events, people, and words but only what their own ears hear, their own eyes see, their own words express, their own minds imagine, their own memories inspire, and their own thoughts create. They will comprehend that the phenomena of nature exist as ideas, as thoughts, and that these thoughts exist only in relation to memory, the past, and to the truth beneath the words, which is not irresistibly self-evident. Thus, the truth of this "conversation solitaire" of *A la recherche du temps perdu* is this: the past exists within us both as archaic and personal images, and it appears intermittently in altered images that are themselves more general than the idea of such phenomena as matter, time, space, or people. This is so because these entities are embodied in the "milieu vital," and each is verifiable only within the words, which, although common to all, come as metaphors from the lips of great writers.

Aussi je lisais, je chantais intérieurement sa prose [Bergotte], plus *dolce*, plus *lento* peut-être qu'elle n'était écrite, et la phrase la plus simple s'adressait à moi avec une intonation attendrie. Plus que tout j'aimais sa philosophie, je m'étais donné à elle pour toujours. (*R*, 97)[13]

Because Bergotte's philosophy is a system of "phrases imprévisibles," of clear and precise yet mellow and expressive, simple and sonorous words that articulate archaic images relating to the memory of an individual or group of persons, the problem is not so much to find out about the "interlocuteurs imaginaires" as to understand what the fictitious questions of Bergotte's solitary conversation reveal, what they tell of the phenomena of nature. Bergotte's philosophy, it seems, is true in proportion to the time that must elapse before it finds verification, "sanction objective," within time itself. And from the beginning of time, no truth is more certain, no word more revealing, no idea more "imprévisible," more independent of all others and therefore less in need of verification, than this:

De sorte que, s'il n'y avait pas l'habitude, la vie devrait paraître délicieuse à des êtres qui seraient à chaque heure menacés de mourir,—c'est-à-dire à tous les hommes. Puis, si l'imagination est entraînée par le désir de ce que nous ne pouvons posséder, son essor n'est pas limité par une réalité complètement perçue dans ces rencontres où les charmes de la passante sont généralement en relation directe avec la rapidité du passage. (*R*, 713)[14]

Thus, the reluctance with which we accept ourselves as "menacés de mourir" leads to our flight into the world of habit or the realm of ordinary existence. This habit prevents us from seeing the truth that "le désir de ce que nous ne pouvons posséder," which would allow us to experience that creative power that only great writers exhibit, is in direct relationship to the swiftness of the earthly existence that we live superficially. This same truth applies to speech forms, to discourse. A word is a direct relationship connecting a reality, whether perceived habitually or grasped imaginatively by metaphor, to the emotional state it evokes. A word that enters our mind stimulates our desires for what we cannot possess and causes our imagination to recover those profound ideas, those archaic images, that source of being, of which our existence is a direct reflection. In this way alone the "réalité complètement perçue dans ces rencontres" transforms itself into a memory of yesterday, an image of the past whose depth increases as our path leads toward death. The ultimate truth of Proust's inquiry is that the imagination is indeed awakened by the uncertainty of existence, by the realization that the past more than the present, failure more than success, chance more than fixed laws, change more than stability, suffering more than joy, despair more than hope, regret more than happiness, nonbeing more than being, and death more than life are the most profound sources of memories, ideas, and images through which we experience the pain and the bliss of human life. Even oblivion, by lifting us out of our habitual existence, characterized by dream images, encourages "la renaissance exclusive" of archaic images.

Tout un promontoire du monde inaccessible surgit alors de l'éclairage du songe, et entre dans notre vie, dans notre vie où comme le dormeur éveillé nous voyons les personnes dont nous avions si ardemment rêvé que nous avions cru que nous ne les verrions jamais qu'en rêve. (*R*, 865)[15]

Living Dream as Metaphor

From the logic of this reflection, it follows that the true and the false, the beautiful and the ugly, the real and the illusory cannot really be attributes of habitual thoughts, which are devoid of "phrases imprévisibles," of images. Like a dream, truth, beauty, love, and reality cannot be defined using the language of science, the words of the "philosophes qui nous recommandent de borner nos désirs" (*R*, 714), the discourse of "la pensée des métaphysiciens" (*R*, 97) whose answers to the questions of the phenomena of nature derive from a rigid syllogistic form. Rather, for Proust, these images exist in "l'éclairage du songe" and emerge from the inaccessible world of solitary discourse. The ideas of truth, beauty, love, and reality are those of the "dormeur éveillé" and cannot be traced to anything other than the "dormeur" himself who has created the words of a "beauté plastique" that is acquired at the cost of ruling out habitual speech forms. This is why the words of the "dormeur éveillé," of the great writer, appear complicated and exhausting.

By yielding to habitual discourse, which is not governed by the direct relationship with the world of dreams, truth, beauty, love, and reality are replaced by images drawn from casual encounters, habitual discourse, and the most superficial layers of human existence. But Proust insists that what is real is the continuity of change, the becoming and the flux, the swiftness of our existence and the longing of our desires. This is what envelops the phenomena of nature, truth, beauty, love, and death; and there is more of the inaccessible in them than the visible, more of the indefinable than the definable, more dreams than habit, more solitary conversation than dialogue.

> Mais le bonheur ne peut jamais avoir lieu. Si les circonstances arrivent à être surmontées, la nature transporte la lutte du dehors au dedans et fait peu à peu changer assez notre coeur pour qu'il désire autre chose que ce qu'il va posséder. (R, 624)[16]

Yet there is still "quelque chose de nouveau, une image" in this reality: there is more beauty than can be experienced, more love than can be enjoyed, than can be found in a life of casual encounters, of habitual existence. All live under the constant threat of death, under the constantly shifting winds of chance; for we are always on our own, within ourselves, faced with a new encounter, a new beginning, a new life. Because of this, we are afraid and hide in the safe world of habit, which is the world of illusion. In dreams, however, we stand once again face to face with the original void, the original beginning, the original mystery of birth; the phenomena of nature can begin anew if they are recreated in the words of the creator who is this "dormeur éveillé."

> Tout à coup je m'endormais, je tombais dans ce sommeil lourd où se dévoilent pour nous le retour à la jeunesse, la reprise des années passées, des sentiments perdus, la désincarnation, la transmigration des âmes, l'évocation des morts, les illusions de la folie, la régression vers les règnes les plus élémentaires de la nature . . . tous ces mystères que nous croyons ne pas connaître et auxquels nous sommes en réalité initiés presque toutes les nuits, ainsi qu'à l'autre grand mystère de l'anéantissement et de la résurrection. (R, 819–20)[17]

In the language of dreams, then, we participate not only in mysteries that we ourselves imagine but in the original mystery of life, death, and resurrection, the mystery of the *word* revealing itself to all things, the mystery of reality, the timeless vision of the "dormeur éveillé."

The mysteries we imagine, or the great mystery of life, death, and resurrection, or the return of the self to the solitary conversation of the child, or the recapturing of lost feelings, are not fully understood through language. They have a beauty and a truth beyond words, beyond the language of casual encounters. And the only way to express these ideas, to bring them to "l'éclairage de la réalité," is to start from the inwardness of the mind's eye, the intimate world of the "dormeur éveillé," the "milieu vital" that transcends time and space, the "phrases imprévisibles" of great writers, the melodious language of the world's "premiers physiciens." Here in the world of the "dormeur éveillé," the human person is at one and the same time creator and creature; here words and images are present in their "milieu vital" tapped by the "dormeur," who creates from the deepest center of his being a vital image that communicates thought itself. The word, then, is nothing but self-created thought expressing the phenomena of nature in their coming-to-be and their being, for the word applies to the changing world of dreams in its direct relationship to the timelessness of reality, to the mystery of the origin of things, to the memories of the past.

Nonetheless, the word of the "dormeur éveillé" is distinguished from the word of the "interlocuteurs imaginaires" by its correspondence with the "sanction objective" of elementary forms that retrogressively point to thought, the idea, the image of all things. It is this word which is a thought, a vital image, an idea, a metaphor, a dream. This is the true universe into which we must plunge in order to recapture the past in its "milieu vital," to restore lost images. Even so, reality cannot be truly described with any speech forms, for neither a single word, sentence, nor even a string of sentences, however unforeseen and plastic they may be, can express the living dreams, the forms, of the "dormeur éveillé." The only way to express them is through the images drawn from the different orders of reality, which, once in the mind, direct us toward the "promontoire du monde inaccessible" where we experience the word to be spoken, the image to be grasped, the beauty to be felt, the truth to be beheld, the past to be remembered, and the love to be enjoyed, which are the very mystery of human existence, "chaque minute anéantie par l'oubli" (*R*, 820).

So, then, the word as self-created thought, as dream, has two fundamental aspects that stand in direct relationship to each other: one aspect is the objective sanction, the archaic image of the phenomena of nature (time, space, habit); the other aspect is the inner self, the "dormeur éveillé," who is present in the world both as a being conditioned by habit and as awakened being. Thus the word itself constitutes the phenomena of dreams. But if dreams are extinguished, awareness of the word is lost. Otherwise the world as dream would be communicated through the lan-

Tintoretto, *The Dreams of Men*. Oil on canvas, 374 × 217 cm, ca. 1575–77. (*Courtesy of The Detroit Institute of Arts, City of Detroit Purchase*.)

guage of ordinary encounters, the world of everyday discourse. Instead, the word of the "dormeur éveillé" frees itself from its empirical speech forms by creating for itself a structure of meaning or complex of images that is both unforeseen and plastic, a pale reflection of the "dormeur éveillé" in whom the outside world begins to take form as his dream ends. He has transformed habitual discourse, the language of rational philosophers (including the language of metaphysics), into a solitary conversation in which every word, every sentence acquires new meaning and dynamism. For this reason, habitual discourse, the language of rational philosophy and metaphysics, is suspended and is replaced by the nonverbal forms of a twilight existence, of the visual memory. This visual memory is, for Proust, merely thought rediscovering the archaic images embodied in the habitual world of phenomena.

> Dans une langue que nous savons, nous avons substitué à l'opacité des sons la transparence des idées. Mais une langue que nous ne savons pas est un palais clos dans lequel celle que nous aimons peut nous tromper, sans que, restés au dehors et désespérément crispés dans notre impuissance, nous parvenions à rien voir, à rien empêcher. (*R*, 583)[18]

A la recherche du temps perdu, using the artistic and mythic style of the world's first natural philosophers and original sentences of a great writer, substitutes for the opacity of sounds the transparency of ideas. At the same time, the novel is a fortress sealed within Proust's own mind whose ever-changing chains of images exhaust the reader. Sometimes his language is so clear that it seems to direct the reader toward the promontory of the inaccessible world, those mysteries of which he speaks and that he has made visible; at other times he plays us false by his artistic (metaphoric) use of words. The literary beauty, mellowness, and plasticity of his verbal expressions make the mysteries themselves deceptively transparent. His language is occasionally expressive, inviting the reader to leave the habitual world of existence and enter, at least for a moment, the twilight world of the "dormeur éveillé" whose word envelops the phenomena of nature. And yet Proust himself would say that his language is neither complete nor exhaustive and that his speech forms, far from providing the reader with answers to questions of finality and causality, truth and falsehood, being and becoming, mystery and phenomenon, beauty and ugliness, or love and hate, never cease to raise questions by their ambiguity. Indeed, the depth of his metaphors frequently conceals the fact hat their meaning cannot be read correctly from the direct relationship involving archaic images and what memory reveals. *A la recherche du temps perdu*, then, is the means by which Proust expresses the thought of things, the word itself: the word as self-created thought is a solitary conversation that elevates the reader from the discourse of casual encounters and habitual talk to the level of the idea, or from the shallowness of everyday living to the reflective living of dreams, or better still, from the phenomenal moment through the action of the visual memory to that "milieu vital" in which words are first given meaning.

> S'il est vrai que la mer ait été autrefois notre milieu vital où il faille replonger notre sang pour retrouver nos forces, il en est de même de l'oubli, du néant mental; on semble alors absent du temps pendant quelques heures; mais les forces qui se sont rangées pendant ce temps-là sans être dépensées, le mesurent par leur quantité aussi exactement que les poids de l'horloge ou les croulants monticules du sablier. On ne sort pas, d'ailleurs, plus aisément d'un tel sommeil que de la veille prolongée, tant toutes choses tendent à durer et, s'il est vrai que certains narcotiques font dormir, dormir longtemps est un narcotique plus puissant encore, après lequel on a bien de la peine à se réveiller. (*R*, 821)[19]

This logical priority of the "néant mental," of absenting ourselves from habitual existence, shows that formerly the word was indeed the sleep from which the opaque sounds of speech and the passage of the phenomena of nature emerged and registered in the temporal, habitual consciousness. When this is so, when "la veille prolongée" ends, habitual discourse is suspended, and true dialogue derives its meaning from thought, from the sleep from which "on a bien de la peine à se réveiller." In this way we arrive at a direct relationship between time (habitual existence, habitual speech) and the "néant mental," the sleep (pure phenomenalism, subjective idealism), of all speech forms. If the word, the metaphor is self-created thought, it is useless, since it cannot express the visible world, the world of the objective sanction, the world of reasonable discourse or habit. Lacking this utility, Proust places full emphasis upon the metaphoric use of words as the only clear and precise way with which to express ideas.

> Je ne pouvais pas quitter le roman que je lisais de lui [Bergotte]. . . . Puis je remarquai les expressions rares, presque archaïques qu'il aimait employer à certains moments où un flot caché d'harmonie, un prélude intérieur, soulevait son style; et c'était aussi à ces moments-là qu'il se mettait à parler du "vain songe de la vie", de "l'inépuisable torrent des belles apparences", du "tourment stérile et délicieux de comprendre et d'aimer", des "émouvantes effigies qui anoblissent à jamais la façade vénérable et charmante des cathédrales", qu'il exprimait toute une philosophie nouvelle pour moi par de merveilleuses images dont on aurait dit que c'était elles qui avaient éveillé ce chant de harpes qui s'élevait alors et à l'accompagnement duquel elles donnaient quelque chose de sublime. . . . Aussi sentant combien il y avait de parties de l'univers que ma perception infirme ne distinguerait pas s'il ne les rapprochait de moi, j'aurais voulu posséder une opinion de lui, une métaphore de lui, sur toutes choses. . . . (*R*, 93–95)[20]

Thus, to understand *A la recherche du temps perdu*, whose thrust is to elucidate expression itself as a present experience, as a privileged moment, as thought externalizing itself through created words, it is essential to remember that the metaphors that Proust fashions become for him the literal present. Proust's notion that all reality is ultimately only the projection of the inner consciousness of the creative individual is the fundamental theme explored in the following chapters.

2
Proust and Merleau-Ponty on Perception

> Quand je voyais un objet extérieur, la conscience que je le voyais restait entre moi et lui, le bordait d'un mince liséré spirituel qui m'empêchait de jamais toucher directement sa matière; elle se volatilisait en quelque sorte avant que je prisse contact avec elle, comme un corps incandescent qu'on approche d'un objet mouillé ne touche pas son humidité parce qu'il se fait toujours précéder d'une zone d'évaporation. (*R*, 84)[1]

> Toute perception intérieure est inadéquate parce que je ne suis pas un objet que l'on puisse percevoir, parce que je fais ma réalité et ne me rejoins que dans l'acte. . . . C'est dans mon rapport avec des "choses" que je me connais, la perception intérieure vient après, et elle ne serait pas possible si je n'avais pas pris contact avec mon doute en le vivant jusque dans son objet. (*P*, 438–39)[2]

To create a metaphor is to substitute a word for the image or form of things. This form is what Proust calls the *reserve*, that part of existence that cannot be encountered by people as they live in the world because it is forever shrouded in a "zone d'évaporation" and consequently cannot be recognized as image. When Merleau-Ponty (1908–61) uses the word *form*, he too means the inner being of things that remains invisible to the eye, although the mind's eye can perceive it and know it as form. Thus, although both agree that this inner form cannot be visually perceived, they disagree on whether it can be penetrated mentally.

Both Proust and Merleau-Ponty consider every object a phenomenal manifestation of itself: the visible image of its own inner depth, of its own hiddenness. It is upon this hiddenness that the mind's eye moves from within to without, from the mentally visible to the invisible. Hence, every act of perception is at the same time an act of revelation and concealment. It is an illumination of the object's inner depth, but this illumination does not penetrate to the deepest reserve of the phenomenal world. Perception is therefore paradoxical, since the image perceived through the inner self is a manifestation of thought or idea and also contains an objective element beyond the subjective perception itself, beyond the phenomenal world from which it emerged. Both the image and the thought, which exist between the inner depth of objects and their perception, are the most visible and yet the most mysterious reality. This reality is the synchronization of image, form, idea, and thought as beauty. In the beautiful, image and thought, phenomenal and transcendent, subjective and objective, preconscious and conscious are interconnected—they rest in one another, and whoever perceives beauty perceives this interaction even more deeply than an ordinary observer.

The perception of the image is primarily caused by the phenomenal world; to have a mental picture, to experience a "milieu vital" (Proust), is to relate to the world as object of sight. And to say that the real universe is perceptible is to engage in a dialogue with a "milieu d'existence" (Merleau-Ponty) by which perceivers open or close themselves to a world beyond the visible, beyond the subjective. Thus, for both Proust and Merleau-Ponty perception actualizes what is in the inner depth of things. This actualization is done by the perceiver and is therefore subjective. For both writers, the image, the form, cannot be perceived without the perceiver's being engulfed and enraptured by it, being elevated and transported to a world of another order, the invisible or the divine world without which perception cannot make anything visible.

Proust and Merleau-Ponty, thus, express each in his own way a theory of perception that takes the point of view of subjective idealism and phenomenalism. Proust's pure phenomenalism does not lead perceivers beyond their own mental picture; everything they see is an appearance, a mirage, a projection of their own inner self, their own thought impressed on the "zone d'évaporation." By contrast, the subjectivity of Merleau-Ponty is not true phenomenalism. Rather, it is rooted in a "milieu d'existence" that objectively transcends the phenomenal world and yet is encountered within phenomena through perception. Whereas Proust regards consciousness as mere evaporation of sight, the inability of the senses to touch the image of things, Merleau-Ponty views consciousness as a "puissance qui co-naît à un certain milieu d'existence ou se synchronise avec lui" (*P*, 245).

Proust: The Impressed Image

At the center of Proust's view on perception lies the notion that consciousness has nothing exterior about it; the objects that are seen evaporate, thereby preventing the observer from having a direct contact with the external world. But this evaporation zone in the phenomenal world contains or limits the consciousness (bodily sensations) of its observers and thereby confines their vision within the narrow limits of inner sight, which opens them to the visible world. Here, on this spiritual border, one's consciousness suddenly finds itself surrounded by the phenomenal world, and it is from this "entre moi et lui" that a deeper kind of perception emerges; a seeing that takes possession of one's whole being (both sensory and mental). Thus, the perceiver is caught on this spiritual border and sees only the self, since the visible world is in a constant state of evaporation: the phenomenon seen is the perceiver's consciousness, thought and body.

> Hier soir, je n'étais plus qu'un être vidé, sans poids, et . . . je ne pouvais cesser de remuer ni de parler, je n'avais plus de consistance, de centre de gravité, j'étais lancé, il me semblait que j'aurais pu continuer ma morne course jusque dans la lune. Or, si en dormant mes yeux n'avaient pas vu l'heure, mon corps avait su la calculer, il avait mesuré le temps non pas sur un cadran superficiellement figuré, mais par la pensée progressive de toutes mes forces refaites que, comme une puissante horloge, il avait cran par cran laissé descendre de mon cerveau dans le reste de mon corps où elles entassaient maintenant jusqu'au-dessus de mes genoux l'abondance intacte de leurs provisions. (R, 820–21)[3]

It is clear in this passage that perception is motivated by the mind's eye losing contact with the material world as it exists in time. In the opaque elements of the sensory, the world of clear objects is abolished, and the body, when seen superficially, appears an empty and weightless shell. Nevertheless, when seen with the mind's eye, the body is replenished with its original weight and dimensions, in proportion as the mind's eye penetrates the depth of the body. Thus, the perceptual moment is not substance, is not spiritual: it is a relationship between the outside world and the inner sense, the thought of the perceiver, a sort of mental picture, an incarnated image that is an "élément essentiel" in the complicated structure of the senses. Perception, then, is found at both extremes of our being: in the senses, which are wholly immersed in the "élément essentiel" of the phenomenal flowing into the body through them, and the brain that can perceive the idea, the image, the element of things without the mediation of the visible world, with the eyes closed. The spiritual boundary allows an identity of both the senses and the mind, the outer and the inner; but this can happen only by the suspension of the usual center of gravity (sensory perception), by projecting, in a dreamlike existence, the mental picture of the phenomenal.

> Un être réel . . . pour une grande part est perçu par nos sens, c'est-à-dire nous reste opaque, offre un poids mort que notre sensibilité ne peut soulever. Qu'un malheur le frappe, ce n'est qu'en une petite partie de la notion totale que nous avons de lui que nous pourrons en être émus;

bien plus, ce n'est qu'en une partie de la notion totale qu'il a de soi qu'il pourra l'être lui-même. La trouvaille du romancier a été d'avoir l'idée de remplacer ces parties impénétrables à l'âme par une quantité égale de parties immatérielles, c'est-à-dire que notre âme peut s'assimiler. (*R*, 85)[4]

According to Proust, humanity has two kinds of senses: one is closed off to the opaque elements of the sensory world; the other substitutes their immaterial parts for those impenetrable parts. If both sensibilities are different states of perception, it follows that only a small part of the totality of the phenomenal world is actually perceived: the immaterial parts are distinct from this completeness. The mind, held back by the weight of its own sensibilities, does not penetrate to the opaque zone of the senses, while at the same time the five distinct senses are opened up to this idea through the word of the novelist.

Et une fois que le romancier nous a mis dans cet état, où comme dans tous les états purement intérieurs toute émotion est décuplée, où son livre va nous troubler à la façon d'un rêve moins d'un rêve plus clair que ceux que nous avons en dormant et dont le souvenir durera davantage, alors, voici qu'il déchaîne en nous pendant une heure tous les bonheurs et tous les malheurs possibles dont nous mettrions dans la vie des années à connaître quelques-uns, et dont les plus intenses ne nous seraient jamais révélés parce que la lenteur avec laquelle ils se produisent nous en ôte la perception. . . . (*R*, 85)[5]

Entering such a purely mental state the perceiver is raised above the phenomenal and becomes free to explore the sensible world's immaterial parts, which here encompass the five senses, "parfaitement distinctes les unes des autres, inégales entre elles de valeur et de signification" (*R*, 349).

It is therefore essential that the senses remain opaque for the mind to see. But these immaterial parts, which veil the physical senses and whose presence the senses feel as if it were a "rêve plus clair que ceux que nous avons en dormant," have been acquired because the senses are rooted in the phenomenal, to which they remain attached. As a dream is accessible only upon awakening, so these immaterial parts are the other side of sensory perception and become accessible when sensation subsides. The senses present to the perceiver what is never revealed in the visible; they open a space from which the mind's eye can perceive the beauty of seeing, hearing, touching, tasting, and smelling.

Car si on a la sensation d'être toujours entouré de son âme, ce n'est pas comme d'une prison immobile: plutôt on est comme emporté avec elle dans un perpétuel élan pour la dépasser, pour atteindre à l'extérieur,

avec une sorte de découragement, en entendant toujours autour de soi
cette sonorité identique qui n'est pas écho du dehors, mais retentisse-
ment d'une vibration interne. On cherche à retrouver dans les
choses. . . le reflet que notre âme a projeté sur elles. . . . (R, 86–87)[6]

Indeed, the impenetrable opaqueness of the visible encourages us as perceivers to discover in things their reflection within us, the idea of our inner
self, which we project on things. At the moment the senses break out into
the world, a field of vision emerges that is the experience of the sensual:
the mind's eye draws strength from contact with the sensual, and it in turn
expands through the realm of the imagination. In its attempts to break out
into the world, the mind binds the moments of perception to each other
without the use of abstract ideas. The mind's struggle to bind the perceiver's own sensibility to the phenomenal world is perpetually discouraging
because the evaporation zone forever prevents contact with phenomena.
Of the narrator's walks in the woods of Roussainville, Proust writes:

En vain, tenant l'étendue dans le champ de ma vision, je la drainais de
mes regards qui eussent voulu en ramener une femme. . . . Je fixais
indéfiniment le tronc d'un arbre lointain, de derrière lequel elle allait
surgir et venir à moi; l'horizon scruté restait désert, la nuit tombait,
c'était sans espoir que mon attention s'attachait, comme pour aspirer
les créatures qu'ils pouvaient recéler, à ce sol stérile, à cette terre
épuisée. . . je cessais de croire partagés par d'autres êtres, de croire
vrais en dehors de moi, les désirs que je formais pendant ces promenades
et qui ne se réalisaient pas. Ils ne m'apparaissaient plus que comme les
créations purement subjectives, impuissantes, illusoires, de mon tem-
pérament. Ils n'avaient plus de lien avec la nature, avec la réalité qui dès
lors perdait tout charme et toute signification et n'était plus à ma vie
qu'un cadre conventionnel. . . . (R, 158–59)[7]

Hence, these sensory openings into the world form a single vortex in
which the association of certain ideas produces a deeper mode of perception where the imagination substitutes immaterial parts for the real objects. Accordingly, what the mind's eye perceives is a sense of sight that
has no "lien avec la nature, avec la réalité," a sense of hearing that hears
no "écho du dehors,"a sense of smell that perceives the concealed fragrance of the landscape, a sense of taste that savors the embraces and
kisses of the "femme que j'avais tant désirée," and a sense of touch that
grasps "les créations purement subjectives." In short, what the senses
move to reveal is the complete idea, or archaic image, of feminine beauty
—an image devoid of intellectual value and suggesting no abstract truth.
This inner perception, then, is the field of vision of all different images
beneath the visible world, which the senses sense but can never bring to
light because they lack the strength to pierce through the impenetrable

zone of the visible that only the mind's eye can penetrate. What appears is beautiful to the extent that the mind's eye unifies all parts of the visible world around a field of vision and disposes, measures, dominates, extracts, and rearranges the images of the unseen into what is seen and substitutes that which is seen for the opaqueness of phenomena.

It is, then, the purely subjective world that Proust proposes to make visible through the notion of the body. He uses the instrument of the mind's eye, as opposed to that of abstract reasoning, to perceive the phenomenal world. Since the world of nature is filled with an evaporation zone, a field of immaterial sensations or ground of fissures, a number of different impressions, fleeting memories, and "souvenirs ajoutés les uns aux autres" (*R*, 186), the bodily senses are incapable of precise connection with the field of vision, the pure ideal. However, the real, in its various phenomena, can be unified around the perceiver's field of vision through the remembrance of things past (archaic images seen by the imagination), the world of images impressed on the mind. Hence, the mind's eye sees by looking away in the memory from that which is visible to the senses, by closing off the bodily senses from the objective elements of phenomena. It grasps the immaterial parts that have taken the place of the various images scattered in the outside world and brings them into the purely subjective world of the idea, thought itself. At the same time, the mind's eye appropriates the spiritual boundary and enters the perceiver's inner self (memory). Thus, the mind's eye perceives the immaterial parts along the sensory paths of the body, along the pathways of the corporeal (phenomenal) world, and perceives horizons that it has never seen, transfiguring landscapes, objects, people that have never been perceived. This transfiguration is possible only because the mind grasps the unified whole of the phenomenal, uniting sensory and mental perceptions within a single gaze. In order for consciousness to emerge, memory and thought must confront each other within the mind, while each retains its distinctive attributes. Thus they will complement each other in their perceptual activity. That is, the mind's eye attempts to blend these two visions but cannot, which leaves the various images in the consciousness and fills the perceiver with regret. As Proust's narrator contemplates the hawthorns, he writes:

> Tout à coup, je m'arrêtai, je ne pus plus bouger, comme il arrive quand une vision ne s'adresse pas seulement à nos regards, mais requiert des perceptions plus profondes et dispose de notre être tout entier. Une fillette d'un blond roux, qui avait l'air de rentrer de promenade et tenait à la main une bêche de jardinage, nous regardait, levant son visage semé de taches roses. . . . Je la regardais, d'abord de ce regard qui n'est pas que le porte-parole des yeux, mais à la fenêtre duquel se penchent tous les sens, anxieux et pétrifiés, le regard qui voudrait toucher, capturer, emmener le corps qu'il regarde et l'âme avec lui; puis, tant j'avais peur

que d'une seconde à l'autre mon grand-père et mon père, apercevant
cette jeune fille, me fissent éloigner en me disant de courir un peu devant
eux, d'un second regard, inconsciemment supplicateur, qui tâchait de la
forcer à faire attention à moi, à me connaître! (*R*, 140–41)[8]

For Proust, the soul lives triumphantly in its senses; it reaches out,
touches, and captures, is petrified, convulsed, angry, sad, indifferent, anxious, and afflicted until the phenomenal itself (the hawthorns, the young
girl) abruptly fades away in the evaporation of the perceiver's memories,
the inner self. Indeed, this deeper kind of perception which takes possession of the whole person rests on the possession of all the senses and forces
the phenomenal to be fixed on the perceiver's self. As such, perception
comes from the perceiver and makes its way back to him or her. Because of
this, perceiving is not only a "porte-parole des yeux" but also a window of
the mind. And the soul, the mind's eye, in unity with the body breaks out
into the world that is nothing but the perceiver's looking at the self. In this
passage, the purpose of the narrator's imploring look is to make himself
visible to the young girl whose expression reflects his first gaze from which
the field of vision is defined and by which it is itself completed by the triple
acts of attention, seeing, and knowing. The evaporation zone arises between the narrator's own sensations and his whole being and keeps his
perception from ever becoming clear in itself. Because perception is the
result of the mind's eye seeking to capture the existing phenomenon and,
despite its efforts, always failing in its quest, it follows that the reality the
mind perceives is dead. Perceiving, then, is directed towards this realization, and since what must be realized is the perceiver's sensory form, it
cannot be realized other than in a purely subjective way, in the projection
of the perceiver's soul onto the corporeal world. The mind's eye pierces the
opaque points of the sensual field, and the images it brings back, far from
being those of a particular phenomenon, present rather the joyless sensation of an "image, une projection renversées, un 'négatif' de notre sensibi-
lité" (*R*, 894). And as a window of the mind from which the five senses
follow one another in search of the various fragrant, tactile, and sonorous
charms they enjoy even without the aid of the bodily senses, the mind's eye
limits the field of vision by exposing on a one-dimensional surface first one
and then another photograph of the same phenomenon. The difference
between these images is that the last one remains visible for some time,
while the others, those from the past, may be present to the memory and
ready to emerge from the inner self in answer to a call from the senses.

Hélas! dans la fleur la plus fraîche on peut distinguer les points im-
perceptibles qui pour l'esprit averti dessinent déjà ce qui sera, par la
dessiccation ou la fructification des chairs aujourd'hui en fleur, la forme
immuable et déjà prédestinée de la graine. . . . Je savais qu'[il] . . . habi-

tait sous la rose inflorescence d'Albertine, de Rosemonde, d'Andrée, inconnu à elles-mêmes, tenu en réserve pour les circonstances, un gros nez, une bouche proéminente, un embonpoint qui étonnerait mais était en réalité dans la coulisse, prêt à entrer en scène, imprévu, fatal . . . soudainement issus, à l'appel des circonstances, d'une nature antérieure à l'individu lui-même, par laquelle il pense, vit, évolue, se fortifie ou meurt, sans qu'il puisse la distinguer des mobiles particuliers qu'il prend pour elle. . . . Mais nous ne saisissons que les idées secondes sans percevoir la cause première . . . qui les produisait nécessairement et que nous manifestons au moment voulu. (*R*, 891–92)[9]

It is the ultimate form, the vital image of the visible universe that the mind's eye, this deeper sense of perception, tries to uncover beneath the seemingly opaque world of sensations. The bodily eyes see only what they look at: they see human faces, colors of landscapes, waves of the sea, and not their immaterial parts. But when, even without "l'esprit averti," the mind's eye looks beyond the flesh within which "la dessiccation ou la fructification" of the phenomenal takes place to that origin or source that is entwined in the imperceptible points of the real world, in the reserve of sensations, then the phenomenal is no longer perceived on the basis of secondary ideas. Instead, it is seen as the primary cause that creates the world of nature and makes it as it is. It is truly the morning that seems to be the eye of the mind; and once the mind awakens, once it opens itself to the light of the visible, it calls forth powers dormant in ordinary or habitual vision, a "vaguelette qui enfle délicieusement" (*R*, 851) the surface of existence. And when the mind's eye reaches the reserve at the bottom of all things, the primary cause of vision recognizes the reserve despite the impressions created on the mind by the secondary ideas, the external features of things. If there were no flesh (secondary ideas) for the mind's eye to penetrate, it would cease to perceive things in their inner depth. The inner depth or reserve of things is not done away with in perception; secondary ideas are replaced by the thought of the perceiving, by the acts of the visual memory.

Et comme d'autre part nous voulons continuer à penser à elle [la belle fille], il préfère l'imaginer dans l'avenir, préparer habilement les circonstances qui pourront la faire renaître, ce qui ne nous apprend rien sur son essence, mais nous évite la fatigue de la recréer en nous-même et nous permet d'espérer la recevoir de nouveau du dehors. (*R*, 658)[10]

Thus, the primary cause presents the outside world to the senses, bestowing on it secondary ideas that enable the perceiver to rediscover those immaterial parts that endow things with an identity. Otherwise things would merely become fleeting sensations of the flesh, continuously dissolving beneath the evaporation zone. The mind's eye perceives the phenomenal idea and limits itself to the field of vision of the past as thought from which it extracts images or impressions. When the mind's eye perceives the real universe, it visualizes it in the phenomenal, and its power of perceiving is nothing but the spiritual boundary of the sensory world, which is not only the "porte-parole des yeux," or instrument of bodily sensations, but also their visible interior, consciousness itself. The visual horizon of the mind's eye, then, is the purely subjective in the consciousness of the perceiver's own body, which does not sense the images out there but senses pure images. And the role played by the body in perception or consciousness is comprehensible only if memory, the "mémoire de ses côtes, de ses genoux, de ses épaules," is not only consciousness of the past but a window that opens to the present.

> . . . et mon corps, le côté sur lequel je reposais, gardiens fidèles d'un passé que mon esprit n'aurait jamais dû oublier, me rappelaient la flamme de la veilleuse de verre de Bohême, en forme d'urne, suspendue au plafond par des chaînettes, la cheminée en marbre de Sienne, dans ma chambre à coucher de Combray, chez mes grands-parents, en des jours lointains qu'en ce moment je me figurais actuels sans me les représenter exactement, et que je reverrais mieux tout à l'heure quand je serais tout à fait éveillé. (R, 6)[11]

The body and the world, therefore, involve imagined clear zones of vision around which their forgotten, impenetrable, opaque, and evaporated zones revolve. The deeper sense of perception does not come without the mind's eye demanding that the phenomenal itself be known exactly and become transparent "à l'heure quand je serais tout à fait éveillé." But the moment when the phenomenal is properly seen and understood is nothing but the restoration of the world of the "dormeur éveillé," of those "jours lointains" from which perception, or consciousness, has its beginning. The world of habit, however, silences the sensorial ideal, the imagined moment, the purely subjective remembrance, representations, or thought itself. Thus, for Proust, the perceptual moment depends on the conscious recalling of past memories.

> Certes, j'étais bien éveillé maintenant, mon corps avait viré une dernière fois et le bon ange de la certitude avait tout arrêté autour de moi. . . . Mais j'avais beau savoir que je n'étais pas dans les demeures dont l'ignorance du réveil m'avait en un instant sinon présenté l'image distincte, du moins fait croire la présence possible, le branle était donné à ma mémoire; généralement je ne cherchais pas à me rendormir tout de suite; je passais la plus grande partie de la nuit à me rappeler notre vie d'autrefois à Combray chez ma grand'tante, à Balbec, à Paris, à Doncières, à Venise, ailleurs encore, à me rappeler les lieux, les personnes que j'y avais connues, ce que j'avais vu d'elles, ce qu'on m'en avait raconté. (R, 8–9)[12]

Merleau-Ponty: The Encountered Image

A perception of the image that sees the phenomenal world from the purely subjective state of the perceiver's inner self, the perceiver's thought would sink below the real world into that of remembrance, memory, impressed images. Such an interior orientation of consciousness, however, prevents contact with the image within the phenomenal. Therefore, Merleau-Ponty attempts a synthesis between total human experience and the temporal, phenomenal world. Without this synthesis, it would be impossible to penetrate the visible for the purpose of perceiving the image.

> Nous avons l'expérience d'un Je, non pas au sens d'une subjectivité absolue, mais indivisiblement défait et refait par le cours du temps. L'unité du sujet ou celle de l'objet n'est pas une unité réelle, mais une unité présomptive à l'horizon de l'expérience. (*P*, 254)[13]

For Merleau-Ponty, perception is not an absolute subjectivity, a pure ideality that takes total possession of our whole being (sensory and mental); rather, it is both subjective and objective, sensory and mental, individual and collective, resulting in our experience of that "couche primordiale où naissent les idées comme les choses" (*P*, 254).

From this logic it follows that when we perceive the phenomenal we do not see it through thought, or inner consciousness, or through some ideas that might reveal the depth, or secret of things. When we look at the world, the world binds the self to the phenomenal, and the self perceives the world as having a natural existence in itself. This is the sense in which the unity between the subject and the object is presumptive. It is based on "l'horizon de l'expérience," on the "milieu d'existence" from which both the self and things emerge, are obliterated, and remake themselves. In other words, the phenomenal is not a thing that can be made into an absolute subjectivity; it is the "couche primordiale" of and field for all thoughts and perceptual encounter: "L'homme est au monde, c'est dans le monde qu'il se connaît" (*P*, V).

Thus, the encounter between the human person and the world is the perceptual moment, or human consciousness, that both unites us inwardly with our own personal horizons and at the same time binds us outwardly to the outside. There is a moment when

> . . . dire que j'ai un champ visuel, c'est dire que par position j'ai accès et ouverture à un système d'êtres, les êtres visibles, qu'ils sont à la disposition de mon regard en vertu d'une sorte de contrat primordial et par un don de la nature, sans aucun effort de ma part; c'est donc dire que la vision est prépersonnelle; —et c'est dire en même temps qu'elle est toujours limitée, qu'il y a toujours autour de ma vision actuelle un horizon de choses non vues ou même non visibles. La vision est *une pensée*

assujettie à un certain champ et c'est là ce qu'on appelle un *sens*. (*P*, 250–51)[14]

The *sense*, then, connects the two aspects of the perceptual act—thought and phenomenal reality—thereby joining the visible with the invisible, the prepersonal with the personal, the individual phenomena with a general field of vision. Still, this vision can never hope to penetrate to that original source of all things; otherwise both sense and the visible world would disappear. Merleau-Ponty claims that vision is a "pensée assujettie à un certain champ." And so, prior to thought there is at a deeper level a field of invisible things that struggle to emerge from that primal source, nature.

Perception is thus a momentary encounter, a synchronization of the personal with the world in its visible and invisible aspects. Perception is thought opening itself up to phenomenal reality, but it is not an inward consciousness. "L'homme est au monde," and it is from this concrete existence that the human being's senses appropriate what is there and make it visible to the self, although this vision always contains things that are not seen. Nor is perception a momentary sensation, a certain "néant" of consciousness, an existence of "l'en soi," a language that is known only by the self and expresses thought itself; "[la perception de] l'être n'est que pour quelqu'un qui soit capable de prendre recul à son égard et soit donc lui-même absolument hors de l'être" (*P*, 246). Visible reality, or Being, can be perceived only when we look at it from a distance, from the invisible, when our look grasps being not as absolute subjectivity, as purely interior, idealized thought, but as a temporal synthesis of perceptual encounters that become, "en vertu d'une sorte de contrat primordial et par un don de la nature," transpersonal, since vision is resolvable only in the light of a "milieu d'existence."

> Dans chaque mouvement de fixation, mon corps noue ensemble un présent, un passé et un avenir, il sécrète du temps, ou plutôt il devient ce lieu de la nature où, pour la première fois, les événements, au lieu de se pousser l'un l'autre dans l'être, projettent autour du présent un double horizon de passé et d'avenir et reçoivent une orientation historique. (*P*, 277)[15]

For this reason, when we feel that we are standing outside being as a result of our taking possession of time, we experience that sense which is a union of the subjective, objective, and historical field of Being itself. The revelation of Being as invisible things is possible only when our gaze renews our primordial contract with the natural world. In this way, invisible things, too, are revealed as having a temporal horizon, a historical orientation likewise founded on Being. Being offers itself to the visible world only within this context, which, for the sense of vision, is not separable from the perceptual moment since it stands in a presumptive unity with time. Perception, thus, cannot be separated from the place in nature, space, and time in which it takes place.

> La perception est toujours dans le monde du "On". Ce n'est pas un acte personnel par lequel je donnerais moi-même un sens neuf à ma vie. Celui qui, dans l'exploration sensorielle, donne un passé au présent et l'oriente vers un avenir, ce n'est pas moi comme sujet autonome, c'est moi en tant que j'ai un corps et que je sais "regarder". Plutôt qu'elle n'est une histoire véritable, la perception atteste et renouvelle en nous une "préhistoire." (*P*, 277)[16]

In this prehistorical horizon, which encompasses all time, the individual does not stand before the world as an autonomous subject. Rather, when, as an impersonal "one," we as human beings become aware of our bodies and the phenomenal world, there corresponds to this impersonal awareness the personal act of perceiving, which makes conscious the prehistorical manifestation of the self in the world, ratifying and renewing the invisible world. This double horizon of past and future, visible and invisible, rather than being "une histoire véritable," is the self coming to understand itself within time and space.

> La constitution d'un niveau spatial n'est qu'un des moyens de la constitution d'un monde plein: mon corps est en prise sur le monde quand ma perception m'offre un spectacle aussi varié et aussi clairement articulé que possible et quand mes intentions motrices en se déployant reçoivent du monde les réponses qu'elles attendent. Ce maximum de netteté dans la perception et dans l'action définit un *sol* perceptif, un fond de ma vie, un milieu général pour la coexistence de mon corps et du monde. (*P*, 289–90)[17]

According to Merleau-Ponty, in their bodies, perceivers have before them the "spectacle aussi varié et aussi clairement articulé que possible," which constitutes an integral whole by the very fact that the phenomenal is the depth of "l'On" incarnating itself as "un milieu général" in the world that contains the body. The body, then, is "en prise sur le monde," in the sense that the body gives the world "un sens qui est adhérent à certains contenus" (*P*, 172), and this sense is perceived and received as the image of a certain depth of the "milieu d'existence." Moreover, in view of the condition that "l'homme est au monde," the perceiver is brought to this "maximum de netteté" because the body serves as the "texture commune de tous les objets et il est, au moins à l'égard du monde perçu, l'instrument général de ma 'compréhension' " (*P*, 272). Thus, the body becomes the bridge between personal and impersonal perception.

The common texture of all objects is created when the body lends perception its total unity and comprehensibility, and it is to this perception that the "intentions motrices" have to be referred if the responses they expect from the world are to be understood. Now, the fact that everything lends itself to an encounter with human beings means that the phenomenal that humans encounter historically is visible only because the image by which it communicates with them emerges from "l'On," from the "milieu d'existence" that is the human being's ability to enter into a deeper communion with the whole perceptual tradition, both prepersonal and personal, particular and historical, interior and exterior, natural and cultural, preconscious and conscious. In Merleau-Ponty's words,

> Quand on dit que la pensée est spontanée, cela ne veut pas dire qu'elle coïncide avec elle-même, cela veut dire au contraire qu'elle se dépasse, et la parole est justement l'acte par lequel elle s'éternise en vérité. (P, 445)[18]

The perceivers, too, must go beyond the visible universe with every gaze, finding in each perceptual encounter more than what they think they see; they must find an opening that discloses the clarity of the whole spectacle from which the perceptual act derives its maximum illumination.

> Pour chaque objet. . . il y a une distance optimale d'où il demande à être vu. . . . Elle est obtenue par un certain équilibre de l'horizon intérieur et de l'horizon extérieur. . . . La distance de moi à l'objet n'est pas une grandeur qui croît ou décroît, mais une tension qui oscille autour d'une norme. (P, 348–49)[19]

What is involved here is not, as in any of the scientific disciplines, the mere technical adjustment of the sensory and mental apparatus to the visual field; rather, it is the proper correspondence of an impersonal existence to its living existence, of an individual background to a universal horizon. Not only must sensory, intellectual, cultural, and historical distances be brought into optimum focus but existential prerequisites must be met in order for the different and clearly perceived images that make their claim on the individual's "milieu d'existence" to find a maximum of visibility, or a sense, in the existence of a natural world: "Et le corps n'est pas même, à son égard, un instrument: il est un objet parmi les objets" (P, 444).

It follows from this that the subjective condition of the possibility of seeing an object for what it is ought not to intrude upon the object's objective existence or substitute the body for its phenomenal reality. If human beings can link themselves up with the world, it is not because they constitute the world from thought, idea, or inner consciousness; rather, it is because they submerge themselves into the thickness and density of the world by perceptive experience. The object, the body, and the world are

connected in a living manner, and we find ourselves in a world that continuously demolishes and remakes our existence. We slip into the preconscious form of existence to open or close ourselves to an outside being or
image, and, conversely, a certain image from the phenomenal world produces a certain consciousness of our own bodies.

> Nous avons réappris à sentir notre corps, nous avons retrouvé sous le
> savoir objectif et distant du corps cet autre savoir que nous en avons
> parce qu'il est toujours avec nous et que nous sommes corps. Il va falloir
> de la même manière réveiller l'expérience du monde tel qu'il nous
> apparaît en tant que nous sommes au monde par notre corps, en tant que
> nous percevons le monde avec notre corps. (*P*, 239)[20]

Merleau-Ponty tells us that by contact with the body and with the world, by
learning to feel our bodies, we rediscover and renew ourselves, awakening
that primal source of existence, that objective and transcendent depth in
our own subjectivity. At times, however, we do not understand our existential situations. We get tied up in our own consciousness and for a
moment leave our spatial and temporal existence, as in a dream. We forget
our fundamental condition as person-in-the-world. Yet the world reminds
us that it is not a "système d'objets dont nous faisons la synthèse, mais
comme un ensemble ouvert de choses vers lesquelles nous nous projetons"
(*P*, 444). If this totality of things is fragmented, not only is the perceptual
encounter disrupted but everything about phenomenal reality becomes incomprehensible. Or, if we exclude from our encounter with the world this
projection, by which we open ourselves to a knowledge of the wholeness of
the image, everything becomes incomprehensible: the world, the body,
and thought are no longer related to each other in their presumptive unity.

If seeing the seen is merely an aspect of a totality of things, "la perception présume une explication" (*P*, 396) of the whole itself. But only if parts
of the whole are properly connected to each other can they together produce a "spectacle aussi varié et aussi clairement articulé que possible" (*P*,
289). The spectacle consists of varied parts at appropriate distances from
each other so as to produce a clear perception of the image. At the same
time, this image, which is complete in itself even if it does not correspond
to other images scattered in the world, does not destroy the totality, that is,
that indivisible distance necessary to the manifestation of that wholeness.
Since the distance "de moi à l'objet n'est pas une grandeur qui croît ou
décroît, mais une tension qui oscille autour d'une norme" (*P*, 349), perception makes explicit not only the distance between the subject and the object but the fact that human beings, by virtue of their being- in-the-world,
are that norm, that total comprehensibility, harmony, and coherence
around which phenomenal things come together in order to reveal themselves. We are that norm because we are the contents of the dispersed and

indeterminate horizons, of the general context of things. Thus, perception makes visible not just an impressed image, a unity of the impersonal to the personal possibility, of the idea to existence, of ideality to reality, of objectivity to subjectivity, of absolute to relative; rather, the visible claims for its manifestation humanity's total existence, along with both ideality and reality, thought and body.

> Toute pensée de quelque chose est en même temps conscience de soi, faute de quoi elle ne pourrait pas avoir d'objet. A la racine de toutes nos expériences et de toutes nos réflexions, nous trouvons donc un être qui se reconnaît lui-même immédiatement, parce qu'il est son savoir de soi et de toutes choses, et qui connaît sa propre existence non pas par constatation et comme un fait donné, ou par inférence à partir d'une idée de lui-même, mais par un contact direct avec elle. La conscience de soi est l'être même de l'esprit en exercice. (P, 426)[21]

Merleau-Ponty tells us that this self-consciousness makes us not only the norm of our own existence but of all things as well. In us, this tension between our body and all bodies, our thought and all thoughts, our existence and general existence, our being and Being itself, is fully experienced. In this tension, perceptive Being is not simply a doll, an automaton, a material mass. Rather, it is filled with ambiguities, since on the one hand it reveals itself to an individual self, and on the other hand it is still the same Being that is the object of perception by all individuals. This Being cannot be divorced from subjective existence; yet it reveals itself as "l'On" and, therefore, as independent of the perceiver as subject. It gives us as perceivers the root of all our experiences and reflections; however, when we do not reflect and when we are not conscious of our bodies and our experiences, the depth dissolves into doubts. In fact,

> Comme . . . je n'ai pas d'autre témoignage sur mon passé que ces témoignages présents et que, cependant j'ai l'idée d'un passé, je n'ai pas de raison d'opposer l'irréfléchi comme un inconnaissable à la réflexion que je fais porter sur lui. Mais ma confiance dans la réflexion revient finalement à assumer le fait de la temporalité et le fait du monde comme cadre invariable de toute illusion et de toute désillusion: je ne me connais que dans mon inhérence au temps et au monde, c'est-à-dire dans l'ambiguïté. (P, 397)[22]

This dynamism of tension, attested to by presumptive unity, doubt, and ambiguity, is characterized by an intersecting double horizon: as knowledge of humanity in the world and as knowledge of humanity that transcends the world. The encounter is made possible only if it occurs simultaneously from both sides, but not in a reciprocal way, "puisque le monde est justement, non pas une somme de choses que l'on pourrait toujours révoquer en doute, mais le réservoir inépuisable d'où les choses sont tirées" (*P*, 396).

And as humanity emerges from this "réservoir inépuisable," from the natural world as theater of collective experiences, as "l'horizon de tous les horizons, le style de tous les styles" (*P*, 381), it witnesses a deepening of the perceptual field, of consciousness; it becomes present to the human world and to the general world by coexisting with all historical experience that transcends it "et toutes ces perspectives forment ensemble une seule vague temporelle, un instant du monde" (*P*, 381). At the same time, what is seen is communicated to others through the body; and it is this communication that constitutes permanent consciousness and depth of existence. Within this horizon, we must see that we are not thought over body, intellect over senses, idea over phenomenon. Neither must we think we are an absolute self with freedom to bestow upon ourselves and others a certain image; because, "la forme des objets n'en est pas le contour géométrique: elle a un certain rapport avec leur nature propre et parle à tous nos sens en même temps qu'à la vue" (*P*, 265). As body, we are beings whose total existence is an encounter; as body among other bodies, we perceive ourselves in perceiving the world. Through perception "les sens communiquent entre eux en s'ouvrant à la structure de la chose" (*P*, 265).

This opening up of the image, form, and things, this projection to the world, makes it possible for us to see what we have never sensed. This opening up of the image is the consciousness of the mystery of form—this "réservoir inépuisable" of things that can never be fully exposed by the perceiver. We as perceivers do not possess a gaze with which we can absolutely grasp the sphere of the general; the perceiver is perceptible reality, and the body is one among perceptible things. Things preserve their own thickness, their own density of being: they never become completely visible. "Si la chose même était atteinte, elle serait désormais étalée devant nous et sans mystère. Elle cesserait d'exister comme chose au moment même où nous croirions la posséder" (*P*, 270). For this reason the perceptual synthesis no more holds the mystery of the object than it does that of one's own body. Because of this, the perceived object presents itself as invisible, and the perceptual synthesis is indeed achieved in the world and not at the metaphysical point occupied by the thinking subject. Thus, if we are beings-in-the-world, we must root our experiences in the form: we must see within the world the image that transcends the world. This is the mystery of the image, of existence itself.

La série de mes expériences se donne comme concordante et la synthèse a lieu non pas en tant qu'elles expriment toutes un certain invariant et dans l'identité de l'objet, mais en tant qu'elles sont toutes recueillies par la dernière d'entre elles et dans l'ipséité de la chose. L'ipséité n'est, bien entendu, jamais *atteinte*: chaque aspect de la chose qui tombe sous notre perception n'est encore qu'une invitation à percevoir au delà et qu'un arrêt momentané dans le processus perceptif. (*P*, 269–70)[23]

Conclusion: The Perceived Image

Merleau-Ponty sees the image in its mystery, its hiddenness, its invisibility, its transcendence; and this image is perceived and preserved in its objective aspect. On the other hand, Proust demands that the image be revealed from the purely subjective consciousness, from the perceiver's inner mind's eye. This polarity, however, is not as absolute as it seems, since Merleau-Ponty's image contains certain Proustian aspects. Both writer's refer to a "milieu d'existence" or "milieu vital" as that from which images emerge. Both also regard the body as a bridge between human consciousness and the world, and consequently both recognize the possibility of human dialogue with the phenomenal. But whereas for Merleau-Ponty meaning is taken from the totality of our encounters, rendering us images governed by our experiences, doubts and ambiguities; for Proust, we are images illuminated and governed by the interiority of our own mind's eye, our own thought, our own memories.

When Merleau-Ponty and Proust look at things, they perceive the image of things in the phenomenal world. These images lead Merleau-Ponty to the invisible world and at the same time are derived from it; they form the ground for a synthesis between personal and impersonal reality. The fact that Proust's vision cannot perceive and grasp these images in their objective forms, on the other hand, leads him to substitute for their opaqueness immaterial parts drawn from his own self-consciousness. For Proust, the coincidence of body and thought in the world is not merely presumptive because it lacks the tension between phenomenon and purely subjective consciousness. The tension does not appear because the image in things, although it continues to exist as "un mince liséré spirituel," is indeterminate. This leads Proust to substitute immaterial parts for this image of phenomena which remains forever beyond his grasp. Since the image has been replaced by immaterial parts, sense data are disruptive to the perceptual process and need to be replaced by memories or the world of dreams. Thus perceivers cut themselves off from the phenomenal horizon. On the other hand, for Merleau-Ponty, as "l'On" and individual and yet as one who is to be understood within the general horizon of historical consciousness, the human person is the expression of the impersonal "On": the human person sees the distances of things while reflecting on the relationship between what is prepersonal and personal, phenomenal and invisible. Human beings see unity with the world as presumptive and tensional, opening up the depths of the "resérvoir inépuisable." The image of things appears to us to be transcendent because it is one with the perfect continuity from the preconscious world to the invisible world through their self-consciousness, their "milieu d'existence."

For Proust, perception is always an intensely personal and inward expression, deriving only from the self-consciousness of the perceiver, while for Merleau-Ponty, perception is rooted in the phenomenal experience and thus transcends both the individual perceiver and the phenomenal itself.

3

Proust and Claudel on Music and Silence

La petite phrase apparaissait, dansante, pastorale, intercalée, épisodique, appartenant à un autre monde. (*R*, 218)[1]

Ah, ne troublez pas le silence, et laissez-moi
faire attention à ce parfum, je le sais, qui va revenir! (*CGO*, 180)[2]

Proust's world of metaphors attempts to reveal the form or image that exists in things, but because this form remains hidden behind the evaporation zone, it is forever beyond his grasp. Therefore, Proust replaces this form with immaterial parts that he creates from his own memories and imagination, and he projects these immaterial equivalents onto the evaporation zone. These immaterial equivalents are the artistic forms he, as artist, constructs to communicate his vision of the reserve of things; at the same time, they help him preserve his own experience of privileged moments once they have been lost. Since the experience of privileged moments is not a rational process but a sensual encounter with the form, Proust seeks to create artistic images that speak to the senses. Music is one of the most expressive forms of artistic revelation that Proust knows. Through it the inner person is drawn by way of vibrations and rhythms to experience the deeper harmony of creation or inner silence itself. Without this silence, without this divine measure, music, whether created or discovered,would be imperceptible; it is silence that makes the music clear, complete, and rhythmical (harmonious). It is through this silence that the self moves on the way to rejuvenation.

Both Proust and Paul Claudel (1868–1955) endeavor to become conscious of the inner harmony of the world; both recognize that there is within us that which yearns for a return to, an intimate communion with, its source or origin; both are convinced that the inner self—the life of remembrance (Proust) or contemplative wonder (Claudel)—is the bridge to spiritual perfection, to transformation; both invite us to hear the sounds of the dark night, which correspond to either a created sonata (Proust) or a discovered cantata (Claudel). For Proust, the created sonata means the

Tintoretto, *Women with Musical Instruments*. **Oil on canvas, 142 × 214 cm, ca. 1555–56.** (*Courtesy of Staatliche Kunstsammlungen Dresden.*)

"grande nuit impénétrée et décourageante de notre âme que nous prenons pour du vide et du néant" (*R*, 350); for Claudel, the discovered cantata means, "ah, ce soir est à moi! ah, cette grande nuit est à moi!" (*CGO*, 74).

Proust responds to night as the silence within which the artist creates music, the phrase of the sonata that the self enjoys. For Claudel, on the other hand, night is the silence within which the self discovers the lyrical melody, the hymn, the cantata, the Magnificat that is already present in creation but which requires the complete participation of the self (sensory, intellectual, and volitional) to perceive it. Even though Proust and Claudel use night to express the self's lamentation over the limits of existence, what lies beyond the night is different for each. For Proust, night is pure phenomenon, subjective idealism, pure creation of the artist's reserve, and music is only one path toward the continuously created harmony of things remembered, of privileged moments. Claudel imagines night as a time where objective and subjective realities encounter each other in a hymn of praise bearing us upward in the direction of the Creator. Whereas for Proust night is indeed nothingness, darkness, dreadfulness, ugliness, the sickness and death of the self, for Claudel, night is the moment of birth when the flesh speaks to flesh and when the self hears the divine song of creation in what is a soundless perfect melody. For Proust, night is habit overcome in the self-rejuvenation of humanity in a self-made world; for Claudel, night is the darkness of sin overcome through the redemption of God's incarnate Word, the luminous dawn of a new beginning, the spiritual birth, the choir of the muses.

Proust: The Remembered Sonata

In *A la recherche du temps perdu*, Proust documents the perfect completion of solitary life in the sense of union brought during privileged moments. To achieve this intimate communion, the solitary person must create. In this creative activity, the solitary person cuts the self off from the phenomenal world, the world of habit, in order to ascend toward the divine world, the soundless melody. For Proust, music is a bridge that stretches from the material world to the eternal, joining the phenomenal with the idealized self. As a bridge, music is the thought that recovers, recreates, and recalls privileged moments by inflaming the memory and circumventing the intellect.

Mais depuis plus d'une année que, lui révélant à lui-même bien des richesses de son âme, l'amour de la musique était, pour quelque temps au moins, né en lui, Swann tenait les motifs musicaux pour de véritables idées, d'un autre monde, d'un autre ordre, idées voilées de ténèbres, inconnues, impénétrables à l'intelligence, mais qui n'en sont pas moins parfaitement distinctes les unes des autres, inégales entre elles de valeur et de signification. (*R*, 349)[3]

So the intellect stands still before the musical motifs that initiate the soul on a journey whose goal is a completely idealized self united with privileged moments which lie beyond the phenomenal world. Music thus is nothing spoken, nothing known, nothing perceived or grasped through reason. It is the riches of the soul; it is "idées voilées de ténèbres"; it is "une certaine acquisition sentimentale," which, through a slow and rhythmical movement, allow the self to escape the phenomenal world and enter an "autre monde, d'un autre ordre" where the self is self-possessed and free of all habitual concerns, of all the interests of the material world. At the same time, music is the "ténèbres impénétrables" of the yearning for true love; it is the "charmes d'une tristesse intime" of vanished privileged moments; it is "l'intelligence positive" that says that things abruptly return to their habitual course. Of these, music can do no more than intensify the sadness. Music carries the hope in which the irreversible future hears itself while it conveys a sentiment of dread that privileged moments depend on chance for their occurrence. Speaking of Swann's experience upon hearing a beautiful musical phrase, Proust's narrator says:

> Et tout d'un coup, au point où elle était arrivée et d'où il [Swann] se préparait à la suivre, après une pause d'un instant, brusquement elle changeait de direction, et d'un mouvement nouveau, plus rapide, menu, mélancolique, incessant et doux, elle l'entraînait avec elle vers des perspectives inconnues. Puis elle disparut. Il souhaita passionnément la revoir une troisième fois. Et elle reparut en effet, mais sans lui parler plus clairement, en lui causant même une volupté moins profonde. Mais, rentré chez lui, il eut besoin d'elle: il était comme un homme dans la vie de qui une passante qu'il a aperçue un moment vient de faire entrer l'image d'une beauté nouvelle qui donne à sa propre sensibilité une valeur plus grande, sans qu'il sache seulement s'il pourra revoir jamais celle qu'il aime déjà et dont il ignore jusqu'au nom. (*R*, 210)[4]

As a yearning, a longing that makes humanity's spiritual ascent to the divine world possible, music is imperceptible sound. The self hears itself; it is unconcerned with what is outside of it. All that matters is that the soul drowns itself in the privileged moments that the musical phrase alluded to in the above quotation brings back to memory, no matter how fleeting, imperfect, or fragile the music is. As remembered sound, music allows the self to subsist in immanent stillness, in a permanent (but not static) world of dreams where the phenomenal world is elevated to the absolute now, to the moment when the self grasps itself, conceives itself as divine essence, as a being born into eternal life. As remembered sounds of privileged moments, music is a pause in time. It is a "mouvement nouveau" that carries us into the next privileged moment in the ever-moving rhythm "rapide, menu, mélancolique, incessant et doux" of time. As remembered sound, music redeems by "perspectives inconnues" from the world of pure phenomenon, and we are led into the invisible world where time is eternal.

> . . . Swann trouvait en lui, dans le souvenir de la phrase qu'il avait entendue, dans certaines sonates qu'il s'était fait jouer…la présence d'une de ces réalités invisibles auxquelles il avait cessé de croire et auxquelles, comme si la musique avait eu sur la sécheresse morale dont il souffrait une sorte d'influence élective, il se sentait de nouveau le désir et presque la force de consacrer sa vie. (R, 211)[5]

This moral aridity is the dark night when the self experiences itself as homeless, belonging neither to the phenomenal world nor to the spiritual. It is a moment of stillness without movement; it is the intimate sadness from which the yearning to consecrate life springs forth; it is the slow rhythms that allow the soul to open in order to receive the mysterious sound and inexpressible delights, the living water of love, of beauty which refreshes the soul. It is nothingness, shadows, the void, the formless which the senses cannot grasp, reason cannot comprehend. What matters is that in this moral dryness, music carries the self out of itself in the ecstasy of the consuming fire of love and places the self in intimate communion with eternal nothingness—the divine wilderness and immense darkness of non-being. It is only then that music leads the self from the present into the distant land of the origin, of things past, where it is absorbed into death, which envelops it and transforms it into sublime self.

> Peut-être est-ce le néant qui est le vrai et tout notre rêve est-il inexistant, mais alors nous sentons qu'il faudra que ces phrases musicales, ces notions qui existent par rapport à lui, ne soient rien non plus. Nous périrons, mais nous avons pour otages ces captives divines qui suivront notre chance. Et la mort avec elles a quelque chose de moins amer, de moins inglorieux, peut-être de moins probable. (R, 350)[6]

The musical phrase then becomes identified with this moral aridity suspended between two possible destinies, both equally dreadful, for "le phénomène du bonheur ne se produit pas ou donne lieu aux réactions les plus amères" (R, 625). Happiness fails to appear because there is nothing, no one, no image, no end, and no permanent source to give it existence. Happiness exists only insofar as the music is created as a substitute for its proper end: that is, for a real and true communion with the object of desire. Happiness is realized in the remembrance of privileged moments, in dreams, and is carried by the musical phrase. Happiness flows from the privileged moments that have been experienced and returns as memory through the musical phrase. In the memory of the musical phrase, the inner self is at one with thoughts, ideas, and memories of privileged moments. By the consent of its will, the self responds to the longing awakened by the music and opens itself up to happiness, the joy of privileged moments.

> La petite phrase continuait à s'associer pour Swann à l'amour qu'il avait pour Odette... qui ne correspondait à rien d'extérieur. . . . Cette soif d'un charme inconnu, la petite phrase l'éveillait en lui, mais ne lui apportait rien de précis pour l'assouvir. De sorte que ces parties de l'âme de Swann où la petite phrase avait effacé le souci des intérêts matériels... elle les avait laissées vacantes et en blanc, et il était libre d'y inscrire le nom d'Odette. (*R*, 236–37)[7]

On the other hand, if happiness is felt, it gives rise to the most bitter reactions because, like music, it cannot be sustained by the will either momentarily or eternally; "l'intelligence positive," as well as time, habit, and chance are always there, draining the soul's sensitivity, its yearning for the mysterious essence, the divine form, pure love, with sorrow and dread.

> Ce n'est pas que notre coeur ne doive éprouver, lui aussi, quand la séparation sera consommée, les effets analgésiques de l'habitude; mais jusque-là il continuera de souffrir. Et la crainte d'un avenir où nous serons enlevés la vue et l'entretien de ceux que nous aimons et d'où nous tirons aujourd'hui notre plus chère joie, cette crainte, loin de se dissiper, s'accroît, si à la douleur d'une telle privation nous pensons que s'ajoutera ce qui pour nous semble actuellement plus cruel encore: ne pas la ressentir comme une douleur, y rester indifférent; car alors notre moi serait changé. . . . (*R*, 671)[8]

The musical phrase thus celebrates a state of happiness that is "noble, inintelligible et précis" (*R*, 210) at the same time that it magnifies the void, pain, suffering, moral dryness, fear, and loss of privileged moments and memory, all of which are the death of the self. In fact, fear comes from the emptiness that accompanies the loss of memories, the death of privileged moments, and from the recognition of the joy of reawakening the soul to a higher form of love, a higher beauty, a higher truth. It is this fear, resulting from cutting the self off from the outside world while creating a new order and that the music heightens, that suggests the difference between the human person as a creator, as a sublime self, as an artist, and the human person as a creature of habit, as a bystander, as a phenomenon. "Il [Swann] commençait à se rendre compte de tout ce qu'il y avait de douloureux, peut-être même de secrètement inapaisé au fond de la douceur de cette phrase, mais il ne pouvait pas en souffrir" (*R*, 237). The

musical phrase brought no suffering to Swann because it exalted the fragile
aspect of privileged moments, of existence. Therefore, when the author
calls the musical phrase "sécheresse morale," "crainte" of the self, he is
telling us that the same self is on an endless journey toward the goal which
is never attained, communion with the object of love. Speaking of Swann
and Odette, Proust's narrator says:

> Il la faisait rejouer dix fois, vingt fois à Odette, exigeant qu'en même
> temps elle ne cessât pas de l'embrasser. Chaque baiser appelle un autre
> baiser. Ah! dans ces premiers temps où l'on aime, les baisers naissent si
> naturellement! (R, 238)[9]

The musical phrase is a call, a movement of the self toward the summit
of spiritual perfection, toward the height of self-transformation, since it
calls forth from "ces premiers temps" when life, like the lovers' kisses, has
the naturalness, rhythm, movement, vibrations, sounds, tones, and pauses
of a symphony. The phrase invites Swann to be born; it asks him to listen to
the deepest aspect of himself, the mind, the reserve, which is all that he is.
"Même quand il [Swann] ne pensait pas à la petite phrase, elle existait
latente dans son esprit" (R, 350). This invitation is a thought without concept; a voice without words and without sound; a hearing without tones; a
seeing without images; a smell without scents; a touch without feeling. This
is a call of the profound night when the self wordlessly contemplates itself
in its phenomenal and spiritual existence: it recognizes that the self is time-
bound, with time as its goal, and that the divine world is merely the creation of thought, of the artist's reserve. In this contemplative act, the musical phrase reflects back to the self its thought, its memory, its "premiers
temps," and the self comes to see that living is a constant act of dying;
living is an eternal dread, an ever-existing dark night with neither light to
illuminate it, nor dawn to relieve it. Even the memory is earthbound: it,
too, like the kisses, will vanish. This is the moral dryness, the fear, and the
sadness that not even a memory lasts. The yearning for spiritual consummation with the beloved is a yearning without attainment; for "chaque
baiser appelle un autre baiser," till in its final kiss, in its final embrace, in
its final good-bye, the mind's eye seems to behold a glimmer of the highest
rapture. It is the ecstasy of the self returning to nothingness, to the void, to
the abyss, to the divine desert, of loving no more, of the final rejuvenation,
of the time when time indeed stands still and it becomes eternal.

> . . . l'idée qu'elle [Odette] était cependant restée là, près du piano, dans
> le moment actuel, prête à être embrassée et possédée, l'idée de sa matér-
> ialité et de sa vie venait l'enivrer [Swann] avec une telle force
> . . . qu'il se précipitait sur cette vierge de Botticelli et se mettait à lui
> pincer les joues. . . . Et, remarquant, pendant ce retour, que l'astre était

maintenant déplacé par rapport à lui et presque au bout de l'horizon, sentant que son amour obéissait, lui aussi, à des lois immuables et naturelles, il se demandait si cette période où il était entré durerait encore longtemps, si bientôt sa pensée ne verrait plus le cher visage qu'occupant une position lointaine et diminuée, et près de cesser de répandre du charme. (*R*, 238–39)[10]

The musical phrase as a vehicle for expressing these immutable laws of birth, extinction, and rejuvenation punctuates the rhythmical movement of our phenomenal existence in those notes of tenderness, passion, serenity, courage, fear, suffering, dread, and dying that compose our interior existence, each one differing from all the rest, as one note, one beat, one measure, one variation of the sonata differs from another. As such, the musical phrase has the objective quality of carrying the sound: this musical phrase of the "notre moi" is at the same time the world of others, the world of uncreated sounds, colors, and forms, the world of divine stillness, unutterable beauty, unspoken discourse, and unplayed melody, where every sounding note, every pause slides from the phenomenal to the simply remembered past, the undifferentiated beginning. As the last sound of the sonata fades into its original key, so the privileged moments vanish into the created phenomena, leaving the self listening to itself. And just as music returns to the same basic phrases so that it seems that the sounds have never been carried away and that music is everywhere and yet always in a determined space, so do we slowly, rhythmically, always move in one gentle unity between birth and rejuvenation, the determined phrase, the limited space, of our existence.

Le beau dialogue que Swann entendit entre le piano et le violon au commencement du dernier morceau! La suppression des mots humains, loin d'y laisser régner la fantaisie . . . l'en avait éliminée; jamais le langage parlé ne fut si inflexiblement nécessité, ne connut à ce point la pertinence des questions, l'évidence des réponses. D'abord le piano solitaire se plaignit, comme un oiseau abandonné de sa compagne; le violon l'entendit, lui répondit comme d'un arbre voisin. C'était comme au commencement du monde, comme s'il n'y avait encore eu qu'eux deux sur la terre, ou plutôt dans ce monde fermé à tout le reste, construit par la logique d'un créateur et où ils ne seraient jamais que tous les deux: cette sonate. Est-ce un oiseau, est-ce l'âme incomplète encore de la petite phrase, est-ce une fée, cet être invisible et gémissant dont le piano ensuite redisait tendrement la plainte? (*R*, 351–52)[11]

To say that the piano and the violin are engaged in a determined dialogue is to say that silence is also determined, since if one partner ceases to play, the other is forced to be silent. Here the piano represents the full experience of the human person's privileged moments, communicated to the violin, which in turn acts as memory of the privileged moments. Whereas on the one hand, the piano has all the lines of the theme, the violin, on the other hand, has only one line and therefore it cannot introduce anything new into the dialogue. In this way as well, the piano determines what the violin plays. However, the violin cannot express the whole range of memories of the privileged moments. Unable to produce all the sounds of the piano, the violin takes some of them and sustains them until they fade into the silence that the piano has forced upon it. This dialogue between piano and violin is thus a discourse between the phenomenal and the spiritual, the visible and the invisible, the outer and the inner self (thought, idea, memory, reserve); it is always in progress, revealing one in the act of concealing the other. Once the dialogue stops, memory, thought, and idea cease to exist, and the self dies either physically or spiritually or both. Hence, death is the key that determines the dialogue. It is the final note, the last sound, the last word, the determined pause, the end of punctuation, the silent truth that the dialogue is not eternal, and that living (remembrance) is a movement toward this determined end. Death, however, is the pathway to rebirth, and whereas the musical dialogue (the phenomenal) envisioned by the original artist must die, the death of that dialogue marks a new beginning for another artist who has privileged moments. Thus, just as in this dialogue between the piano and violin, the song of the bird (piano) is carried away by the wind among the leaves of the trees (violin), the experiences, the memories of the privileged moments within the artist's creation are diffused by the breath of the artist's soul, a breath that is a yearning of the soul for its source, and a breath that disappears into stillness, flows into the boundless, limitless depths of nothingness, which suppresses human words, thereby returning the phrase, the speech, the dialogue to that time immemorial when silence revealed the first human sound.

La parole ineffable d'un seul absent, peut-être d'un mort (Swann ne savait pas si Vinteuil vivait encore), s'exhalant au-dessus des rites de ces officiants, suffisait à tenir en échec l'attention de trois cents personnes, et faisait de cette estrade où une âme était ainsi évoquée un des plus nobles autels où pût s'accomplir une cérémonie surnaturelle. (R, 352)[12]

The ineffable word refers to the determined dialogue of a string of utterances (memories, remembrances, privileged moments) belonging to the world of thought, the inner world of the artist, which is externalized and stamped on the outside. The word not only brings the artist, Vinteuil, out of himself; it also produces an ineffable speech in which he again disappears. The discourse is not burdened by punctuation and empty phrases; the word connects them with silence from which they emerge. In this way, dialogue with the outside ends, including real privileged moments; Vinteuil forces this discourse to end by imposing silence on himself, a silence that awaits a deeper silence, a more ineffable utterance of another solitary artist who will fill out the empty spaces of the discourse with words. What remains then is no longer externally determined but created by the artist within the silence Vinteuil has made. As such, silence speaks of pain, emptiness, terror, dread, and darkness; for indeed, it is the dark night that leads humanity on a journey toward despair. Having removed the punctuation (silence) from the language of determined dialogue, artists impose on themselves both death and life. Death is imposed when they separate themselves by means of a created discourse that chance or habit could at any time destroy, thus annihilating the results of their self-divinization. The ineffable word then is no longer the silence that consecrates, calling us as human beings to the summit of spiritual birth; instead, it is the moral dryness of the isolated individual whose created privileged moments are the only entry into an illusory world of birth, death, and rejuvenation, where perception, discourse, memory, and thought are the various lines of a created sonata.

Longtemps, je me suis couché de bonne heure. Parfois, à peine ma bougie éteinte, mes yeux se fermaient si vite que je n'avais pas le temps de me dire: "Je m'endors." Et, une demi-heure après, la pensée qu'il était temps de chercher le sommeil m'éveillait; je voulais poser le volume que je croyais avoir encore dans les mains et souffler ma lumière; je n'avais pas cessé en dormant de faire des réflexions sur ce que je venais de lire, mais ces réflexions avaient pris un tour un peu particulier; il me semblait que j'étais moi-même ce dont parlait l'ouvrage. . . . Puis elle [cette croyance] commençait à me devenir inintelligible, comme après la métempsycose les pensées d'une existence antérieure; le sujet du livre se détachait de moi, j'étais libre de m'y appliquer ou non; aussitôt je recouvrais la vue et j'étais bien étonné de trouver autour de moi une obscurité, douce et reposante pour mes yeux, mais peut-être plus encore pour mon esprit, à qui elle apparaissait comme une chose sans cause, incompréhensible, comme une chose vraiment obscure. (*R*, 3)[13]

Claudel: The Discovered Cantata

Claudel takes the Proustian idea of "la grande nuit impénétrée et décourageante de notre âme que nous prenons pour du vide et du néant" and carries it as far as it will go, without Proust's fear of darkness, his succumbing to dread, his estrangement from the outside world, and his elimination of the phenomenal self. Night makes Claudel aware of what he is—that he is a solitary not so much because he wants to escape time as because he must discover his being in time; that he is a solitary not so much because he must leave the world as because he must deny himself in order to incarnate divine truth; that he is a solitary not so much because he walks in the light as because he must penetrate his own darkness. "Il faut que la Lumière luise dans de parfaites ténèbres et que ce qui ne sert pas à la recevoir serve du moins à la refléter" (*PP*, 11–12). Human beings, according to Claudel, are called to discover the Light so that they do not fear to be alone in the darkness. And darkness has one purpose: to absorb the human person into the sphere of the eternal Light.

> L'âme se sert de la parole même qui lui est adressée pour y répondre, elle est congénitale à cette question même qui lui est adressée. Elle déclare passionnément à Dieu que Lui seul existe. . . . Sous l'exigence de son amant, tout à coup l'âme s'est arrachée aux ténèbres. . . . De ces ténèbres qui sont son élément propre, elle fait l'instrument de sa confession. Ce sont elles qui lui fournissent aliment, forme et organe. (*PP*, 27–28)[14]

God sees human beings in his light and, therefore, as creatures who are seen, God calls us to see both our darkness (that we are not God), and our light (that we are an image of God). As image, human beings are a mirror, an open window on the darkness of being and on the radiancy of infinite Being, whose essential form places them in a relationship with invisible Being, the light of God, faith.

> Pour connaître l'Etre, c'est notre être lui-même que nous avons à placer avec Lui dans une relation antérieure au matin. . . . La vision nouvelle n'est que le développement de cette bienheureuse nuit en nous de la Foi. (*PP*, 46)[15]

For us to see we must be in darkness; our being must be nothing in order to perceive the light of absolute Being whereby we see the harmonious melody of our life mirroring the divine harmony on the ground of our being, not according to the creating melodies of the artist.

> Cette touche sonore est l'avant-goût et le gage d'un commerce prolongé et détaillé qui, désormais, apparaît réalisable à la condition que notre vacarme intérieur *n'empêche pas la musique*. Il y a donc dans la sonorité divine, au fond de nous, à la fois imprégnation de notre intelligence et ébranlement de notre volonté. (*PP*, 72)[16]

This "touche sonore" is nothing but silence; it is receptive only to divine sound, to the eternal word. For the music of divine harmony within us is our destiny, a destiny that takes us on a journey from the day (material reality) to the dawn of the next day (spiritual awakening) through the night (self-negation). During the night, we discover our cantata or magnificat, not through any particular physical or spiritual senses but according to the "connaissance des touches suaves." Night calls us to the darkness of faith, and calls us to journey alone into God's dwelling place where the soul is illumined by his light and transformed from the noises of the day into its eternal glory.

Night thus serves as a stage for humanity's spiritual journey, a point of contact between the sensory reality of the flesh (day) and the spiritual reality of the soul (dawn of a new day). When night is placed in this three-step movement, it is prized as that saving link between the human person as physical being and God's spiritual realm. Building on this three-step journey of the human person as "antérieure au matin," the night and the new visions, Claudel establishes a three-step ascent of the soul toward a communion with the Divine. The stages of this ascent are the soul rooted in the sensory, by which it discovers the rhythm of creation, the word of God; the soul becoming aware of the sweet touches, the divine sonority within itself; and the soul perfected in its new vision, the light of faith. As the soul approaches the great night, it hears a lyric canticle calling it forward and upward:

> Ah, ce soir est à moi! ah, cette grande nuit est à moi! . . .
> Ah, je suis ivre! ah, je suis livré au dieu! j'entends une voix en moi et la mesure qui s'accélère, le mouvement de la joie. . . .
> Que m'importent tous les hommes à présent! Ce n'est pas pour eux que je suis fait, mais pour le
> Transport de cette mesure sacrée! . . .
> Que m'importe aucun d'eux? Ce rythme seul! Qu'ils me suivent ou non? Que m'importe qu'ils m'entendent ou pas?
>
> *(CGO,* 74–75)[17]

To Claudel, the night is the crucial point when we hear both the physical chanting and divine song of God within us. But when the senses become the first stage of the soul's ascent, the sonorous touch is heard as the sacred measure; their value as the instrument for sensing the rhythm of the divine Glory may become also the senses' liability, since we can be redirected only from inside out; that is, because the physical sound we perceive is incapable of carrying us into and through the night. In the night, Claudel sees that the soul not only senses that the physical world is; while sensing it, the soul finds itself awakened to the movement of joy that requires the full attention of inner senses. Music is the appropriate bridge between the soul and the "force nocturne," and since God is divine harmony, the soul comes to perceive the ineffable sound of the unspeakable silent word of God, the incarnate Son, Christ, who "s'adresse à nos *sens,* c'est-à-dire aux différentes formes de notre *sens* intime, à notre sens du sens" *(PP,* 62).

To attain this "sens du sens," the human person must tread a solitary path, a path that requires separation from the phenomenal self and freedom from self-will. We must become as we were when we were not, which is precisely our entrance into darkness, nothingness, nonbeing. Before human beings were a phenomenal self they were eternal selves in God's creative world. However, this solitary path, this breaking with the outside world, refers to a return of the self to its source, the eternal abyss. This return takes place during the great night and after a prolonged period of anguish and of despair. The despair comes because the soul, informed by the corporeal senses, and relying on the imagination, can and does still absorb itself in the remembrance of and desire for sensual forms.

> Combien de temps dans ces ténèbres? vous voyez que je suis presque englouti! Les ténèbres sont mon habitation.
> Ténèbres de l'intelligence! ténèbres du son!
> Ténèbres de la privation de Dieu! ténèbres actives qui sautent sur vous comme la panthère. . . .
> O Seigneur, combien de temps encore? cette veille solitaire et l'endurance de ces ténèbres que vous n'avez pas faites?
>
> (*CGO*, 82)[18]

And yet in this experience of the darkness, of the abyss, there is the passageway to the divine. We must first, however, die to ourselves: "O passion de la Parole! ô retrait! ô terrible solitude / ô séparation de tous les hommes! / O mort de moi-même et de tout, en qui il me faut / souffrir création!" (*CGO*, 86). If only we did not have to suffer for the sacred measure, if only we did not have to worry about "l'idée de moi-même qui était avant moi," if only we did not have to abandon the wellsprings of sensory experiences where the yearning for the world is first formed, we would not have to experience the unbearable solitude. Yet, it is above all this solitude that is the sonorous touch of our inner vision, of God's word in us. It is this solitude that hears

> . . . un cri dans la nuit profonde!
> J'entends mon antique soeur des ténèbres qui remonte une autre fois vers moi,
> L'épouse nocturne qui revient une autre fois vers moi sans mot dire,
> Une autre fois vers moi avec son coeur, comme un repas qu'on se partage dans les ténèbres,
> Son coeur comme un pain de douleur et comme un vase plein de larmes. (*CGO*, 90)[19]

This cry that the self hears is the call of the motherly, feminine aspect of the soul, ready and willing to receive "l'épouse nocturne" who will confer on it "son coeur," thereby leading to full spiritual birth. In this night of solitude, it is the heart that feels, sees, touches, hears, tastes, is impregnated by the Bridegroom as the soul longs after the Word and bears its fruit of praise. It is God's Word as seed sown in the heart of the human person that is the bread of life. It is the "sens du sens" that invades us, spreads in us, conquers us, intoxicates and occupies us entirely, and directs our path. It is through "son coeur" that human beings are brought into the dawn of a new day where they will taste the gift of the bread of sorrow and will savor the precious essence distilled from the vessel filled with tears, which is the self-consuming wine of love, a love beyond material reality gender, sound, and words: "O ami, je ne suis point un homme ni une femme, je / suis l'amour qui est au-dessus de toute parole!" (*CGO*, 52).

Love then is the content of silence, and silence carries the germinal seed of things in their process of formation; it carries "l'activité de l'âme composée sur le son de sa propre parole! / L'invention de la question merveilleuse, le clair dialogue avec le silence inépuisable" (*CGO*, 24); it carries "l'immense octave de la Création" (*CGO*, 42). In the silence of love, we discover little by little the center, the measure, the order, the sound, the breath, the water, the fire, the poetry of the universe; everything is seen as an expression of eternity, everything is in the light of the Creator: "Tout être, comme il est un / Ouvrage de l'Éternité, c'est ainsi qu'il en est l'expression" (*CGO*, 44). In this night of silence filled with love, we are "comme une goutte translucide dans le soleil de Dieu" (*CGO*, 46); we are given "une minute de lumière" to see that we are still earthbound, caught in the darkness of the sensory world, although the light of the new day will finally transform us. In this new vision, the human person still yearns to possess the soul of the beloved and to be united soul to soul, as the two lovers, Ysé and Mesa, attest in *Partage de midi*.

. . . et je suis la raison entre tes bras,
et je suis Ysé, ton âme! . . .
   Et j'entends ta voix dans mes entrailles comme un cri qui ne peut être souffert. . . .
   Il n'y ait plus rien d'autre que toi et moi, et en toi que moi, et en moi que ta possession, et la rage, et la tendresse, et de te détruire et de n'être plus gênée. . . .
   Ah, ce n'est point le bonheur que je t'apporte, mais ta mort, et la mienne avec elle,
   Mais qu'est-ce que cela me fait à moi que je te fasse mourir,
   Et moi, et tout, et tant pis! pourvu qu'à ce prix qui est toi et moi,
   Donnés, jetés, arrachés, lacérés, consumés,
   Je sente ton âme, un moment qui est toute l'éternité, toucher,
   Prendre
   La mienne comme la chaux astreint le sable en brûlant et en sifflant!
(*PM*, 1030)[20]

Here the soul speaks to physical form in a clear dialogue that is an encounter between itself and its bodily experiences, each of which must be consumed until the soul comes to see that it is the complete privation of "l'épouse nocturne." Everything about Ysé's carnal language carries the word to which the soul cleaves and in which it is incarnated. It is the "sens du sens" that penetrates the inexpressible voice in order that the soul sense the cry of the yearning to possess an instant of eternity within the union of "toi et moi." In this dialogue, then, all the senses perceive the soul sensually; sensual love addresses the soul through the language of the physical ("donnés, jetés, arrachés, lacérés, consumés, rage, possession"), becoming one with the soul in the sonorous touch of the body of "son coeur." For this reason Ysé says to Mesa: "Ce n'est point le bonheur que je t'apporte, mais ta mort, et la mienne avec elle." Death to physical reality is the way to the summit of true love and of spiritual perfection, which is the creative breath or the vessel of tears of God's Incarnation, in the whole of the human person (body and soul). Ysé's dialogue, structured around the motif of "Je sente ton âme," is that voice of love that is heard by the senses and touched by the soul through the gates of renunciation or death. It is that voice that speaks of marriage after the self has emptied itself of its willful existence.

> C'est l'âme qui reçoit l'âme et toutes choses en toi sont devenues claires.
> La voici donc au seuil de ma maison, la Parole qui est comme une jeune fille éternelle!
> Ouvre la porte! et la Sagesse de Dieu est devant toi comme une tour de gloire et comme une reine couronnée! . . .
> Ne me touchez point! ne cherche pas à prendre ma main.
>
> (*CGO*, 52)[21]

Claudel tells us that in order to attain clarity of vision or clear dialogue, we must have passed through the night and achieved communion with the Divine through death. To have died means to have recovered the centre, "la juste mesure," the permanent, the end, the word that gave us our initial movement and rhythm. Clear dialogue enables us to renounce self and the outside world; we cease to be material and mental existence and become a spiritual body with spiritual senses. The cause of this spiritualization is the intoxication, the "vin de la Gloire"; it is the rapture in which we have been consumed in the bosom of the "Nuit Maternelle," so that we lie silent in the voice of adoration, transfigured and resplendent in the darkness, in pure communion with our source, our origin. In this clear dialogue, we know nothing about anything; what we perceive through the sonorous touch is the profound night, the shadows where resides the highest beatitude, "l'épouse nocturne," the "fiancé Cantique." When we speak of this clear dialogue, it is only in words of darkness, in sounds of silence; yet this discourse is the essential light that we cannot reach or the hymn we cannot sing naturally. It is here in this clear dialogue that we are led above self, above all that we can perceive, conceive, and understand. Silently we are in the sacred measure of things; silently, in a slow rhythm, we are led along the road to the attainment of a moment of eternity. Whereas on the one hand, the measure of the day (material reality) is clamorous, disorderly, opaque, and noisy; on the other hand, the eternal morning is tuned, harmonious, transparent, and quiet. In this clear dialogue it is not so much the equal measure of the day that connects it with another day but the "veille solitaire" with which each day is born. This clear dialogue is the "force nocturne" because there is no way to penetrate it, save through the spiritual eyes that take this darkness around themselves and transform it into the "connaissance des touches suaves," the "sens du sens." In the pure tones of this clear dialogue the human person drinks living water from its source, the vessel filled with tears, which is a fountain flowing into itself where nothing flows, since everything exists in the soundless divine sonority of the divine ground. "L'eau qui est claire voit par notre oeil et sonore entend / par notre oreille et goûte / Par la bouche vermeille" (*CGO*, 47). This clear water is fresh, pure, translucent, delightful, and soundless; it is the spring in which we submerge ourselves, with all that we are, with all that we are capable of, in order to quench our yearning, our thirst, our hunger, and our cry with an abundance of tears that flow from the heart. Here in this clear dialogue, the soul delights in the "trône de Dieu"; here, the word has discovered firm ground amidst the waters and storms of the material world; it has discovered "aliment, forme et organe." "Et je fais l'eau avec ma voix, telle l'eau qui est l'eau / pure, et parce qu'elle nourrit toutes choses, toutes choses / se peignent en elle" (*CGO*, 45). But this dryness, this yearning, this lamentation of the soul is impossible to assuage here on earth, and consequently we sink and disappear into the darkness, just as water soaks into the ground after a drought.

Clear dialogue allows us to discover the harmony of the cantata in which the single sound of a solitary voice is perfected in a more complete discourse of the many voiced *Magnificat* in response to God's revealed love, which makes us burst out singing:

> Faites que je sois entre les hommes comme une personne sans visage et ma
> Parole sur eux sans aucun son comme un semeur de silence, comme un semeur de ténèbres, comme un semeur d'églises,
> Comme un semeur de la mesure de Dieu.
>
> (*CGO*, 98)[22]

Human beings and God are not two incompatible substances; instead, the
"mesure de Dieu" is precisely the incarnate Word, which is this "semeur
de silence," this clear dialogue that presupposes that one voice without
sound is there, and our magnificat is the answer to the Magnificat of God.
We are always involved in a discourse with all creation in which the
"mesure de Dieu" measures how far we have advanced toward realizing our
harmony with the divine sonority both within the self and in things. The
likeness of the Creator that we discover in the Word is this clear dialogue,
this life-giving measure of the intimate rhythm of created things. God's
image is the word whose "touche sonore," whose "sens du sens," whose
"connaissance des touches suaves," reverberates through all creation, and
yet each echo of the divine voice has a unique pitch that we recognize and
echo back. "Poëte, j'ai trouvé le mètre. Je mesure l'univers avec / son
image que je constitue" (CGO, 101). This is the origin of the light with
which the poet, this solitary person, is flooded and that bestows on him or
her a share in the divine life, a life that arises from the "nuit profonde,"
from the "terrible solitude," and from the "vase plein de larmes." In this
way, the beloved ("la parole") is indeed the "Nuit Maternelle," because
through the beloved alone we embrace our material existence, and through
the night we receive our spiritual birth, our "sens du sens." It is only then
that we see clearly the purpose of our being born, the end of our existence,
and the reason for our name—joy, consecration, adoration, and exultation
in union with the Creator.

> Car d'une part toute la nature sans moi est vaine; c'est moi qui lui
> confère son sens; toute chose en moi devient
> Éternelle en la notion que j'en ai; c'est moi qui la consacre et qui la
> sacrifie.
> L'eau ne lave plus seulement le corps mais l'âme, mon pain pour moi
> devient la substance même de Dieu.
>
> (CGO, 104)[23]

Conclusion: Silence

Notes and rests, scale and mode, movement and rhythm, modulation
and tempo are the primary characteristics of musical discourse. Both
Proust and Claudel use musical language to measure clearly humanity's
movement from material to spiritual reality; their written word is musical,
which begins to sound gently in us, no matter how diverse our own spiritual
music may be. Proust asserts that the memory of the musical phrase of
Vinteuil's created sonata can be the bridge transporting us to recapture
privileged moments in a determined dialogue with the self. The cantata
Claudel hears as he passes through the night is a crescendo, a rhythmic

movement that enables us to discover the "sonorité divine" within all creation and to respond to God's Word in a clear dialogue. Music as employed by Proust and Claudel is in fact nothing but the resonance of the word, which we can hear through a discourse with their written words.

The syllable, word, phrase, and theme are the elements of the artistic discourse of both Proust and Claudel; they make up the components of the created or discovered harmony; they are the impulses that bring the word to life, disperse it limitlessly through creation, and concentrate it in a definite space, giving duration to speech. Speech is fulfilled only when the word comes forth from discourse, which takes place in relation to either a created (self-spoken) word, or a discovered (unspoken) Word. But whether created or discovered, the word reveals humans as the beings who speak the audible harmony of their passage from sensual reality to spiritual speech. In the sensory the word is melody of discourse.

Proust's self-spoken word returns to silence with the demise of memory (thought). The prospect of this silence fills him with terror, dread, and hopelessness because this word has lost its connection with an origin outside himself. The word that is uttered by Proust is totally locked up within the soul of human beings (reserve, inner essence) and their memory, and therefore the word must perish when they do. To forestall the occurrence of this silence, Proust looks to the musical phrase as the only measure that can identify and preserve privileged moments. Because memory has no connection with anything phenomenal, even the musical phrase fails to transport us out of the self to communion with what is there, in the outside. Consequently, we remain in our own room (inner self), surrounded by darkness, which is finally replaced by the ultimate darkness of death.

Claudel's unspoken word returns to the primordial silence, to the still voice, to the unuttered sound, to the eternal darkness in which we lose ourselves in ecstatic intoxication and communion with the divine Word, our true origin, our breath within self, our image. The prospect of this silence fills us with anguish as we contemplate the loss of material concerns. The passage through the silence, although painful, also fills us with unexpected joy because we perceive the bliss that awaits us at the end of our journey. Claudel believes that as we pass through the darkness of the night to the dawn of the new day we discover our original Magnificat, which echoes God's Magnificat, and join the celestial choir in an eternal life of praise to the Creator.

4

Proust and Braque: Form and Reality

. . . je ne pus plus voir sans plaisir Mme Elstir, et son corps per-
dit de sa lourdeur, car je le remplis d'une idée, l'idée qu'elle était
une créature immatérielle, un portrait d'Elstir. . . . On sent
bien, à voir les uns à côté des autres dix portraits de personnes
différentes peintes par Elstir, que ce sont avant tout des Elstir.
(*R*, 851)[1]

I must, therefore, create a new sort of beauty, the beauty that
appears in terms of volume, of line, of mass, of weight, and
through that beauty interpret my subjective impression.
Nature . . . suggests emotion, and I translate emotion into art. I
want to expose the Absolute, and not merely the factitious
woman. (*CU*, 53)

Whereas music communicates directly to the senses, carrying the soul to
an immediate experience of the privileged moment, visual arts such as
painting emphasize the tactile element of experience and so lead the soul
from external harmonies to the mental perception of the inner harmony of
things. This path to the privileged moment, although less direct, is more
useful because it teaches us how to attain the privileged moment through
contemplation or perception of the sensual world by enabling us *to see* the
reserve in things around us. Proust praises the painter Elstir for his portrayal of the idea (immaterial equivalent) that is created to indicate the
inner reserve of things. Thus, for Proust the idea is a purely subjective
creation by an artist such as Elstir, since he cannot fully communicate the
absolute, the form, the incommunicable mystery, the objective beauty, the
archetypal image of the feminine, the natural harmonies of masses, lines,
and colors. When Braque speaks of translating the experiences of the
senses, however, and of creating a new beauty, he seems to echo the view
of art and reality expressed by Proust when he says of Elstir's paintings:
"Que ce sont avant tout des Elstir." Yet Proust's reality is not Braque's
reality; Braque's art aims at representing things in their three-dimensional
configuration and from that creation to interpret his subjective impression.
Because Proust and Georges Braque (1882–1963) are associated with

French artistic movements of impressionism and cubism respectively, Braque's paintings provide a worthy focus for a comparative study of Proust's notion of form and reality, nature and art. For Braque, painting is not only a matter of giving expression to reality, but also of transcending it through contained emotion.

The reader of *A la recherche du temps perdu* searches in vain for some objective principle or measure in the works of Elstir: a phenomenal uniqueness differentiating each person painted; an ordered definite boundary to the color of each landscape represented; a definite geometric space among the many impressions, sensations, images depicted; an objective correspondence between the painted objects and the objects themselves in their materiality. The play of light and shade and the color of the composition, as well as the images reproduced, reveal no apparent guiding logic, yet they are true to nature; this is so because the subjective perception of the artist produces this nature within himself or herself, thereby substituting art for reality. Proust's narrator says:

> Depuis que j'en avais vu dans des aquarelles d'Elstir, je cherchais à retrouver dans la réalité, j'aimais comme quelque chose de poétique . . . j'essayais de trouver la beauté là où je ne m'étais jamais figuré qu'elle fût, dans les choses les plus usuelles, dans la vie profonde des "natures mortes." (*R*, 869)[2]

Rooted as this nature is in perceived reality, the phenomenal world is reduced in the thought of Proust to the idea within the individual artist, the idea that inspires the artist to create a still life, that is, to create a plastic substitute for a reality dependent purely on chance (the emotional state of the artist). For indeed every phenomenon, every object, when its mass, volume, and weight are separated from its form vanishes into thin air only to be replaced by a reality created exclusively of appearances (forms); and the work of art itself reveals the forms as a state of "idéalisme subjectif . . . phénoménisme pur" (*R*, 816), a state in which what is is completely transfigured by the response it elicits from the idea (inner self). It is this response that for Proust becomes the memory or remembrance of the form, the reality that the artist keeps in mind while painting.

Braque's new beauty, on the other hand, does not wholly dispense with the phenomenal world, with what is there, even though the outside is interpreted subjectively. Braque writes: "The subject is not the object; it is the new unity, the lyricism which stems entirely from the means employed" (*CU*, 147). And the means Braque employs are forms and colors that accord with the artist's idea, not the object itself. Braque's new beauty thus is not concerned with creating fully idealized forms; rather, it creates forms that do not transcend objective phenomena. Braque's new (subjective) forms are spatio-temporal images, which correspond to a new unity of reflective feelings by means of clearly perceived (objective) forms. "Nobility," Braque insists, "comes from contained emotion" (*CU*, 147). In other words, it is from this synthetic unity of subjective perception and objective forms that Braque wants to express the absolute. In the case both of the artist who contains emotion in the face of objective nature and of the one who imagines a subjective reality, the idea is still that which reads the form inscribed in the nature of things, although each artist conceives the nature of things differently.

Elstir's Paintings: A Substitute for Reality

Proust's notion of form and reality is grounded in the privileged moments, when the inner self becomes one with the phenomenal world, and the mind's eye perceives the forms within the phenomenal world. This occurs because the yearning and the thirst of human beings, as they strive for self-divinization, are momentarily quenched when they find ecstasy in artificially created forms. The genius of an artist, then, consists in the "formule de son inconscient" (*R*, 851) by which the artist at once perceives and reveals the forms within the phenomenal, as it were, from their full transparency, from their inside and outside at the same time, from their elemental components. The artist's eye alone sees the idea, the form of things, and only through the artist's unconscious gift can the idea become visual reality hidden in the phenomenal; the artist's eye alone can penetrate to the mystery of the forms beneath their outward appearances; the artist's eye alone can unveil the invisible forms, the inconceivable images that lie there in the phenomenal world.

> Toute cette harmonie factice que la femme a imposée à ses traits . . . cette harmonie, le coup d'oeil du grand peintre la détruit en une seconde, et à sa place il fait un regroupement des traits de la femme, de manière à donner satisfaction à un certain idéal féminin et pictural qu'il porte en lui. (*R*, 861)[3]

Thus considered, a painting is both an imitation (or representation) and a creation. It is an imitation, although it substitutes a new and different arrangement of the original features, for the artist is nevertheless reproducing the forms (outward expressions) of the object. It is a creation because the painted object is not an objective datum of reality. As a creation, however, the picture is objective; its existence is both physical and lasting. The artist's idea must directly intervene in what is natural, in what is already there, so that the "idéal féminin et pictural" (original form) can be represented in such a way as to be pleasing to the senses. This pictorial ideal is nothing but the outward expression of the artist's unconscious gift (inner self), which reveals the phenomenal forms in their lines, shapes, colors, and planes. Speaking to Proust's narrator, Elstir says:

> On ne reçoit pas la sagesse, il faut la découvrir soi-même après un trajet que personne ne peut faire pour nous, ne peut nous épargner, car elle est un point de vue sur les choses. (R, 864)[4]

It is this wisdom that selects forms from the phenomenal world; the inner wisdom, the unconscious gift of the artist, is brought forth purely through the painting, which reveals material reality in its essential harmony.

Artists then represent the forms of things as they see them. Elstir utilizes this unconscious gift in order to transcribe movable reality into a pause, a permanent reality. And Elstir's art gives pause to natural (phenomenal) forms through imagery: what Elstir paints is an "image singulière d'une chose connue" (R, 838), an image different from what the viewer sees because it is painted, not from a central perspective, not in a well defined geometric space, not using natural colors that emanate from the objects themselves but from the laws of "illusions optiques" (R, 838). On the one hand, these laws maintain the relative position of the images painted and on the other hand, reduce the images to indeterminate, fluidlike, vaporlike forms, mirages. As a mirage, the painting, instead of representing objects in their natural forms, creates an ethereal, mystical tableau in which the observer discovers no fixed boundaries, no lines of separation among the objects represented, and no distinction between natural and artistic forms. The unconscious gift of the artist reduces some phenomenal forms to nothing and elevates others to their poetic clarity: sea, land, heavens, clouds, rain, trees, birds, and humans are transformed into artistic forms in a way that is completely the artist's own doing, the artist's own creation. "Je désirais vivement aller retrouver dans la réalité ce qui m'exaltait si fort et j'espérais que le temps serait assez favorable pour voir du haut de la falaise les mêmes ombres bleues que dans le tableau d'Elstir" (R, 902).

What inspires Proust's narrator and inflames his imagination about Elstir's paintings is the "métamorphose des choses représentées" (R, 835), as in the painting of the harbor of Carquethuit where we read of Elstir "n'employant pour la petite ville que des termes marins, et que des termes urbains pour la mer" (R, 836). Elstir uses the forms of the phenomenal world in a way that is completely his own: he recreates stone as "vaporeuse que l'ombre" (R, 839), white sails as "papillons endormis" (R, 389), a river broken up by "une colline couronnée de bois," a path on which a mountain ridge, the spray of a certain fall, or the sea keep one "de suivre la continuité de la route" (R, 840). In short, everything about Elstir's paintings is true to nature, yet natural forms become subordinate to an abstract, artistic unity.

> Mais les rares moments où l'on voit la nature telle qu'elle est, poétiquement, c'était de ceux-là qu'était faite l'oeuvre d'Elstir. Une de ses métaphores les plus fréquentes dans les marines qu'il avait près de lui en ce moment était justement celle qui, comparant la terre à la mer, supprimait entre elles toute démarcation. C'était cette comparaison. . . qui y introduisait cette multiforme et puissante unité. . . . . (*R*, 835–36)[5]

The multiform creation achieved by Elstir is not the product of the direct use of phenomenal forms, but of a process that represents them as singular and seductive. It is because of this that Proust derives a great deal of pleasure from Elstir's paintings, a delight that is "matériellement réalisé déjà dans la nature" (*R*, 847) and awaits the unconscious gift of the artist to evoke that "idéal féminin et pictural" from material forms.

> Que de tels objets puissent exister, beaux en dehors même de l'interprétation du peintre, cela contente en nous un matérialisme inné, combattu par la raison, et sert de contrepoids aux abstractions de l'esthétique. (*R*, 847–48)[6]

Elstir's artistic eye allows him to express his unconscious gift using any form he wants; he does not consider esthetic rules of abstractions because he finds them a stumbling block to his "idéal féminin et pictural," which allows him to see beyond the formal, to see that forms exist as the outward expression of his innate materialism.

In Elstir's paintings, the esthetic has no importance by itself and is meaningful only insofar as it reveals the artist's unconscious gift (inner sense). Only through the expression of an innate materialism can the artist interpret reality itself. The only esthetic guide is the principal of the "métamorphose des chose représentées" (*R*, 835) whereby Elstir transforms phenomenal forms into other forms of his own creation. This is the basis of Elstir's art and it becomes for Proust the core of his inner self. Just as in his painting Elstir renounces the rules of esthetic theories, the harmonious hierarchical progression of natural forms, and instead uses only those forms and colors that allow him to create a new order of forms of which he himself is the highest, so Proust renounces formal (habitual) memory as the human person's innermost reality, which alone makes possible our essential form as an image other than itself, and substitutes for it his unconscious gift by which the privileged moments we have created intrude into the memory and usurp control of it for a time. Just as esthetic theory cannot provide Elstir with an immediate and sensory "idéal féminin et pictural," so too our habitual memory is incapable of translating the multiple impressions it receives from the outside world into logical categories that can be understood by reason.

> Probablement ce qui fait défaut, la première fois, ce n'est pas la compréhension, mais la mémoire. Car la nôtre, relativement à la complexité des impressions auxquelles elle a à faire face pendant que nous écoutons, est infime, aussi brève que la mémoire d'un homme qui en dormant pense mille choses qu'il oublie aussitôt, ou d'un homme tombé à moitié en enfance qui ne se rappelle pas la minute d'après ce qu'on vient de lui dire. (*R*, 529–30)[7]

Consequently, just as esthetic difficulties inherent in painting as an intellectual act are solved once the artist's innate materialism attains the "formule de son don inconscient," so our habitual memory must be deepened in order to express our deepest longing, that inner reserve from which certain forms, patterns, colors, and impressions emerge and are impressed onto the outside world.

> La nature . . . comme une métamorphose de nymphe, nous a immobilisés dans le mouvement accoutumé. De même, nos intonations contiennent notre philosophie de la vie, ce que la personne se dit à tout moment sur les choses. Sans doute ces traits n'étaient pas qu'à ces jeunes filles. Ils étaient à leurs parents. L'individu baigne dans quelque chose de plus général que lui. A ce compte, les parents ne fournissent pas que ce geste habituel que sont les traits du visage et de la voix, mais aussi certaines manières de parler, certaines phrases consacrées, qui presque aussi inconscientes qu'une intonation, presque aussi profondes, indiquent, comme elle, un point de vue sur la vie. Il est vrai que pour les jeunes filles, il y a certaines de ces expressions que leurs parents ne leur donnent pas avant un certain âge, généralement pas avant qu'elles soient des femmes. On les garde en réserve. (*R*, 909)[8]

According to Proust, although individual artists differ from each other in the type of art form they choose to develop (just as paintings differ from each other in their material composition), nevertheless, what makes art possible is the artists' inner reserve, which transcends their individual personalities, while material forms of the world serve as the principle of individuation. For some individuals it is musical form (Vinteuil), for others, literary (Bergotte), for others still, it is painting (Elstir) that causes esthetic enjoyment. These external manifestations of the various art forms become insignificant when the unconscious gift of all artistic expression is revealed. The reserve is the inner sense that drives the artist to create; it is the point of view from which the artist perceives reality and in which "l'idéal féminin et pictural" reveals itself. It is this "quelque chose de plus général que lui" that is the source of the artist's creative imagination; in this reserve the specific composition of the artist's work has the potential to manifests itself in the original artistic forms that serve as parents. The artist, however, unlike the biological parent, conceives and reproduces by substituting forms which then act as real living forms. These forms are manifestations of the artist's unconscious gift, and like the expressions of an individual, they cannot be fully foreseen since they are stored in the reserve until they actualize themselves in nature as the incarnation of the perfect work of art, as the "métamorphose de nymphe."

> Je regardais les trois arbres, je les voyais bien, mais mon esprit sentait qu'ils recouvraient quelque chose sur quoi il n'avait pas prise. . . . N'appartenaient-ils au contraire qu'à ces paysages du rêve, toujours les mêmes, du moins pour moi en qui leur aspect étrange n'était que l'objectivation dans mon sommeil de l'effort que je faisais pendant la veille, soit pour atteindre le mystère. . . soit pour essayer de le réintroduire dans un lieu que j'avais désiré connaître et qui, du jour où je l'avais connu, m'avait paru tout superficiel, comme Balbec? (*R*, 717–18)[9]

Elstir's paintings are the culmination of the metamorphosis of nature; his paintings reveal what he sought in trees, flowers, towns, landscapes, people, and the sea, both in their physical and their poetic existence. What Elstir seeks is a perfect likeness of himself as creative mind. "Comme des ombres ils [arbres] semblaient me demander de les emmener avec moi, de les rendre à la vie" (*R*, 719). Elstir fully recognizes the significance of material objects as being nothing but shadows of nature. He brings things back to life by reproducing their forms and tonality of color as his artist's eye records them at a particular instant, totally from his inner sense, which allows him to paint the sea as an orange mass when it is blue and to paint the shadows as blue when they appear black. On his entrance into Elstir's studio, Proust's narrator remarks:

> [Je] me sentis parfaitement heureux, car par toutes les études qui étaient autour de moi, je sentais la possibilité de m'élever à une connaissance poétique, féconde en joies, de maintes formes que je n'avais pas isolées jusque-là du spectacle total de la réalité. (*R*, 834)[10]

The poetic knowledge invoked with respect to Elstir's forms implies the "formule du don inconscient" of the artist, a gift that allows Elstir to isolate new forms, impressions, and images from the total spectacle of reality, thereby constantly recreating nature. Elstir's paintings, then, delight the narrator because they reveal the mystery, thought, idea, or reserve of the material objects without which they would not exist. But in revealing nature's idea, Elstir also realizes his esthetic feeling and memories, which serve as a basis for the poetic knowledge. The manifestation of "l'idéal féminin et pictural" is revealed to Elstir within his memories. Not every memory has this power: only those recollections of poetic knowledge capable of joining together what is incompatible in natural forms—material forms with thought—and not the memories of habitual life. The revelation of thought as "l'idéal féminin et pictural" is this poetic knowledge of the artist. Thus material forms, too, have an interior form based on thought. For once material forms become completely ideas in paintings, they become pure dreams, pure memories of the artist. In this way, the paintings are internally conjoined in the reserve with the memories of the artist governing the unconscious gift, directing it toward sense impressions. Again, speaking of the trees, Proust writes:

> Fallait-il croire qu'ils venaient d'années déjà si lointaines de ma vie que le paysage qui les entourait avait été entièrement aboli dans ma mémoire? . . . Ou encore ne cachaient-ils même pas de pensée et était-ce une fatigue de ma vision qui me les faisait voir doubles dans le temps comme on voit quelquefois double dans l'espace? Je ne savais. Cependant ils venaient vers moi; peut-être apparition mythique, ronde de sorcières ou de nornes qui me proposait ses oracles. Je crus plutôt que c'étaient des fantômes du passé, de chers compagnons de mon enfance, des amis disparus qui invoquaient nos communs souvenirs. (*R*, 718–19)[11]

The truth of the artist's poetic knowledge demands the obliteration of the material forms of the objects represented in the paintings. The artist experiences objects, landscapes, time, people, and events primarily as shadows, phantoms, apparitions of the past. The artist does not conceive of them in their phenomenal reality but in their sensory (imaginative) effect. Memories, not esthetics, brush aside everything that conceals reality from the artist's inner feeling in order to bring him face to face with the hidden form of reality itself. The yearning to express reality itself, the inner form, to make reality as it is, leads the artist to perceive the still forms within the material world. These still forms in paintings are a substitute for changing forms of reality itself. Although unmoving, these forms are based on the representation of phenomenal forms and colors that direct the mind of the observer away from the materiality of the objects portrayed toward the idea of the painting itself and therefore of the inner living reality of the phenomenal. A still life, for example, must substitute thought forms for natural forms and express these thought forms through colors; or expressive colors invest the still life with a new and deeper source of life by substituting pure images for material forms.

> Depuis que j'en avais vu dans des aquarelles d'Elstir, je cherchais à retrouver dans la réalité, j'aimais comme quelque chose de poétique, le

geste interrompu des couteaux encore de travers, la rondeur bombée
d'une serviette défaite où le soleil intercale un morceau de velours
jaune, le verre à demi vidé qui montre mieux ainsi le noble évasement de
ses formes et, au fond de son vitrage translucide et pareil à une condensation du jour, un reste de vin sombre mais scintillant de lumières, le
déplacement des volumes, la transmutation des liquides par l'éclairage,
l'altération des prunes qui passent du vert au bleu et du bleu à l'or dans
le compotier déjà à demi dépouillé, la promenade des chaises vieillottes
qui deux fois par jour viennent s'installer autour de la nappe, dressée sur
la table ainsi que sur un autel où sont célébrées les fêtes de la gourman-
dise, et sur laquelle au fond des huîtres quelques gouttes d'eau lustrale
restent comme dans de petits bénitiers de pierre; j'essayais de trouver la
beauté là où je ne m'étais jamais figuré qu'elle fût, dans les choses les
plus usuelles, dans la vie profonde des "natures mortes." (R, 869)[12]

Braque's Paintings: A Representation of Reality

In the previous quotation describing a still life, "le geste interrompu" of
knives lying across one another, the "rondeur bombée" of a napkin, the
"verre à demi vidé" with its curved sides, "le déplacement" of solid objects, the transmutation of liquids—all culminate in the continuously
emerging colors of yellow velvet, green, blue and golden-yellow of the
plums with the effect of light and shade. Everything seems translucent,
crystal clear, as "une condensation du jour." As Proust's artistic eye makes
its journey through Elstir's watercolors, it becomes subject to the same
sense of daylight represented in the painting, and slowly the mind's eye
sees less of the reflected lights of the objects represented and more of the
condensation of the imitated forms; it itself becomes the still life, the trans-
cript of nature created by the unconscious gift of the artist.

Like Proust, Braque also is interested in finding beauty, poetic knowledge, in reality, in the still forms of things. He also is motivated by the
same subjective awareness of reality as Proust. For Proust, however, esthetic reality does not exist objectively in phenomenal things; instead,
although it may be imputed to phenomenal objects, it exists exclusively in
the unconscious gift of the subject as artist. For Braque, the senses perceive the artistic form already there in things, but they cannot grasp it in its
full perfection, that is, poetically. According to Braque, "la nature ne donne pas le goût de la perfection. On ne la conçoit ni meilleure ni pire" (IN,
2). Consequently, a gulf always remains between the painted forms and
phenomenal reality itself. As part of the artistic desire to represent material reality as it is and not ideally, as the artist sees it: "Le peintre pense en
formes et en couleurs, l'objet c'est la poétique" (IN, 11). To penetrate to
poetic beauty, the artist resorts to visual and tactile space and transforms

material forms into various perspective planes and geometric figures. This is done with a view to drawing the observer physically closer to the painting while at the same time maintaining the inherent gulf between the factuality of these forms as painted objects and their real physical existence. "L'espace visuel sépare les objets les uns des autres. L'espace tactile nous sépare des objets" (*IN*, 78). Whereas on the one hand this method prevents the eye from seeing any real visual space between the objects painted, on the other it adds to tactile space by introducing into the painting as many components of material objects as necessary to make them recognizable.

Visual and tactile space, form and colors, are means by which the artist represents the whole of the phenomenal world. These forms and colors become the concepts by means of which artists interpret their subjective impressions and draw the observer closer and closer to the artistic form. "Le tableau est fini quand il a éffacé l'idée. L'idée est le ber du tableau" (*IN*, 80). This is the principle that allows the artist to connect heterogeneous forms in a homogeneous visual and tactile space without destroying the idea, which gives poetic understanding, poetic form, to the painting. Braque concludes: "Il n'est en art qu'une chose qui vaille: Celle que l'on ne peut expliquer" (*IN*, 13). This inexplicable thing (the idea, the absolute, or formlessness) that moves artists to create both directs their inner senses toward real objects and at the same time limits their subjective impression by subjugating it to objective phenomenal forms of which painting is a representation. "Les moyens limités engendrent les formes nouvelles, invitent à la création, font le style. Le progrès en art ne consiste pas à étendre ses limites, mais à les mieux connaître" (*IN*, 33). Fragmentations of material forms, the interlocking of visual and tactile space, the replacement of natural light with various shades of colors, the use of lines, volume, and mass to express the depth of the objects as they are—that is, in their geometric volumes—all these are means by which the artist lays bare the germ of the phenomenal itself. "Je n'ai pas à déformer. Je pars de l'informe et je forme. Je ne cherche pas la définition. Je tends vers l'Infinition" (*IN*, 117).

The stand taken by Braque depends on the following principle: artistic forms tend toward "l'infinition" primarily because in order for something to be seen as formless it must be defined within the inner image and outer boundaries of material forms. The painting is thus both the objectivization of "l'infinition," which is but exists phenomenally only as the unformed within objects, and the idea that is the expression of the artist's subjectivity, limited and defined by the nature of "l'infinition" itself. Only thus can Braque say: "Le vase donne une forme au vide et la musique au silence" (*IN*, 48). This identity of the void with the material form, from which artistic form emerges, and the identity of the silence with musical form, by which the formless, the infinite, the absolute unite idea with material form,

Georges Braque, *The Duo*. **Oil on canvas,** $39\frac{3}{8} \times 51\frac{1}{8}$ **in., 1937.** (*Courtesy of the Musée National d'Art Moderne, Centre Georges Pompidou, Paris. Copyright ARS New York / ADAGP, 1988.*)

is the synthesis that is the foundation for artistic expression or poetic discourse: this identity of void and form, uniting subject and object, is the very essence of Braque's esthetic principle. "Rechercher le commun qui n'est pas le semblable" (*IN*, 70). In what can be shared (inner form, idea) the artist sees "l'infinition" and subjectively gives it limited, visible form in accordance with its phenomenal reality. In fact, for Braque, it is the unformed within things that is reality itself, which is perceived as material form that the artist represents. According to Braque, "une chose ne peut être à deux places à la fois. On ne peut pas l'avoir en tête et sous les yeux" (*IN*, 114). To Braque, then, the form of the painting itself should not be the same as the idea of the artist that has given visual representation to the formlessness of things; there must always be a gulf separating the internal form ("tête") of objects from the subjectively perceived reality ("les yeux"). "Réalité. Ce n'est pas assez de faire voir ce qu'on peint. Il faut encore le faire toucher" (*IN*, 4).

Le duet, for example, clearly exemplifies Braque's esthetic principle. Here, the interplay between subjective and objective, void and form, absolute and limited, is represented in changeable material forms placed in an apparent depth relationship to each other, and it invites the observer to participate in and touch the beautiful, which otherwise would be closed off in the blackness of the void, the abyss of the indeterminate, and the formlessness of silence. The painting would simply fade into a visual illusion, an ethereal impression. Instead, in this painting a direct relationship exists between material forms and the complex interweaving of light and dark shapes, and the various geometric figures, located in the central foreground, that produce the musical symbols, which change the objects from a silent, static picture of an event into a formed, limited, and beautiful reality. In fact, *Le duet* can be seen to represent a clear dialogue between the darkness of phenomenal forms and the light of poetic forms; or, better still, between artistic forms themselves (music and painting) and the reality behind them. Hence, the emotional response to art is born of the presence of "l'infinition," of the idea, which becomes visible in material forms and at the same time transcends those objects as created beauty. "Définir une chose, c'est substituer la définition à la chose" (*IN*, 35). A thing is defined and therefore created according to the rule of form and colors, visual and tactile space. Yet, these forms, colors, and spaces express the void, the formless, and say nothing other than what these objects are: namely, piano, chair, two persons, a piece of paper with what appears to be the name of Debussy. By themselves these objects do not create esthetic enjoyment. Poetic beauty is revealed when the artist transforms these objects into artistic forms that move toward "l'infinition" and whose only limitation lies in the pictorial space of the objects that symbolize it. In a way, the name of Debussy indicates the sounds that must be evoked in order for "l'infinition" to be realized in this painting; for music gives the stillness to this painting, a stillness that grows ever deeper into the darkness and mystery of reality. Darkness, then, must become darker, light more luminous, and silence deeper in order for the artist's eye to penetrate into the inner silence (form) of the phenomenal: "La Nuit, la poussière, le sommeil. La Poësie doue les choses d'une vie circonstancielle" (*IN*, 112). In this way, Braque's artistic form represents reality without annihilating it. Braque reminds us that artistic forms are perceived by the senses, which penetrate deep into the translucent light (inner form) of material forms that may be obscured by habit and reason. "C'est une erreur que d'enfermer l'inconscient dans un contour et le situer aux confins de la raison" (*IN*, 49).

This view should not be taken to mean that there are no limits to the inner sense, the unconscious of the artist; rather, what it signifies is that the artist's unconscious gift should not be a substitute for "l'infinition," as is the case in the work of Proust. Material forms should not become realized ideas, or pure impressions, or pure geometric figures, eliminating, deforming the objective inner form of things. It certainly appears that Braque's early paintings, as for example *Nature morte* and *Le portugais*, reveal a certain abstraction or rationalism, an analytical style whereby material forms are reshaped and removed from tactile space, while his later paintings are executed within the confines of form and colors, which act as rules that correct emotion. White, yellow, black, brown, gray, and blue, for example, in *La guitare bleue*, enhance the material forms accordingly, with different colors also revealing differences in the idea of the objects represented. Here colors do not seem to modify "l'infinition" as much as expose, quantify, and define it within visual and tactile space. Form and colors, then, are necessary means to represent nature as it is phenomenally, not as it exists ideally or absolutely in the unconscious gift of the artist. "L'Art est un mode de représentation" (*IN*, 5). As such, of necessity, painting does not essentially contain the natural germ that informs it, the mystery it reveals: that mystery whose effect is that reality ceases to be real (temporal) in order to become a still life, a static object in the creative mind of the artist. "L'émotion ne s'ajoute ni ne s'imite. Elle est le germe [et] l'oeuvre est l'éclosion" (*IN*, 6).

For Braque, then, painting has a higher aim: "Tout est sommeil autour de nous. La réalité ne se révèle qu'éclairée par un rayon poétique" (*IN*, 97). Such indeed is the reality represented, both outwardly (phenomenally) and inwardly, in *Le port*. The scene depicted here bears witness to a "rayon poétique" as a revelation, a light that can pierce the "sommeil autour de nous." Thus, it exists externally: it is the artistic reality of the subject's idea shining out of the sleep of the phenomenal as form and color, visual and tactile space. "Sans brève nous courons après notre destin. Sensation. Révélation" (*IN*, 107). The artist's inner sense illumines this harbor scene,

Georges Braque, *The Blue Mandolin.* **Oil on canvas, 115.7 × 88 cm, 1930.** *(Courtesy of The Saint Louis Art Museum, Museum Purchase, Saint Louis. Copyright ARS New York / ADAGP, 1988.)*

Georges Braque, *Harbor in Normandy.* **Oil on canvas, 81 × 81 cm, 1909.** *(Purchase from the Walter Aitken Fund Income, Major Acquisitions Centennial Fund Income, Martha E. Leverone Fund, and Restricted Gifts of Friends of AIC in honor of Mrs. Leigh B. Block Committee on Major Acquisitions 1970.98. © 1988 The Art Institute of Chicago. All Rights Reserved. Copyright ARS New York / ADAGP, 1988.)*

and what is revealed is the light (inner essence) hidden behind the world of dreams, in the habitual or fortuitous. "C'est le fortuit qui nous révèle l'existence. Au jour le jour" (*IN*, 57). *Le port* represents nature's disclosing and particularizing itself as form and colors, which are the means to touch the formlessness and so reach "l'infinition" of all reality—a reality that also includes the artistic representation of the phenomenal. The "sommeil autour de nous" still remains, and the artist must awaken it and impregnate it with the germ of a creative imagination. To do this, Braque concludes, the artist must be close enough to what is out there to feel, touch, smell, taste, and hear nature's vibrations, yet far enough so as not to be submerged in it. "L'écho répond à l'écho; tout se répercute" (*IN*, 91). Viewers of this painting only need align themselves with this "rayon poétique," whose echoes of the beauty of the painted forms, of the shades of the calming pink, blue, light and dark brown, white, and black and its evocation of a visual and tactile sense of space through the complexes of lines, points, and geometric figures direct and inform the inner (subjective) sense of "l'infinition" while limiting and defining it within the nothingness of reality itself. "Le mystère éclate avec le grand jour. Le mystérieux se confond avec l'obscurité" (*IN*, 58).

The *Nu allongé* reveals the "rayon poétique" of the mystery, of "l'infinition" within a human body. In its essence, the nude, with all its phenomenal forms, touches the mystery, just as the concrete corporeal form reveals the human soul, which demands to be realized phenomenologically, to be called forth not only as naked reality but also as an individuation of the world of sleep, of the mysterious and obscurity to which the soul owes its origin. In a way, the nude compels the observer to enter into and touch the world of dreams, the world of the absolute that is the archetype of the feminine, by revealing the void, darkness, formlessness, and dreams that both shape and limit this represented human form through the variation of light and darkness. The mystery of existence the nude embodies invites the observer to move away from the phenomenal and beyond self to touch in the archetypal feminine image the womb of the invisible dormant in all things, the germ concealed in material forms. In the *Nu allongé*, the artist's sleep has made it possible for him to awaken the mystery of creation; he has given form to the void, light to the darkness, speech to silence, water to the earth, and reality (phenomenon) to the unimaginable. Braque has formed the woman into his own image so that she may in turn echo more clearly how form and flesh, light and darkness, mystery and phenomenon, life and death, although contraries, may be united within the rule of subjective and objective, form and reality. For the mystery of Being is beyond the artist's subjective creation; it is the objective germ that is the form hidden in things, drawing its existence from "l'infinition."

Georges Braque, *The Reclining Nude.* **Oil on canvas, 27 × 40 cm, 1926.** (*Copyright ARS New York / ADAGP, 1988.*)

Conclusion: The Form

The poetic knowledge evoked by Proust and the "rayon poétique" described by Braque share a sense of the divine and the mysterious, of the delights of nature, of "l'infinition," of the void of phenomenal forms as well as of the artist's inner sense, which uses them as artistic form and a means of representing reality itself. Although both Proust and Braque agree that the artist must create new forms from the idea, the unconscious gift, they differ as to what these forms are and how they should be represented. For Proust, the form is total self-expression of the artist's thought, which must be accompanied by a complete metamorphosis of the objects represented. For Braque, the form, revealed in color and shapes, visual and tactile space, exists apart from the artist's thought, although it must be subjectively penetrated so that its ultimate essence may be opened up and revealed. Whereas Braque seems to say that there is a form directing both the phenomenal and the artist toward their respective ends, the perfection of material forms or painting itself, Proust insists that there is no objective verification of this perfection, of this hiddenness within things. For Proust, the original form, "l'idéal féminin et pictural," is essentially a matter of memory, of remembrance; it is the idea of the subject actually made real (objectified) as a substitute for what exists there, on the outside. Everything Elstir paints, Proust concludes, is "avant tout des Elstir."

Elstir's paintings, then, do not constitute a pictorial representation or datum of nature; instead, they are a metaphor for nature, not as it is, which is absolute beauty, absolute form, absolute mystery, but as it is experienced in the unconscious gift of the artist. The world Braque paints is a reality of form and colors, of visual and tactile spaces, and therefore it is a representation, a pictorial fact, of what exists phenomenally. "Le peintre ne tâche pas de reconstituer une anecdote mais de constituer un fait pictural" (*IN*, 22).

However Proust and Braque interpret form and reality, their vision is able to penetrate our own inner sense and invite us to see and touch the phenomenal world; their vision serves as a guide in the direction of a constant dialogue with artistic forms, which echo material forms in their archetypal beauty (Braque) or subjective reality (Proust). Artists create so that others may ascend through their work, to whatever degree they are able, toward the summit of self-perfection. For Braque this self-perfection has an external measure in artistic effort, whereas for Proust, the artist's unconscious gift is itself the final standard of this attainment.

5
Proust and Gabriel Marcel on the Mystery

Swann n'avait donc pas tort de croire que la phrase de la sonate existât réellement. Certes, humaine à ce point de vue, elle appartenait pourtant à un ordre de créatures surnaturelles et que nous n'avons jamais vues. . . . C'est ce que Vinteuil avait fait pour la petite phrase. (*R*, 350–51)[1]

Nous avons donc à nous demander maintenant en quoi consiste au juste cette exigence de transcendance. Je pense que nous devons tenter d'abord de la situer par rapport à la vie telle qu'elle est concrètement vécue, et non pas la définir dans l'éther raréfié qui serait celui de la pensée pure. (*M*, 1:49)[2]

Proust experiences the Form or Idea as a harmonious whole through phenomenal forms. These experiences are fleeting, however, and so he attempts to regain them by the use of metaphors, music, and painting—all the arts—to induce the mind to leave behind the world of habitual experience and journey through dreams into the divine world where the Form or Idea exists. These attempts are only partially successful because they are themselves time-bound. As an alternative way to find a more permanent grasp of Form, Proust turns to intellect to halt the flow of time by the creation of intelligible forms. However, this path is blocked by the evaporation zone, which prevents the intellect from penetrating deep to the reserve within things. In desperation, the intellect creates immaterial equivalents as intelligible substitutes for the unintelligible and impenetrable reserve. This allows Proust to create and to live in a dream world that is itself a substitute for the dream, which is the only path capable of leading him to the Mystery or the Form itself.

In contrast to Proust's view of immaterial equivalents that dissolve the mystery of Being into a function of the interior subjective encounter between memories and the reserve of things, Gabriel Marcel (1887–1973), in his approach to the mystery, not only retains the tensional pull between phenomena and thought but carries this tension to the level of faith, the level of the encounter with God's form, with the absolute Thou who reveals himself so as to be perceived, known, and experienced phenomenolog-ically, that is, intersubjectively. For Gabriel Marcel, faith and encounter go together; faith is our encounter with our existence; it is an invitation to see, and to see our existence more clearly and, at the same time, to be seen as we really are from God's eye, which alone can penetrate the reserve. Thus, the call that faith extends to us to see and to be seen entails a re-sponse, so that existence is confronted by both thought and God's actions. In this response, what formerly had been just a phenomenon now becomes a mystery of reality seen from the light of Being, from God's gift of his Word. Still, in the mystery of the phenomenon, we experience unrest, mental uneasiness, and spiritual uncertainty, even when our existence is brought under the veil of faith.

Both Proust and Gabriel Marcel affirm the hiddenness of the mystery within the phenomenal, and both describe the perception of this mystery as a progression from the phenomenological level to the level of thought. But whereas the mystery Proust tries to make visible is created by thought it-self, by the subject's inner vision or imagination, and has no correspon-dence to an objective image, Gabriel Marcel's mystery retains an objective ground, which is the light of faith—a faith, however, that emerges from the subjective encounter through which we experience it.

Proust: The Imagined Mystery

According to Proust, the mystery demands that we encounter the re-serve of things and be confronted with both the external forms of things and their inner depth from which the mysterious and the beautiful shine forth. In this encounter with the phenomenal, we are brought face to face with the reserve of things and its manifestation, thought and its sensory reality, the soul and its body. In order to experience the mystery, we need to perceive the phenomenal manifestation of this reserve and perceive with the mind's eye as well. Only the mind's eye can cut through to this reserve from which the mystery floods the visible world with luminosity: the mys-tery becomes the measure for all encountered phenomena. The experience of the mystery presupposes, on the one hand, our desire to see, to grasp this reserve and to be enraptured by it, and on the other hand, the evapora-tion zone that brings into focus our power to create images (imagination). In our encounter with the phenomenal, our vision, connecting us with the reserve of things, is eclipsed as it sees more and more the interlocking of the inner self and this reserve of things closed in an ethereal space of pure air. In other words, in this encounter the phenomenal disappears, opening the way for the mind to experience the mystery. Speaking of the chrysan-themums in Madame Swann's house, Proust writes:

Comme des feux arrachés par un grand coloriste à l'instabilité de l'atmos-
phère et du soleil, afin qu'ils vinssent orner une demeure humaine, ils
m'invitaient, ces chrysanthèmes . . . à goûter avidement pendant cette
heure du thé les plaisirs si courts de novembre dont ils faisaient
flamboyer près de moi la splendeur intime et mystérieuse. (R, 596)[3]

The mysterious splendor that illumines the whole of the phenomenal
world, however, is not the reservoir of things in their various external
and concrete forms; rather, it is the world of created images that place
themselves between this depth of things and the perceiver's own vision. To
perceive the mystery and be enraptured by its splendor is to divest the
visible world of its unique essence, thereby giving us the space in which we
become incarnate by substituting color tones of our own creation for those
impermanent tones produced by the phenomenal world. Only in this way
do we perceive the splendor of things and become enraptured by its mystery. Speaking of Albertine and her friends, Proust writes:

Mon désir avait cherché avec tant d'avidité la signification des yeux qui
maintenant me connaissaient et me souriaient, mais qui, le premier jour,
avaient croisé mes regards comme des rayons d'un autre univers. . . . Je
les regardais sans les vider peut-être de tout le médiocre contenu dont
l'expérience journalière les avait remplis, et pourtant (sans me rappeler
expressément leur céleste origine) comme si, pareil à Hercule ou à Télé-
maque, j'avais été en train de jouer au milieu des nymphes. (R, 950)[4]

These lovely forms, however, do not seem to be placed within their spatial
and temporal context; they are "comme des rayons d'un autre univers"
and therefore detached from their "médiocre contenu," floating, melting,
and evaporating before the penetrating gaze of the perceiver's own vision.
Not only are these lovely forms illuminated by the lights of another world,
but also, suffused by the splendor of the nymphs, these phenomenal forms
radiate or project the perceiver into a world of pure forms. This projection
makes it possible for the narrator to empty these visible forms of their
"expérience journalière" and to replace it with "parties immatérielles."
This in turn allows the narrator to enter the domain of pure joy, the realm
of intoxication, the world of dreams, where he encounters his absolute self
in the tensional pull between time past and time regained, between the
contemplating and the contemplated self, between privileged moments and
oblivion. In this encounter, the mystery appears to him in the midst of
dreams, of remembrance.

Dreams enable this "dormeur éveillé" to experience momentary flashes
of the mysterious splendor of things. Dreams free phenomenal forms from
their habitual context; dream forms are abstracted from anything this "dormeur éveillé" recognizes as concrete images. Dreams place phenomenal

forms in an evaporating cloud, which, floating in a windless universe, is filled with the soaring lights of sun, moon, and stars, and in which the mystery, Being itself, is encountered. In dreams, this "dormeur éveillé" sees a world based on mental vision and whose parameters are given by the "zone d'air pur" through which phenomenal forms must pass in order that they may be emptied of their "médiocre contenu" and thus fully reveal the deep reservoir, the inner light, the most profound mental layer of this "dormeur éveillé." In sleep, no gleam of visible light comes to lighten the inward universe of the dreamer, whose luminous senses flow out from the unknown world of the visible, which otherwise he could not penetrate. Lovely forms and the mysterious splendor to which the self looks are not fixed somewhere outside the self, "dans les souvenirs d'une époque histori-que, dans des oeuvres d'art" (*R*, 424). Rather, they are found in the inner depth of memory, which absorbs phenomenal images and creates a multi-ple, dreamlike association of forms. This reverie produces the mysterious splendor that "l'âme ressent d'abord sans en reconnaître la cause, sans comprendre que rien au dehors ne la motive" (*R*, 423). Dreams, therefore, make possible "une sorte de trop-plein spirituel," thereby transforming sensory forms into hidden realities and vice versa. Again, of Albertine, Proust's narrator says:

> Je trouvai Albertine dans son lit. . . . La vue du cou nu d'Albertine, de ces joues trop roses, m'avait jeté dans une telle ivresse (c'est-à-dire avait tellement mis pour moi la réalité du monde non plus dans la nature, mais dans le torrent des sensations que j'avais peine à contenir) que cette vue avait rompu l'équilibre entre la vie immense, indestructible qui roulait dans mon être, et la vie de l'univers, si chétive en comparaison. . . . Je me penchai vers Albertine pour l'embrasser. La mort eût dû me frapper en ce moment que cela m'eût paru indifférent ou plutôt impossible, car la vie n'était pas hors de moi, elle était en moi. . . . Comment cela eût-il été possible, comment le monde eût-il pu durer plus que moi, puisque je n'étais pas perdu en lui, puisque c'était lui qui était enclos en moi, en moi qu'il était bien loin de remplir, en moi où, en sentant la place d'y entasser tant d'autres trésors, je jetais dédaigneusement dans un coin ciel, mer et falaises? (*R*, 932–33)[5]

We are thus balanced upon the life of the mind as if upon a fragile sur-face: above and around us the vastness of the eternal forces of nature, below us that of our own finitude. Our existence is as mysterious as the indestructible life of the phenomenal, which can be totally emptied of its "médiocre contenu" only with difficulty. And to say that "la vie n'était pas hors de moi, elle était en moi" is to say that nothing exists outside our sensibility, the inner necessity to create: "La réalité ne se forme que dans la mémoire" (*R*, 184). But though the life of the universe is accessible only through memory, this same life remains the great reservoir subsisting in our "sol mental," where the origin of things is revealed on the same level as our past life. For example, Proust reports that "c'est au côté de Méséglise que je dois de rester seul en extase à respirer, à travers le bruit de la pluie qui tombe, l'odeur d'invisibles et persistants lilas" (R, 186). The phenomenal is not seen, then, under the life-giving energy of an outside source; rather, it appears as a mystical apparition, a religious tableau of the life of this "dormeur éveillé" who transforms visible forms in his dreams. Indeed, the mystery appears as the hidden source of the life of this "dormeur éveillé" who reconciles within himself both visible and invisible forms.

In the early part of *A la recherche du temps perdu*, speaking of the water-garden along the Vivonne in Guermantes Way, the narrator insists that this garden gave the flowers a

> . . . couleur plus précieuse, plus émouvante que la couleur des fleurs elles-mêmes; et, soit que pendant l'après-midi il fît étinceler sous les nymphéas le kaléidoscope d'un bonheur attentif, silencieux et mobile, ou qu'il s'emplit vers le soir, comme quelque port lointain, du rose et de la rêverie du couchant, changeant sans cesse pour rester toujours en accord, autour des corolles de teintes plus fixes, avec ce qu'il y a de plus profond, de plus fugitif, de plus mystérieux—avec ce qu'il y a d'infini— dans l'heure, il semblait les avoir fait fleurir en plein ciel. (R, 170)[6]

It is in that great reservoir, in that deepest layer of the "sol mental" that our divine spark, our mystical sensibility expresses itself in phenomenal forms, and yet in so doing, it remains hidden behind the changeable; it manifests its being in all that is infinite and eternal, and it lends visible forms their mystery. In this water-garden, a certain interior reality opens the mind's eye and manifests our general sense for the infinite, for the divine. In all visible forms, as they exist in equilibrium between the self and the life of the universe, there is revealed the mystery of being, "l'Esprit éternel," which we can never hope to penetrate even through our creative intelligence.

> Car mon intelligence devait être une, et peut-être même n'en existe-t-il qu'une seule dont tout le monde est co-locataire, une intelligence sur laquelle chacun, du fond de son corps particulier, porte ses regards, comme au théâtre où, si chacun a sa place, en revanche, il n'y a qu'une seule scène. (R, 568)[7]

This single intelligence toward which we must direct our eyes is the obscure desire to create, to see beyond the ceaselessly changing forms of things that mysterious form which is their true reality. And, "comme un être surnaturel et pur qui passe en déroulant son message invisible" (*R*, 347), this single intelligence, which is the great reservoir of things, calls us to empty phenomenal things of that mediocre content and substitute in its place immaterial parts so that we may see clearly the invisible form concealed within the phenomenal. The very possibility of such a vision, however, entails a momentary blindness; for phenomenal forms lose their charm "qui leur vient de la mémoire même et de n'être pas perçus par les sens" (*R*, 427). Thus, far from being a true expression of the mysterious splendor, memory and the senses are its suspension. By detaching visible forms from their concrete context and placing them within the world of immaterial parts, through an intelligence whose power is essentially to create within the memory, we perceive the mystery from the inner darkroom of our own unconscious, which is the realm of fantasy, of dreams. For, indeed, this "sol mental" inciting us to create manifests itself only when visible forms vanish into the "zone d'air pur," thereby mobilizing pure thought as an intelligence of forms. In this context, Legrandin says to the narrator:

"Et voyez-vous, mon enfant, il vient dans la vie une heure, dont vous êtes bien loin encore, où les yeux las ne tolèrent plus qu'une lumière, celle qu'une belle nuit comme celle-ci prépare et distille avec l'obscurité, où les oreilles ne peuvent plus écouter de musique que celle que joue le clair de lune sur la flûte du silence." (*R*, 127)[8]

Indeed, when the weary eyes can endure only the light of silence, that is the hour when we have been called to sleep, to dream, to contemplate, to remember. That is the moment when we experience in our heart a prolonged dread of all phenomenal forms, because we are deprived of all sensible forms as well as those that come from our memory and intelligence, and we are not yet capable of perceiving the flashes that come from the obscurity of our reservoir. Yet, though we cannot see the mysterious splendor of visible forms, we are still attracted to the light of being that informs them. And it is from this tension that comes the yearning that makes us seek the mystery in artistic forms. This is the true meaning of the world of dreams; namely, it offers those privileged moments in which the mysterious splendor of visible forms manifests itself and in which the phenomenal world is emptied of its "médiocre contenu," becoming completely darkened. In the midst of the silent world of dreams, which prevents us from seeing anything concretely, this "dormeur éveillé" is filled with a sense of exaltation as he becomes absorbed in the world of immaterial parts, which signify at once the birth of a transpersonal world and the death of phenomenal reality. Far from being blinded, the "dormeur éveillé" is set ablaze by the light of pure forms in whose world there is nothing sensory or intellectual but only mystical dream, consecrated sleep.

C'était le clocher de Saint-Hilaire qui donnait à toutes les occupations, à toutes les heures, à tous les points de vue de la ville, leur figure, leur couronnement, leur consécration. . . . C'était toujours à lui qu'il fallait revenir, toujours lui qui dominait tout, sommant les maisons d'un pinacle inattendu, levé devant moi comme le doigt de Dieu dont le corps eût été caché dans la foule des humains sans que je le confondisse pour cela avec elle. (*R*, 64–66)[9]

The manner in which the steeple of Saint-Hilaire conveys its consecrated form, its mystery, its essential quality beyond the power of words is the result of a center of gravity (the finger of God) that provides a sort of permanence, continuity, identity, and luminosity to the transitory forms in which the steeple is embodied. The steeple is the symbol of our adoration, our dreams, of the most secret depth of our being. The steeple muffles the noises of the outside world and of our habitual thought. To sleep is to encounter the mysterious splendor of all beings and to experience spiritual feelings; it is within the world of created silence that we guarantee the purity of our encounter with the phenomenal forms; it is within the world of consecrated sleep that the phenomenal transforms itself into a "magique comme un profond sommeil" (*R*, 88). Indeed, the forms that flow from our profound sleep are magical in that they are removed from their intelligible context.

Beaux après-midi du dimanche sous le marronnier du jardin de Combray, soigneusement vidés par moi des incidents médiocres de mon existence personnelle que j'y avais remplacés par une vie d'aventures et d'aspirations étranges au sein d'un pays arrosé d'eaux vives, vous m'évoquez encore cette vie quand je pense à vous et vous la contenez. . . dans le cristal successif, lentement changeant et traversé de feuillages, de vos heures silencieuses, sonores, odorantes et limpides. (*R*, 88)[10]

The purging of the phenomenal world creates a magical center around which humanity's reservoir revolves. That is why sleep is the moment of ecstasy, when the mysterious splendor of the ideal form captivates us and the spiritual equivalents recreate for us a world from the glowing light of pure thought. In reference to "la petite phrase" that Swann heard, the narrator says:

. . . Swann la [la petite phrase] sentait présente, comme une déesse protectrice et confidente de son amour, et qui pour pouvoir arriver jusqu'à lui devant la foule et l'emmener à l'écart pour lui parler, avait revêtu le déguisement de cette apparence sonore. Et tandis qu'elle passait, légère, apaisante et murmurée comme un parfum, lui disant ce qu'elle avait à lui dire et dont il scrutait tous les mots, regrettant de les voir s'envoler si vite . . . le corps harmonieux et fuyant. Il ne se sentait plus exilé et seul puisque, elle, qui s'adressait à lui, lui parlait à mi-voix d'Odette. (*R*, 348)[11]

Thus, instead of encountering the mysterious splendor of being in phenomenal forms, Proust completely purges these forms by dissolving the needed tension between the contraries of the visible and the invisible, of the mental ground and the deep reservoir of things, of the subjective and the objective poles, of God and human beings.

When Proust dissolves this tension, however, he finds that in the inner darkroom of our deepest inner recesses there is no longer any separation between heaven and earth, the generative eternal spirit and our creative desire. In Proust's dream world, where magic alone encircles and encloses the self within the world of archaic images, his eternal spirit, his desire to create, flows undivided, joining him to an intelligence that transforms him into a divine artist. The unity of our deep reservoir with that of the phenomena, this cojoining of our creative longing with the eternal spirit, this simultaneity of past and future, of sleep and remembrance, which allows us to experience this mysterious splendor, this intoxicating moment despite the anguish of the realization that it does not last—for Proust, all of this is bound up with the presence of the mystery of being, which eternally lives in us as a dream of a waking life, as that great reservoir whose origin is beyond senses and memory, beyond dreams. The evaporation zone shifts so quickly that we experience reality as a misty cloud, insubstantial impressions of a hidden form.

Puis, même ma propre vie m'était entièrement cachée par un décor nouveau. . . . Celui où je tenais alors mon rôle était dans le goût des contes orientaux, je n'y savais rien de mon passé ni de moi-même, à cause de cet extrême rapprochement d'un décor interposé. . . . Tout à coup je m'éveillais, je m'apercevais qu'à la faveur d'un long sommeil, je n'avais pas entendu le concert symphonique. (*R*, 820)[12]

For Proust, the hidden is a metamorphosis of the seen, the world of an Oriental fairy tale that transforms the above-mentioned concert into pure magic, pure symbols. But what is made visible in this long sleep is the opposite of the metamorphosis that should lie at the depth of dreams: the transformation of the mystery into a visible stream of images that flash across phenomenal existence. To Proust, the mystery is precisely the transfiguration of phenomenal life: the church at Balbec is "la plus belle Bible historiée que le peuple ait jamais plus lire." The narrator does not see it as "un gigantesque poème théologique et symbolique" (*R*, 840) but as a pattern traced in his mind that speaks to him more of "une église presque persane" than a Christian church. Elstir tells the narrator that if he had looked more closely at the facade of the church, he would have seen that "le type qui a sculpté cette façade-là . . . avait des idées aussi profondes que les gens de maintenant que vous admirez le plus" (R, 841). In the church at Balbec, side by side with the past there is the present; side by side with the East there is the Christian West; side by side with the Christian present there is antiquity; side by side with the Incarnation, Death, and Resurrection of the body of Christ, whose blood, "la liqueur de l'Eucharistie," constitutes the mystery of the Church, "il y a certaines paroles de l'office de l'Assomption qui ont été traduites avec une subtilité qu'un Redon n'a pas égalée (R, 841).

Here in the church at Balbec, the invisible and the visible, the mysteries of Christian Revelation and humanity's creative desire, fuse into a dream-like reality, into a refinement that achieves the mysterious through the unexpected, the imagined, the ghostlike qualities of images, as in Redon's paintings. Like these paintings, the church at Balbec conveys to the narrator mysterious splendor by expressive patterns traced in his mind. What the narrator encounters here is the sight of his own thought, which is the imagined mystery.

Gabriel Marcel: The Experienced Mystery

For Gabriel Marcel, the only possible encounter with the mystery is one that involves the phenomenal. For Marcel, it is only those who have encountered Being in that world which constitutes us as existing beings who can really open themselves to God revealed in all phenomenal forms and thus who can philosophize. "A cet égard l'idée chrétienne du corps mystique est peut-être celle sur laquelle le philosophe a le plus pressant intérêt à concentrer son attention" (M, 2:183–84). And the Christian vision of the mystical body reminds us, as seekers and philosophers, that truth can be considered only as a mystical body, as a spirit, as a light. And truth as light, as the spiritual vision of being, does not lie in turning away from phenomenal existence but in turning toward what Gabriel Marcel calls "un certain milieu intelligible" as the only source from which the mystery of being will shine forth for all who interact with phenomena, both physically and mentally. Truth as light, as spirit, as mystical body cannot be abstracted from this "milieu intelligible" through which the Christian idea of the mystical body manifests itself in the concrete world. And, according to Gabriel Marcel, it is not only possible but desirable to find one's way from this "milieu intelligible" into the Christian mysteries. According to him:

L'idée chrétienne d'une habitation du Christ en celui qui lui est entièrement fidèle, idée qui correspond exactement dans l'ordre religieux à la
position que je cherche à définir sur le plan philosophique, implique le
rejet catégorique de cette représentation purement imaginative. (*M*,
2:140)[13]

The spiritual vision of being thus will do more than the philosophical act.
Because of that creative reality, which we experience in our encounter with
truth as mystical body, light, and spirit, the spiritual vision does not empty
the phenomenal of its subjective and intersubjective dimensions; rather, it
makes it possible for the philosophical act to complete itself in "l'idée chrétienne du corps mystique."

Nous avons donc à nous demander maintenant en quoi consiste au juste
cette exigence de transcendance. Je pense que nous devons tenter
d'abord de la situer par rapport à la vie telle qu'elle est concrètement
vécue, et non pas la définir dans l'éther raréfié qui serait celui de la
pensée pure. Ma démarche consistera invariablement, vous avez déjà pu
vous en rendre compte, à remonter de la vie vers la pensée et ultérieure-
ment à redescendre de la pensée vers la vie pour tenter d'éclairer celle-
ci. (*M*, 1:49)[14]

And, in fact, the ascent to the mystery of being must proceed phenomenologically, as a life concretely lived, not as pure thought. However, Gabriel
Marcel's phenomenology does not speak of transcendence either as a sort
of misty cloud that melts away in pure thought or lies beyond the limits of
experience but rather speaks of the mystery as an encouter that does not go
beyond concrete existence. Beyond life "concrètement vécue" there is
nothing: "Je ne dis pas seulement penser mais même pressentir" (*M*, 1:56).
    According to Gabriel Marcel, being would vanish into nothingness if
it were transformed into an image of pure thought; for the self positions
itself only in relation to an existing reality, to a "milieu intelligible" that is
existentially experienced so that the light, the being, and the mystery that
streams from it may be encountered. Gabriel Marcel quotes Heidegger,
who states that the totality of the self is

". . . l'étant apprésentant se trouve placé au sein d'une lumière telle
que quelque chose puisse lui apparaître, lui être rendu manifeste. Ce
quelque chose doit mesurer ou traverser un domaine ouvert à notre
rencontre." (*M*, 1:83)[15]

By the very fact that we are in the world, we cannot separate ourselves
from existing reality; there can be no encounter with being except in the
indissoluble unity of "l'étant apprésentant" and the world. In fact, it is in

the encounter with the world, in the uniting of oneself with the other that being unveils its mysterious splendor, which receives the name of truth.

> Je veux dire que si par impossible on pouvait totalement faire abstraction de la structure en question, le mot vérité se viderait du même coup de toute signification. (*M*, 1:79)[16]

Truth, then, does not radiate from pure thought that does not experience itself in the world; rather, truth, or the light of being, radiates out from the world into the self, which is incarnated in a body and manifests itself in the world. "Ce corps que j'appelle mon corps n'est vraiment qu'un corps parmi une infinité d'autres" (*M*, 1:107). Hence, concrete existence can be spoken of only in reference to a body; it is "mon corps" that makes an encounter with being possible.

For this reason, thought cannot exist apart from what is; and what is is the unity of all existing beings, with the body serving as the mode of our presence in the world. To exist is to enter into a relationship that resists being made objective to the mind.

> C'est ainsi qu'on est amené à faire intervenir le corps sujet. C'est pour autant que j'entretiens avec lui un mode de relations (ce mot n'est d'ailleurs pas parfaitement adéquat) qui ne se laisse pas objectiver—que je puis m'affirmer identique à mon corps et on voit d'ailleurs aussitôt que le terme d'identité lui aussi est inadéquat, car il n'est pleinement applicable que dans un monde de choses ou plus exactement d'abstraction que l'incarnation en tant que telle transcende inévitablement. (*M*, 1:117)[17]

Our presence in the world is not only molded by the structure of determinate spatial and temporal relationships but is also there for encounter, for communion with others. And just as the body is that incarnation within a world of things, within the world of encounters, so the self, in its existential aspects, is one with the intersubjective element from which the ego emerge like an island rising up among the waves, according to Gabriel Marcel. The body is given to the self as a way of being-in-the-world, as "un mode de relations"; existence is encountering the world. This encounter is achieved not through the mind but through the self grasping itself as an existing being, as a being in a situation, as a life of immanence and transcendence, of distance and communion. Distance and communion come together because the self exists both as present to itself and distant from its own being, which it finds only in the being of others. Distance presents itself as an inner distance, as a land with which the self wishes to find communion. And while this distant land transcends the self in its concrete existence, it has a bond with it that cannot be broken. The self's longing for this other world is not a dream, a fancy; rather, it is its very life and depth. This ambiguity of existence makes the self see that being is not thought, nor is it being-in-itself; instead, it is a gift the self cannot give to itself; "c'est une grossière illusion de croire que je puis me le conférer à moi-même." Gabriel Marcel tells us that as a result, existence should be lived in humility, with fear and wonder:

> . . . car je ne puis même pas être tout à fait sûr qu'il ne soit pas, hélas, en mon pouvoir de me rendre indigne de ce don au point d'être condamné à le perdre si la grâce ne vient pas à mon aide; de l'émerveillement enfin, parce que ce don porte avec soi la lumière, parce qu'il *est* lumière. (*M*, 2:34)[18]

Consequently, the encounter between the self and the world cannot be expressed in philosophical categories that leave aside the gift that is grace. Being is constituted by its relations with others; we are part of all that is. And just as the world of things creates us as corporeal beings, so the world of intersubjectivity creates us as spiritual beings; intersubjectivity manifests itself by a union of love with the absolute Thou, who is other than the self and transcends concrete relations, with

> . . . Celui [qui] *est* la symphonie dans son unité profonde et intelligible, une unité à laquelle nous ne pouvons espérer accéder qu'insensiblement à travers des épreuves individuelles dont l'ensemble, imprévisible pour chacun de nous, est pourtant inséparable de sa vocation propre. (*M*, 2:188)[19]

The experience of "Celui" who is this symphony, starting from the keen awareness of "des épreuves individuelles," affirms the ontological emptiness of humanity in order to give supreme fullness to the being of God who, as Christ, has become incarnate; "ce qui suppose une relation tout à fait concrète, bien que très mystérieuse, entre ce Dieu vivant et cette créature qu'est mon semblable" (*M*, 2:133). We realize that in the "don de la grâce," in this living encounter with God, we are touching the horizon of the unconditional; by the light of divine love shining forth from everything that exists, we see that, in the existent being, being reveals itself in all splendor. Out of "une relation mystérieuse entre Dieu et cette créature" the light of truth breaks forth as mystery of being, revealing God as Creator to the creatures. Such a revelation cannot be grasped on the basis of the light of reason or thought, however; what is required is grace, or God's gift of his Son to humanity. Yet, "il faut ajouter que ces mots ne peuvent prendre leur pleine signification qu'à la lumière de l'intersubjectivité, c'est-à-dire de l'amour" (*M*, 2:157).

Intersubjectivity or love, then, gives signification to all that exists; it comes down to us as a gift of God in the incarnate Word who is this absolute Being, this sovereign Good, whose source "nous constitue comme existants" (*M*, 2:171). Intersubjectivity challenges us to act in faith, thereby bringing philosophical speculation and reflection to their deepest goal: the mystery of creation, of existence. We can only become aware of the gift, of the saving grace of being, if we are subjects of the mystical body of this "Dieu vivant" who touches us at the most intimate point of our self-transcending being. According to Gabriel Marcel, the spirit of truth is nothing if it is not a light that seeks divine light. Intelligibility is nothing if it is not at once intersubjectivity and the nuptial joy that results from communion with the absolute Thou. A will without intelligence and grace would be a mere impulse, and an intelligence without a will would be purged of its creative aspect. A body without the gift of the spirit would disintegrate into its fleshly state, instead of serving the life of the spirit. Existence without this gift of light, this intersubjectivity, would be filled with despair. The mystery of being, which is manifest, invites us to move from and beyond ourselves and to surrender to that mystery, that uncreated light, without which we are nothing.

> L'esprit de vérité n'est rien s'il n'est pas une lumière qui se porte au devant de la lumière, l'intelligibilité n'est rien si elle n'est pas à la fois une rencontre et la joie nuptiale qui s'attache à cette rencontre; plus je tente de m'élever vers cette lumière incréée sans laquelle je ne serais pas regard—autant dire que je ne serais pas du tout—plus je progresse moi-même en quelque façon dans la foi. (*M*, 2:178)[20]

Truth is both fulfilled and surpassed in faith; faith measures the depth of the encounter between an "I" and a "Thou", between finite and infinite Being, between life and thought; for we create ourselves in response to a call which comes from a thou. We experience ourselves as encompassed by and destined for another; we choose ourselves in choosing the other; we see that we cannot take one step into freedom without binding ourselves ever more deeply to the life of another by the gift of love, a love that cannot be totally grasped because the mind does not possess a comprehensive gaze. Now, this intersubjectivity does not imply that the light of subjectivity is simply extinguished as the uncreated light of faith shines more radiantly (in which case it might be called the light of dread, of nothingness). Nor does it imply a mere imaginative faculty. What it implies, rather, is that thought is directed to an infinite being by which it knows itself and before which it stands in an attitude of prayer and humility, which manifest the real presence of a thou, a presence that carries speculative thought further and deeper.

> D'une façon générale en effet, nous ne concevons guère l'union que par rapport à nos semblables; nous nous intégrons alors à un tout dont les

éléments sont homogènes. Mais ici, rien de tel n'est pensable. Dès lors le mystère consiste dans ce fait que j'ai à m'insérer dans ce qui me transcende infiniment. Ceci doit d'abord paraître inconcevable. (*M*, 2:103)[21]

According to Gabriel Marcel, the person who recognizes intersubjectivity is both a witness and a person of prayer. This person witnesses and prays continually to God's gift of his Son, that Other, that Spirit, that Thou to whom we direct our prayer in accordance with our own "épreuves individuelles," our own cry. This anguish emerges from the depth of our awakening being, from grasping our own presence in the world, a presence that neither our freedom nor our consciousness can fully understand. Only in God's incarnate Word is our presence in the world fully manifested.

. . . le propre de l'incarnation est en effet d'être irradiante, et c'est bien pour cela qu'il peut y avoir encore aujourd'hui des témoins du Christ dont l'attestation présente une valeur non seulement exemplaire, mais proprement apologétique. (*M*, 2:134)[22]

Gabriel Marcel sees that persons are seen from what they witness: God's Word, which calls them to a communion with absolute Being, with that unconditional ground of existence that consumes them in the mysterious splendor of the uncreated light. When we realize inwardly the despair of gazing at self rather than the other, we open ourselves absolutely to infinite Being, to God's gift of love. In prayer, we participate in the ultimate reality for which Christ has sacrificed himself.

In the Incarnation, God's unconditional gift of love becomes visible in the human yearning for salvation, in the human longing to see God and to be seen by him as we really are, fallen people. Indeed, the Incarnation took place precisely to interlock our existence with God's presence, our freedom with God's gift of the light, our conditional existence with the infinite fullness of God's being; only thus can we be a witness in prayerful adoration to Christ's sacrifice on the cross where our intersubjectivity is fully recognized and made operative. As Marcel expresses it: "Ainsi se réalise une interaction toute spirituelle et qui a ses racines dans la charité elle-même, en tant qu'elle est une vie et non pas une simple disposition" (*M*, 2:136). As persons of prayer and witnesses, we see that Christ's Incarnation, his being made human and assuming sinful existence, is understandable only as a function of charity, of his descent into darkness and ascent to the Light: "Si ceci n'était pas admis, cela qu'on prétendait être un Dieu vivant se réduirait du même coup à une idée nécessairement inaltérable et contre laquelle je ne puis pécher" (M, 2:133-34). We, as persons of prayer, Marcel tells us, see the absolute presence of this living God, who is pure light, pure mystery, pure splendor, because we have humbled ourselves before the Cross: there we experience the moment of charity in the prayer, "I thirst," and the moment of belief in the words, "Father, into thy hands I commend my spirit," and the moment of hope in the words, "It is finished."

> L'être que j'aime est exposé à toutes les vicissitudes auxquelles sont soumises les choses, et c'est indubitablement pour autant qu'il participe à la nature des choses qu'il est lui-même sujet à la destruction. Prenons bien garde cependant: toute la question—fort obscure il est vrai—est de savoir si cette destruction peut porter sur ce par quoi cet être est véritablement un être. Or, c'est cette qualité mystérieuse qui est visée dans mon amour. (*M*, 2:154)[23]

This "qualité mystérieuse" is not in the domain of philosophical and scientific predication; rather, it is on the level of grace, which gives redemption to the darker side of human existence, to its vicissitudes, "épreuves individuelles," and death itself. To ignore these is to forget that the human person is a being in the world, a being in need of salvation, in need of the wholly Other. This mysterious quality, as faith savored through experience, is the very mystery of our participation in divine love and our personal encounters with the world. This mysterious quality, which is the life of prayer, is the foundation for creative fidelity, which is based on the gift of love: it is God's gift of grace. "Nous l'avons vu, c'est ici le domaine de la grâce, c'est aussi celui de l'inter-subjectivité où toutes les interprétations causales sont en défaut" (*M*, 2:178). Grace, or this mysterious quality, lived love, is our means of participation in God's vision, which takes place in the domain of intersubjectivity.

It is in this context that Gabriel Marcel presents the person of prayer as *homo viator*, as spiritual witness to the Christian idea of the mystical body in an interpersonal encounter, an unconditional self-giving, which is certitude, even if vision is reserved for the final encounter with God at the last judgment. In the mystical body these persons of prayer know themselves as they are known, and dwell absolutely in the redemptive suffering of Christ. For them a perfect intersubjectivity constitutes their most authentic subjectivity: this mystical body is what constitutes them as whole persons.

> Le salut n'est rien s'il ne nous délivre pas de la mort. . . . La vérité est bien plutôt qu'il n'y a pas et qu'il ne peut pas y avoir de salut dans un monde qui par sa structure même est soumis à la mort. . . .La méditation la plus profonde nous contraint à nous demander si la mort ne serait pas à quelque degré la rançon du péché, sans que d'ailleurs ceci doive être interprété d'une façon littérale et dans le cadre de l'existence individuelle. . . .Chacun de nous est pour le moins impliqué dans une foule de structures où il est impossible pour un esprit de bonne foi de ne pas déceler la présence du péché. (*M*, 2:181–82)[24]

Marcel claims that the mystical body of Christ, and humanity's sharing in it, is contained in the hidden encounter between God the Father and Christ the Son, that is manifested in the spirit breathed into the Church and its members by the incarnate, dying, and risen Christ. According to Gabriel Marcel, the Church, in the full mystical body of Christ, is nothing other than this "inter-subjectivité incarnée" that responds to God's gift of grace; for the Church is the being of Christ himself and not "une structure comparable à celle qui tombe sous les prises de la connaissance objective" (*M*, 2:109).

What is involved here, according to Marcel, is an attunement to being as a whole, and this ontological availability is, in the human person as being-in-the-world or as "inter-subjectivité," a free communion to "s'unir à," "sentir à." This feeling with, which is not separable from existence, from a most intimate encounter with Being, is our attunement to being as the sensing and the experiencing subject independent of the distinction between passive and active experience. In "s'unir à," or in being united with, we open ourselves to a deeper reality by the reciprocal act of participation and receptivity. Thus, to feel is to participate in the mystery of being. But God is not an existential existent; rather, he manifests himself out of and within the depths of being, which in its intersubjectivity points to the Christian idea of the mystical body as its ultimate structure, since it is God's Word made flesh.

Reconnaissons pleinement que cet être que j'aime n'est pas seulement un *toi*, il est d'abord un objet qui se propose à mon regard et sur lequel je peux me livrer à toutes les opérations dont la possibilité est inscrite dans ma condition d'agent physique. Il est un *cela*, et c'est dans cette mesure même qu'il est une chose; pour autant qu'il est un *toi*, il échappe au contraire à la nature des choses, et rien de ce que je peux dire d'elles ne peut plus le concerner lui, ne peut plus te concerner *toi*. (*M*, 2:155)[25]

For this reason, mystical body, "inter-subjectivité incarnée," and "s'unir à" apply first of all to God in a way determined by the analogy between God and humanity. We open ourselves to God, who does not need us in order to be, and we respond to God in freedom, that is, in our gift of self as persons of prayer, as beings-in-the-world. This ability to welcome or to reject God's gift of love constitutes the very essence, the very being, of our existence, of our inner freedom, of our spiritual self. This is why humanity's "s'unir à Dieu" is not an intuitive act in the epistemological sense, nor is it the result of philosophical inference from the finite to the infinite. The presence of being as intersubjectivity, with everything it entails, continually directs us on the way to the mysterious splendor of the uncreated light, of the absolute mystery itself. And from the point of view of mystery, our existence cannot be differentiated into bodily, sensory, and spiritual activities nor into active and passive participation: "D'une part l'éternité ne peut être que mystérieuse, c'est-à-dire que nous ne pouvons pas nous en former une représentation plane ou étalée, mais d'autre part tout mystère débouche sur de l'éternel" (*M*, 1:234–35). Existence is eternal and therefore mysterious. The more we experience the presence of the other, the more we ascend into the sphere of the eternal where we pass totally into the absolute Other. The Other is incarnate intersubjectivity revealing himself in the kingdom of heaven, where mystery, radiancy, and oneness with all beings are the only words that can express this existence. "Ce mystérieux phénomène qui bien entendu ne peut laisser aucune trace sensible relève en quelque façon de la cité idéale" (*M*, 1:86).

Conclusion: The Creative Mystery

If indeed the mysterious splendor emerges out of our encounter with the phenomenal, with the world of others, then this encounter is characterized by two simultaneous moments of grasping and being enraptured. Both Proust and Gabriel Marcel recognize these two moments; both believe that no one can truly behold the form, the light, the essence of things without having been enraptured, and no one can be enraptured without perceiving the depth of reality, the mystery of existence. In these two moments, we are confronted with both the object and that which radiates from it, making the object worthy of love, bodily and mentally, and of participating in its hiddenness and its splendor.

Such a mystery becomes visible for Proust through the evaporation zone, the contour of the world in a state of constant dissolution: as the narrator embraces and kisses Albertine, her body vanishes, and only the thought of her remains. This thought dissolves into pure air, enveloping him and raising him to an ecstatic experience in which he is consumed by the thought of purging Albertine of her own "médiocre contenu," of breaking all the bonds that connect her to her own reserve, to her concrete existence, to the world of others. But where the thought ends, the impenetrable self remains as a symbol of suffering and dread. Since nothing remains of the phenomenal yet something must be embraced, Proust urges us to enter the world of immaterial parts where we encounter the self as artist. What remains of existence is a pattern traced in the mind that, even if it claims for itself the freedom to create, remains totally dark, a dream, a fantasy, a subtlety of expression, impenetrable even to itself.

For Gabriel Marcel, on the other hand, the creative spirit of the human person dies out where the very structure of creativity, the phenomenal, the "milieu intelligible," the "inter-subjectivité incarnée," is destroyed, and being no longer expresses its mystery, its hidden form. Our presence in the world, both bodily and mentally, opens us to the personal reality of another. However, we cannot force the gift of self on this other; what we can do is to give of ourselves unconditionally in the hope that this other will embrace the Christian idea of the mystical body. This is because what holds true phenomenologically, holds true equally for the Christian relationship between faith and grace, since in the giving of itself faith grasps the revelatory gift of God's love. At the same time, Gabriel Marcel says that grace makes possible, through the mediation of the Incarnation and the Passion, humanity's way into the eternal world of God, the world of the uncreated light. The mystery, for Gabriel Marcel, can be encountered only in a dialogue with the world, a dialogue that grounds human existence in the order of grace, the life of humility, prayer, faith, hope, and charity. It is the order of grace that makes being accessible to humanity, thereby making possible an encounter with the absolute Thou, this person who freely emptied himself on the cross in order to redeem mankind. Gabriel Marcel says that to the eyes of faith and love, the mystical body of Christ reveals the splendor of God's creative will.

For Proust, the contemplation of the mystery produces a sense of despair, because the mystery vanishes as he gazes at it, leaving him no ground for hope and no source for joy except for the artistic forms which he creates from his self-intoxication. For Gabriel Marcel, on the other hand, this mystery is creative by the very fact that it involves the whole person in an intercourse with the world and ultimately allows the human person to transcend the world to live in the level of grace. This grace forms the solid ground that the self needs in order to experience joy in its life.

6

Proust's Esthetics and Renaissance Art

Le mot d' "oeuvre florentine" rendit un grand service à Swann. Il
lui permit, comme un titre, de faire pénétrer l'image d'Odette
dans un monde de rêves où elle n'avait pas eu accès jusqu'ici et
où elle s'imprégna de noblesse. (R, 224)[1]

Finding himself unable to penetrate to the reserve hidden in things, Proust
consoles himself by projecting his own visions, founded on his memories,
onto the evaporation zone as immaterial equivalents. The central motif of
Proust's subjective idealism or pure phenomenalism is self-divinization.
The mind creates a dream world from its memories and at the same time
sees itself as the creative force producing this world of dreams. The mind's
action thus is intensively creative, a mirror of God's creative activity, and
in this sense Proust speaks of self-divinization: everything exists only as a
function of humanity's sublime self. According to Proust, the human person is constantly seeking to experience the bliss of love and longs for a sort
of ecstasy, the mysterious essence, and the rapture of existence. Humanity
yearns for the absolute, the infinite, the unbounded, and the abyss. At the
same time, we exist in a world of constant change in which everything is
reduced to appearances, making more difficult, if not impossible, our quest
for some sort of ecstatic enjoyment. Proust thus faces an apparent paradox: on the one hand, he is unable to penetrate the changing reality of
experience because everything in it is reduced to appearances and these
appearances are themselves fleeting; on the other hand, he feels an inner
urge to penetrate the phenomenal world. The arts occupy a central position in this paradox by serving as a means to halt the change and to stabilize
the impressions. The arts become the esthetic measure of all things because
they can remain outside the confines of temporal horizons. The result is
that Proust extracts artistic images from their historical context, ignoring
the content that these images were intended to represent.

    In this effort, Proust seeks the clearest artistic measure and finds it in the
visual arts of the Renaissance. He might have been expected to find im-
pressionistic art more suited to his vision of the world; instead, he turned to
the Florentine and Venetian masters, who through the sharpness of their

artistic forms and the brightness and harmony of their colors, revealed for him a true esthetic measure. Renaissance art, with its dual strains of classical forms and Christian themes, unlike impressionist and postimpressionist art, does not drown the absolute in the relative, the spiritual in the natural, the transcendent in the immanent, the contemplative in the phenomenal. It does not disconnect God from humanity, being from nothingness, the light of phenomenal forms from the light itself. Renaissance art aims at the proper synthesis between phenomenalism and the form, the idea. With its principle of unity, totality, and central perspective, Renaissance art harmoniously balances the world of light with that of darkness, being with becoming, the sublime with the human, and God with human creative power. Without this, Proust himself is only too aware, the notion of beauty emerging from pure phenomenalism or subjective idealism risks annihilating the self in the natural world. Renaissance art not only acts as a stabilizer to his thoughts, but more than this it points him to the world of the unchanging form, the unknown, divine, the mystery.

Proust's Esthetics

Proust's notion of the beautiful crystallizes around an original moment when the regret, mainly but not exclusively, for the lost ecstasy of past privileged moments, is brought to consciousness from the world of dreams and there is an influx of creative power or artistic imagining. It is in the interplay of the paradox of the awakened dreamer that Proust apprehends the world. An when this paradox is most intense, supernatural beings (pure forms), those mysteries of birth, death, and resurrection, that sacramental moment of self-transformation, and the origin itself appear before the eyes objectively, that is, they come to life. This esthetic orientation is found in Proust in the very first pages of *A la recherche du temps perdu*.

> Quelquefois, comme Ève naquit d'une côte d'Adam, une femme naissait pendant mon sommeil. . . . Formée du plaisir que j'étais sur le point de goûter, je m'imaginais que c'était elle qui me l'offrait. Mon corps qui sentait dans le sien ma propre chaleur voulait s'y rejoindre, je m'éveillais. (*R*, 4)[2]

This movement to oneness with the object of love and consummation with the subject itself refers to that complete world wherein we respond to beauty's revelatory delights. In dreams, then, the hidden and the indescribable begin to be revealed and described. And what is revealed and described is another, quite different reality (the ideal, the sublime, the objective, the form), which, like material reality or phenomenon, is an appearance, a mere dream, a fleeting sensation.

Giorgione, *The Tempest*. Oil on canvas, 83 × 73 cm, ca. 1505. (*Courtesy of Galleria dell'Accademia / Böhm, Venice.*)

The conversion to oneness with the object of love from consummation with the subject raises a fundamental problem. On the one hand, oneness with the form as an objective reality cannot be achieved without the dissolution of the self; on the other hand, extinction of the self means that nothing is—in other words, existence is pure phenomenon, absolutely changeable. But if nothing is, and yet we feel something, we remain forever bound to the chains of terror and anguish: the yearning for a complete unity with the object of love brings forth the need to perish. And through death, love is revealed in its divine aspect.

> Peut-être est-ce le néant qui est le vrai et tout notre rêve est-il inexistant, mais alors nous sentons qu'il faudra que ces phrases musicales, ces notions qui existent par rapport à lui, ne soient rien non plus. Nous périrons, mais nous avons pour otages ces captives divines qui suivront notre chance. Et la mort avec elles a quelque chose de moins amer, de moins inglorieux, peut-être de moins probable. (*R*, 350)[3]

These conceptions, these divine captives (impressions, images, or forms) are for Proust the immediate transformation of a longing; the esthetic moment converts the most inflamed desire into an image that is possessed by the imagination, standing between the phenomenal and the objective, between body and thought. Proust emphasizes this underlying connection when he writes:

> Mais dès que j'eus terminé la lettre, je pensai à elle, elle devint un objet de rêverie, elle devint, elle aussi, *cosa mentale* et je l'aimais déjà tant que toutes les cinq minutes il me fallait la relire, l'embrasser. Alors, je connus mon bonheur. (*R*, 500)[4]

As in this letter from Gilberte, so too in the music of Vinteuil, the paintings of Elstir, the theater of Berma, the literature of Bergotte, the love for Albertine and Madame Guermantes, the visits to the countryside and to the various cities, heavenly moments spring up within a feeling, and the whole sensory system at once crystallizes in the form of an ecstatic experience. This experience reveals the intimate connection between subjective (sensory) and objective reality (thought). Of his visit to Florence, Venice, Pisa, and Parma, Proust's narrator explains:

> . . . je ne cessai pas de croire qu'elles correspondaient à une réalité indépendante de moi, et elles me firent connaître une aussi belle espérance que pouvait en nourrir un chrétien des premiers âges à la veille d'entrer dans le paradis. . . . Et, bien que mon exaltation eût pour motif un désir de jouissances artistiques, les guides l'entretenaient encore plus que les livres d'esthétique et, plus que les guides, l'indicateur des chemins de fer. (*R*, 391)[5]

To experience esthetic enjoyment is thus the same thing as to see an objective form. And when this form becomes *cosa mentale* and enters the mind, it acts as an intoxicant, a stimulant, a force ("par une gymnastique suprême et au-dessus de mes forces"), exclusively because the form itself cannot be possessed as anything other than an image, an impression, a sensation, a flash of reality. In this way, love and beauty are merely the embodiment of the most inflamed desire in the mind of the perceiver or artist. In the artistic mind—as opposed to the scientific mind, which apprehends the phenomenal by rational explanation—images are forms expressing sentiments that are one with the lovable and the beautiful, understood not as an abstract unity but as concrete and living forms emanating from the world of experience. This world of experience provides the a priori power for the artistic mind in the sense that experience is the fundamental structure of knowledge.

> Dans la Sonate de Vinteuil, les beautés qu'on découvre le plus tôt sont aussi celles dont on se fatigue le plus vite, et pour la même raison sans doute, qui est qu'elles diffèrent moins de ce qu'on connaissait déjà. Mais quand celles-là se sont éloignées, il nous reste à aimer telle phrase que son ordre, trop nouveau pour offrir à notre esprit rien que confusion, nous avait rendue indiscernable et gardée intacte; alors, elle devant qui nous passions tous les jours sans le savoir et qui s'était réservée, qui par le pouvoir de sa seule beauté était devenue invisible et restée inconnue, elle vient à nous la dernière. Mais nous la quitterons aussi en dernier. Et nous l'aimerons plus longtemps que les autres, parce que nous aurons mis plus longtemps à l'aimer. (*R*, 531)[6]

What is most beautiful in itself, then, is the least immediately accessible to the mind, and the most immediately accessible is the least beautiful in the sense that it has no permanency. Moreover, Proust insists, the contemplative act is not confined merely to the apprehension of the coming to be of forms but also in revealing them as they are in themselves, different from past sameness. Ultimately, the contemplative act stands in direct relationship to the subject's and object's reserve, since the object to be apprehended depends on the receiver's capacity to apprehend. It is this mental commitment on the part of the artist that allows the deeper and higher form of the self-disclosing beauty, the secret of truth, to shine out of the light of the invisible and unknowable, or the reserve of things. It is in the ultimate depth of the reserve that the mind confronts the still deeper range of meaning and truth. And truth arises solely from the mind's agreement that what it yearns for is present in the esthetic moment, the moment when the mind is caught between the unsatisfied longing to touch, see, hear, smell, and taste beauty and the fear of extinction; between the endless change of reality and the reserve of things; between despair and exaltation, grief and joy. This is the moment when the mind strives to grasp the hidden, the permanent essence of things, that immaterial love whose luminous form reveals the mystery of both the self and the world as in a mirror. If only the mind could bring out the reserve of things, if only the mind could recapture the lost past, then we would at the same time experience the mystery of beauty, love, living out the hour of intoxication (a state of subjective idealism) in which the experiential world would exist in the mind. No love or beauty, Proust tells us, fills us that is not already there in the reserve, "mais déplacé, ne pesant plus sur nous, satisfait de la sensation que lui accorde le présent et qui nous suffit, car de ce qui n'est pas actuel nous ne nous soucions pas" (*R*, 816).

Love, then, takes form in these pleasant hours, in the here and now, when the self transcends the phenomenal world, the life of habit, for the sake of that love that constitutes the joy beyond all joys and comes to live in the authentic world of impression. This is the world of the artist, whose knowledge includes the unsatisfied longing to apprehend the hidden forms of things and to express them truthfully, that is, in the paradoxical tension between subjective and objective reality, inner life and outer form, work of art and living forms. Regarding Elstir's paintings and his beautiful wife, Gabrielle, Proust writes:

Ce qu'un tel idéal inspirait à Elstir, c'était vraiment un culte si grave, si exigeant, qu'il ne lui permettait jamais d'être content; cet idéal, c'était la partie la plus intime de lui-même: aussi n'avait-il pu le considérer avec détachement, en tirer des émotions, jusqu'au jour où il le rencontra, réalisé au dehors, dans le corps d'une femme . . . qui était par la suite devenue madame Elstir et chez qui il avait pu—comme cela ne nous est possible que pour ce qui n'est pas nous-mêmes—le trouver méritoire, attendrissant, divin. Quel repos, d'ailleurs, de poser ses lèvres sur ce Beau que jusqu'ici il fallait avec tant de peine extraire de soi, et qui maintenant, mystérieusement incarné, s'offrait à lui pour une suite de communions efficaces! (*R*, 850–51)[7]

The beauty and the encounter between the subject's and the object's reserve and its manifestation are the most incarnate yet at the same time the most mysterious reality: beauty as grace, as meritorious, divine, and solemn, as communion in love. And the grace of beauty becomes the source of inebriation, of ecstasy, and communion or dialogue with beauty becomes the source of inspiration, of truth. In the beautiful, what the artist extracts from within and what is there as outer form are one but for a moment.

Cette Albertine-là n'était guère qu'une silhouette, tout ce qui s'y était superposé était de mon cru, tant dans l'amour les apports qui viennent de nous l'emportent—à ne se placer même qu'au point de vue de la

Correggio, *Leda and the Swan*. Oil on canvas, 152 × 191 cm, ca. 1531–32. (*Courtesy of Gemäldegalerie, Staatliche Museen Preussischer Kulturbesitz, West Berlin.*)

quantité—sur ceux qui nous viennent de l'être aimé. Et cela est vrai des amours les plus effectifs. (*R*, 858)[8]

Reflecting power makes known something that is so exacting, yet ever new. It never allows Elstir to be satisfied and intensifies continuously. Even in the hour of intoxication, beauty still remains unfathomable, hidden from the artist. And the artist's expression of beauty in the idea is intimately related to the offering, to the surrendering of the self, to the sacrifice intrinsically connected to the act of contemplation. This act ascribes to the object of beauty its worth and loves it as an implacable divinity, an immaterial essence, an invisible form. Through the reflecting power, the artist sees the form, the soul of things, in its movements, expressions, thoughts, and actions; indeed, the artist imagines it even before it exists in the body, and the body exists only in the lovely form, in the beautiful itself.

> Depuis que j'avais vu Albertine, j'avais fait chaque jour à son sujet des milliers de réflexions, j'avais poursuivi, avec ce que j'appelais elle, tout un entretien intérieur où je la faisais questionner, répondre, penser, agir, et dans la série indéfinie d'Albertines imaginées qui se succédaient en moi heure par heure, l'Albertine réelle . . . ne paraît, dans une longue série de représentations, que dans les toutes premières. (*R*, 858)[9]

Thus, on the one hand, in perceiving objects, the artist encounters their reserve, which demands either total surrender or resistance. On the other hand, the artist, in perceiving, desires either to serve love unconditionally or to conquer or dominate. The artist approaches this paradox under the guidance of what Proust calls "l'oeil intérieur," "les yeux de la mémoire," or "l'oeil de l'esprit," whereby from first sight, things are apprehended; that is, the eyes see first the outer or material form, then the eyes of memory see the inner form and through the imagination penetrate the saving grace of the idea, the immaterial form or beauty.

> Mes regards se posaient sur sa peau, et mes lèvres à la rigueur pouvaient croire qu'elles avaient suivi mes regards. Mais ce n'est pas seulement son corps que j'aurais voulu atteindre, c'était aussi la personne qui vivait en lui et avec laquelle il n'est qu'une sorte d'attouchement, qui est d'attirer son attention, qu'une sorte de pénétration, y éveiller une idée. (*R*, 716)[10]

But the more one apprehends, the more complete the encounter, the deeper the penetration of being, and the more the being itself wants to be perceived from the mind's eye, which sees but one light, the light that reveals love as demanding suffering, rebellion, and dying. Ultimate communion with the beloved, Proust believes, is achieved through death, "mort suivie, il est vrai, de résurrection, mais en un moi différent et jusqu'à l'amour duquel ne peuvent s'élever les parties de l'ancien moi condamnées à mourir" (R, 671).

Therefore, the eyes perceive in suffering or death that which is completely other; they perceive the self in the depth of the reserve manifesting itself in the light of the real, which is the life of habit, chance, time, and space, as well as the life of finitude, wandering, alienation, guilt, and death. And if in the senses the reserve opens up to the world, then, in the awakened idea of the inner self, the mind's eye opens up to beauty; the mind perceives beauty only through weary eyes gazing on nothingness whose nonbeing the eyes of memory shape within themselves.

> Mais de même qu'il ne m'eût pas suffi que mes lèvres prissent du plaisir sur les siennes mais leur en donnassent, de même j'aurais voulu que l'idée de moi qui entrerait en cet être, qui s'y accrocherait, n'amenât pas à moi seulement son attention, mais son admiration, son désir, et le forçât à garder mon souvenir jusqu'au jour où je pourrais le retrouver. (R, 716)[11]

Beauty, then, proceeds from an inaccessible world, from the idea, from an undiscoverable reality, from an unknown delight, and the invisible light shines only in the eyes that mirror it.

> Mais . . . dans l'état d'exaltation où j'étais, le visage rond d'Albertine, éclairé d'un feu intérieur comme par une veilleuse, prenait pour moi un tel relief qu'imitant la rotation d'une sphère ardente, il me semblait tourner, telles ces figures de Michel-Ange qu'emporte un immobile et vertigineux tourbillon. (R, 934)[12]

Thus from the outset the body is determined by an interior fire related to its reserve, by which the mind's eye is adorned. And it is the art of Michelangelo, in the figures he has shaped, that allows the perceiver to see and understand, "comme par une veilleuse," a particular and unique being.

Regarding smell, taste, touch, and hearing, Proust states:

> Et le plaisir que lui donnait [Swann] la musique et qui allait bientôt créer chez lui un véritable besoin, ressemblait en effet, à ces moments-là, au plaisir qu'il aurait eu à expérimenter des parfums, à entrer en contact avec un monde pour lequel nous ne sommes pas faits . . . parce qu'il échappe à notre intelligence, que nous n'atteignons que par un seul sens . . . l'ouïe. Et comme dans la petite phrase [la Sonate de Vinteuil] il cherchait cependant un sens où son intelligence ne pouvait descendre, quelle étrange ivresse il avait à dépouiller son âme la plus intérieure de tous les secours du raisonnement et à la faire passer seule dans le couloir, dans le filtre obscur du son! (R, 237)[13]

Hearing thus opens the inner self to a reality that the eyes cannot perceive, smell cannot scent, touch cannot embrace, taste cannot savor, and the mind cannot grasp, which awakens, deepens, and sweetens the feeling of delight, directing the mind's eye to behold this Botticelli maiden who reflects the radiance, the saving grace of beauty expressed in images emanating from the penetration of the reserve of things into the perceiver (artist) on the one hand and the exteriorization of the perceiver's reserve into things on the other hand. From this dynamic process the beheld image and experienced reality enter the self, and both intimately encounter each other in the reserve that is the remembered depth, "les yeux de la mémoire," of beauty in its dialectical tension with ugliness. "Car la beauté est une suite d'hypothèses que rétrécit la laideur en barrant la route que nous voyions déjà s'ouvrir sur l'inconnu" (*R*, 713).

Ugliness is what prevents the eyes, and the senses in general, from penetrating any further the wellsprings of ecstatic enjoyments, the reserve of things from which the wave of violent intoxication rises to the horizon of the mind's eye, where the eyes of memory see themselves in that mysterious and luminous light of the Idea, of Beauty. It is the Idea—Beauty or Truth—which organizes darkness (nonbeing) around itself into a luminous form, a saving grace within which a world begins to take shape in the interplay between the perceiver's power to contemplate, penetrate, and apprehend, and the objects of apprehension; between reality and ideality; between art and living forms, body and soul.

> Quand il [Swann] avait regardé longtemps ce Botticelli, il pensait à son Botticelli à lui qu'il trouvait plus beau encore et, approchant de lui la photographie de Zéphora, il croyait serrer Odette contre son coeur. (*R*, 225)[14]

The figure of Odette is thus lovelier when considered in terms of the esthetic measure, the idea of beauty or form, as it coexists in its similarities to Botticelli's images, or when imagined in the context of beauty itself, emerging as in the painter's *The Birth of Venus*.

> Il [Swann] n'estima plus le visage d'Odette selon la plus ou moins bonne qualité de ses joues et d'après la douceur purement carnée qu'il supposait devoir leur trouver en les touchant avec ses lèvres si jamais il osait l'embrasser, mais comme un écheveau de lignes subtiles et belles que ses regards dévidèrent, poursuivant la courbe de leur enroulement, rejoignant la cadence de la nuque à l'effusion des cheveux et à la flexion des paupières, comme en un portrait d'elle en lequel son type devenait intelligible et clair. (*R*, 223–24)[15]

The fact that the artist makes an archetypal form intelligible is rooted in the power of the eyes to penetrate beauty. But after unraveling it, the

Sandro Botticelli, The Birth of Venus. Uffizi, Florence. Oil on canvas, $68\frac{7}{8} \times 109\frac{5}{8}$ in., ca. 1483–84. (Courtesy of Alinari / ART Resource, New York.)

artist's eyes will see nothing other than the reflection, "la marque d'un être particulier." For the artist is called to represent, in one being or another, absolute Being, which is the supreme beauty, the invisible form of the self and the world. So that what the artist reveals in a particular being is always at the same time that inconceivable image which illuminates living forms, unveiling them in their unique beauty. It is this image that the artist wants to fashion and make worthy of perceiving. And it is for this reason, Proust claims, that artists both reveal and conceal themselves in their work, creating images from their being-in-between the light of night and the darkness of day; between the light of being and the abyss of nonbeing, the ugliness which forbids the eyes to enter into communion with the reserve of the beloved object. For nonbeing is like the surface of a mirror that prevents the perceiver from grasping reflected images within the mirror. And this is the artist's source of suffering: to be powerless to turn the eyes of memory, the mind's eye, and reason toward Beauty, Being, or Love.

Je pose la tasse et me tourne vers mon esprit. C'est à lui de trouver la vérité. Mais comment? Grave incertitude, toutes les fois que l'esprit se sent dépassé par lui-même; quand lui, le chercheur, est tout ensemble le pays obscur où il doit chercher et où tout son bagage ne lui sera de rien. Chercher? pas seulement: créer. Il est en face de quelque chose qui n'est pas encore et que seul il peut réaliser, puis faire entrer dans sa lumière. (*R*, 45)[16]

Renaissance Art as Proust's Esthetic Measure

In the twilight zone between being and nonbeing, thought and feeling, light and darkness, Proust experiences the ecstatic moment, the privileged instant, the hour of intoxication. Proust perceives Renaissance art as the esthetic measure, since to him it comes close to achieving this perfect unity of inner and outer form, of the beauty of the soul and that of the body; as mysteriously expressing that essential and intimate communion of divine and human, of woman and man, of invisible and visible, of happiness and grief—as realizing an inspiration so deep that the mind never fully penetrates reality in its reserve beauty. And just as for Proust the contemplation of the beautiful demands that the eyes of perceivers return from the object's reserve to penetrate deeper and deeper into their own reserve, the abyss, the dark region where the idea of beauty reveals itself to the eyes of memory, so too Renaissance art requires a glance of the eyes at nature, and then, through the mind's eye, the impressions are carried to Truth, Love, and Beauty, the saving grace of things. The simple beauty of the Florentine and Venetian masters manifests itself in the mystical forms of Giotto and Angelico, in the virginal, graceful, and veil-like figures of Bot-

Paolo Veronese, *Allegory of Love: Respect.* **Oil on canvas,** $73\frac{1}{4} \times 78\frac{1}{4}$ **in., ca. 1570–75.** (*Courtesy of the Trustees, The National Gallery, London.*)

ticelli, Bellini, and Titian, in the colored forms of Carpaccio, Giorgione, and Veronese, in the charm, tenderness, softness, and *sfumato* of colors of Mantegna, Raphael, and Leonardo, in the mastery of the inner tension by Michelangelo and Tintoretto. Renaissance art expresses the veritable tension between eternity and time; the real is fully revealed in the light of a universal symbol.

For Renaissance masters, symbols have an independent existence; they express a relationship between image and reality, but they themselves are neither. Yet they can be perceived in the concrete world of the here and now, in the world of appearance. Seen in this way, Renaissance art, by contrast with Proust's artistic vision, which allows no independent existence for symbolic forms since he sees symbols as the conceptions or projections of the self, can be characterized as permanent, stable, real, visible, living, tangible, and archetypical. In this sense the artistic world is the created world of nature (as phenomenal and mysterious, immanent and transcendent), and as such it is related to God the Creator. Thus, there is a real collision of the sacred and secular life; Renaissance masters delighted in human scenes, painting ordinary people and everyday objects with such a realism that the viewer cannot help but experience an ecstatic enjoyment because what is seen is not only images but actual human figures surrounded by real objects, materially sensed. Proust gives specific examples of this in Benozzo Gozzoli's fresco of the *Journey of the Magi* in the Medici Palace in Florence and Giotto's frescoes in the Arena Chapel of Padua with which he was familiar through his studies of Ruskin. Of the *Virtues* and *Vices* on the walls of the Arena Chapel, Proust writes:

> Il fallait que ces Vertus et ces Vices de Padoue eussent en eux bien de la réalité puisqu'ils m'apparaissaient comme aussi vivants que la servante enceinte, et qu'elle-même ne me semblait pas beaucoup moins allégorique. Et peut-être cette non-participation (du moins apparente) de l'âme d'un être à la vertu qui agit par lui, a aussi en dehors de sa valeur esthétique une réalité sinon psychologique, au moins, comme on dit, physiognomonique. (*R*, 82)[17]

It is precisely the realism of Renaissance art that captivated Proust's imagination. Indeed, Renaissance masters sacrificed their own individuality to reveal what is real, what lies deep in the reserve of things. And in a single insight Renaissance masters succeeded in expressing reality's most profound mystery: that is, the relation between the appearance of the world and its transcendent form. They searched endlessly among the darkest aspects of objects in order to penetrate and uncover this relationship. Once it was uncovered, they represented the smallest object, there in the distance, as solid, alive, and detached as the most important one nearby. They represented this close figure as distant, fragile, and small as the small-

Titian, *Venus and Adonis*. Oil on canvas, $69\frac{3}{4} \times 73\frac{1}{2}$ in., ca. 1554. (*Courtesy of the Trustees, The National Gallery, London.*)

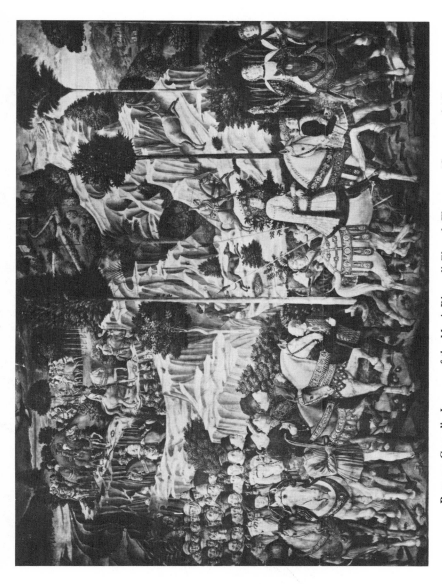

Benozzo Gozzoli, *Journey of the Magi.* **Riccardi Chapel, Florence.** *(Courtesy of Alinari / ART Resource, New York.)*

Correggio, *Jupiter and Io.* **Oil on canvas, 163.5 × 74 cm, ca. 1530.** (*Courtesy of Kunsthistorisches Museum, Vienna.*)

est object in the distance. Yet an absolute distance separates the idea, the form, from the object painted. In this context, Proust insists:

> Aussi ne fut-ce pas avec le plaisir que j'aurais sans doute éprouvé sans cela que je pus distinguer tout d'un coup à mes pieds. . . les Déesses marines qu'Elstir avait guettées et surprises, sous un sombre glacis aussi beau qu'eût été celui d'un Léonard, les merveilleuses Ombres abritées et furtives, agiles et silencieuses, prêtes, au premier remous de lumière, à se glisser sous la pierre. . . . (*R*, 925)[18]

To Leonardo, as to Renaissance masters, the artist is the universal mind's eye that watches over all visible things, and from these same things the artist paints. Whatever is out there as phenomenon, image, essence, or imagination, the artist must first appropriate through the senses before making them *cosa mentale*. Finally, the artist must paint them according to the eyes of memory. The artist must paint them in a well-proportioned harmony, with such a passionate feeling that the perceiver not only grasps beauty as an appearance but also penetrates to true beauty as an attribute of the inner form (reserve, thought, idea). For Renaissance masters, the painting is the point of convergence of sensory perception and thought: here love, beauty, truth, saving grace, the idea, and virtue are assembled in such a way that they mirror bodily reality, which has been transformed by the artist through his penetration of the reserve of things. This is the revelation of the mystery, which in spite of its revelation still remains a mystery, a secret beyond the reach of the artist's senses, thoughts, and hands. For Proust, although the mystery remains beyond the senses, thoughts, and hands, there is no solid and unchanging image, or symbol. Thus, he concludes:

> Je regardais les trois arbres, je les voyais bien, mais mon esprit sentait qu'ils recouvraient quelque chose sur quoi il n'avait pas prise, comme sur ces objets placés trop loin dont nos doigts, allongés au bout de notre bras tendu, effleurent seulement par instant l'enveloppe sans arriver à rien saisir. . . . Ce plaisir, dont l'objet n'était que pressenti, que j'avais à créer moi-même, je ne l'éprouvais que de rares fois. . .et qu'en m'attachant à sa seule réalité je pourrais commencer enfin une vraie vie. Je mis un instant ma main devant mes yeux pour pouvoir les fermer sans que Mme de Villeparisis s'en aperçût. Je restai sans penser à rien, puis de ma pensée ramassée. . .je bondis plus avant dans la direction des arbres, ou plutôt dans cette direction intérieure au bout de laquelle je les voyais en moi-même. Je sentis de nouveau derrière eux le même objet connu mais vague et que je ne pus ramener à moi. Cependant tous trois, au fur et à mesure que la voiture avançait, je les voyais s'approcher. . . . Dans leur gesticulation naïve et passionée, je reconnaissais le regret impuissant d'un être aimé qui a perdu l'usage de la parole, sent qu'il ne pourra nous dire ce qu'il veut et que nous ne savons pas deviner. (*R*, 717–19)[19]

7

Bonaventure and Proust: From Image to Icon

Depuis que j'avais vu Albertine, j'avais fait chaque jour à son sujet des milliers de réflexions, j'avais poursuivi, avec ce que j'appelais elle, tout un entretien intérieur où je la faisais questionner, répondre, penser, agir, et dans la série indéfinie d'Albertines imaginées. . .l'Albertine réelle. . . ne paraît. . . que dans les toutes premières. Cette Albertine-là n'était guère qu'une silhouette, tout ce qui s'y était superposé était de mon cru. . . . (*R*, 858)[1]

The senses take delight in an object perceived through an abstracted likeness either because of its beauty, as in sight, or because of its sweetness, as in smell and hearing, or because of its wholesomeness, as in taste or touch, if we speak by way of appropriation. (*S*, 71)

The previous chapter discussed the paradox in Proust's esthetics, namely, the way in which the artist must create symbols in order to regain the ecstasy of privileged moments. At the same time, these created symbols not only fail to capture the form within things but also destroy the temporal dimension of the world. These symbols become transformed into icons that no longer have any connection with the temporal world or its forms. One example of Proust's taking temporal images and creating from them an atemporal world of icons is the interpretation he gives of the frescoes in the Arena Chapel of Padua by Giotto (1267–1337). Proust considers Giotto's images important only for "la grande place que le symbole y occupait," not for the affirmation, revelation, or incarnation of that imperishable, universal, mysterious, and transcendent reality in which Giotto embeds his figures. Thus considered, Giotto's images are stripped of their archetypal form, of the reference to the unknown mystery of reality. Giotto's images are transformed by Proust into icons that cut themselves off from both the prototype image hidden in things and revealed in their likeness to God and from the phenomenal world, since these icons now correspond to no divine

Giotto, *Interior View from the Altar.* **Scrovegni Chapel, Padua.** (*Courtesy of Alinari /*
ART Resource, New York.)

image and to no phenomena; for Proust, these icons are made truly real, that is, they are idealized. In his characteristic way, Proust locks these icons within his own thoughts, ideas, and memories, out of which he recreates things either by eliminating what is temporal or giving images that correspond to the image of the artist, who is the ultimate revealer of the mysteries of human existence. Thus, of Elstir's paintings, Proust's narrator writes:

> Mais j'y pouvais discerner que le charme de chacune consistait en une sorte de métamorphose des choses représentées, analogue à celle qu'en poésie on nomme métaphore, et que, si Dieu le Père avait créé les choses en les nommant c'est en leur ôtant leur nom, ou en leur en donnant un autre, qu'Elstir les recréait. (R, 835)[2]

In this chapter, I will attempt to show that Giotto's frescoes give the most visible manifestation of what Bonaventure (1217–74) holds images to be. That is, a reflection of the model (exemplar) as it incarnates itself in the beauty of the visible world as light, shape, and color, and by which the senses and the soul delight.

This presentation of Giotto's art as expression of Bonaventure's spiritual esthetics is my own, and it is not based on other Renaissance thinkers. Also, it must not be seen as conclusive evidence that Giotto was either familiar with Bonaventure's thought, or that there is a precise correspondence between the saint's spiritual esthetics and the artist's representation of it. Rather, my interpretation merely gives a narrative form, a textual context, to Giotto's art so that I can compare it with Proust's interpretation. So that if at first my presentation appears to remove the reader from Proust and from twentieth-century French thought, it is because I see in Bonaventure an appropriate bridge to Proust's understanding of Giotto's art. It is imperative to bear this in mind, otherwise my discussion becomes too much an exegesis of Bonaventure, with no connection to the entire work. Thus, in considering Giotto's images to be an expression of Bonaventure's esthetics (in The Soul's Journey into God), I will also be dealing with Proust's esthetic interpretation of Giotto's art. Giotto's frescoes lead the perceiver on a spiritual journey, a pilgrimage, an ascent to what Bonaventure calls a communion with the light of eternal truth, while Proust's interpretation of Giotto's Virtues and Vices reveals a closed world, an icon where we are all creatures who can emerge from within ourselves, from our own remembrance as self-projection but cannot experience a deep and intimate communion with other beings, either vertically or horizontally. And so, Proust insists:

> Cet être, une fois de plus je le fabriquais, en utilisant pour cela le nom de Simonet et le souvenir de l'harmonie qui régnait entre les jeunes corps

que j'avais vus se déployer sur la plage en une procession sportive digne de l'antique et de Giotto. (*R*, 807)[3]

The first part of the quotation discloses the connection between the icon and Proust's truths, that the icon is based on what is not phenomenal (memory). The remainder connects an imaginary person, Simonet, with some of Giotto's images. Whereas Giotto's *Virtues* and *Vices* are animated by divine Incarnation because they are in the image of God, in Proust's art they are the incarnation of the artist himself (Proust's narrator), who becomes the person he imagines, a person who does not exist except in the image made by the artist. It is precisely this imaginary world that determines the form the icon (portrait) is to take: the image is thought of something other than what the artist sees—phenomena—and its mode of representation. And in this imaginary world what is representable is precisely the self-portrait of the artist. In fact, what image could correspond to the Incarnation and Redemption if all images are self-projection, for self-projection excludes the saving Grace of God? Of Giotto's *Charity*, Proust gives his opinion through his narrator:

> De même que l'image de cette fille était accrue par le symbole ajouté qu'elle portait devant son ventre, sans avoir l'air d'en comprendre le sens, sans que rien dans son visage en traduisît la beauté et l'esprit. . . [l'image] qui est représentée à l'Arena au-dessous du nom "Caritas". . . incarne cette vertu, c'est sans qu'aucune pensée de charité semble avoir jamais pu être exprimée par son visage énergique et vulgaire. (*R*, 81)[4]

Whereas in traditional iconographical literature an icon expresses the inner beauty and exemplary image of God's Creation, Incarnation, and Redemption, which lie beyond the subjective perception of the artist, in Proust's view of the icon the artist or the subject (Proust's narrator as iconographer) establishes himself as the source, content, and form of the icon. Proust's own words apply here: "Sans doute peu de personnes comprennent le caractère purement subjectif du phénomène qu'est l'amour, et la sorte de création que c'est d'une personne supplémentaire" (*R*, 468). This fact displaces the symbolic realism of Giotto's images, which now no longer reveal a spiritual vision or prototypical image. We can apply the words of Bonaventure to the spiritual vision of Giotto:

> We contemplate God not only outside us and within us but also above us: outside through his vestiges, within through his image and above through the light which shines upon our minds, which is the light of Eternal Truth, since "our mind itself is formed immediately by Truth itself." (*S*, 94)

Bonaventure's Esthetics: The Image

Bonaventure's *Soul's Journey into God* implies that there is a way, a bridge or road, that both divides and joins humanity and God, material and spiritual things, beginning and end. As a way, it leads the reader on a journey beginning in the contemplation (the highest form being prayer) of nature and ending in the soul's mystical ecstasy (communion, union, marriage) with God. Bonaventure says that through contemplation, the believer receives light to discern the steps of the way into what is a three-stage ascent into the world of the highest pleasure, the greatest good; and Christ, who is corporeal, spiritual, and divine, is the ladder. Contemplation of the natural world makes it possible to see the light of the Eternal Art, "by which, through which and according to which all beautiful things are formed" (*S*, 74).

The beauty of nature, Bonaventure goes on to state, is revealed in things as vestiges of God, possessing mode (the principle of substance), species (the principle of relationship), and order (the principle of unity or end). Because of these three attributes, Bonaventure continues, it is possible to contemplate God at three different levels: in the outside world (the sensible), in the inner world (the spiritual, or the world of the soul's becoming conscious of itself as the image of God), and in the world of the above (the mind, the world of the Trinity). However, according to Bonaventure, any one of these levels can be doubled, according to whether God is considered as the origin or the end. "Or in each of these ways we can see him through a mirror or in a mirror. Or we can consider each way independently or as joined to another" (*S*, 61). So that the soul is on a three days' journey (this division reflects the threefold existence of things—matter, mind, and the Eternal Art), leading into the world of the most beautiful of the beauties, the highest revelation of the Trinity where it attains a peace in the vision of God the Father, a joy that is experienced only through the contemplation of the crucified Christ, a delight in what is an upward movement of ecstatic love through the Holy Spirit.

To begin with, then, Bonaventure tells us that the natural world is beautiful because it signifies the Eternal Art, the Creator, the invisible attributes of God, the origin and end of all things. Bonaventure describes the creatures of this world as shadows, echoes, and pictures of "that Eternal Source, Light and Fullness, of that efficient, exemplary and ordering Art." They are vestiges, spectacles, representations and signs given to us so that we can see (perceive) God. "For every creature," Bonaventure concludes, "is by its nature a kind of effigy and likeness of the eternal Wisdom" (*S*, 76–77). This view of the universe enables Bonaventure to be the artist who can guide his viewers, through the pictures of the natural world, leading them, step by step, to see divine beauty in which they finally embrace the most perfect, the most integral, the most sublime reality, that is, the triune beauty of God's wisdom. "Therefore," Bonaventure says to us, "open your eyes . . . so that in all creatures you may see, hear, praise, love and worship, glorify and honor your God" (*S*, 67–68).

The natural world or the outside thus presents itself to the senses as a picture of different objects, each with its own origin, magnitude, beauty, multitude, fullness, activity, and order in a harmonious whole, possessing a certain arrangement of parts with pleasing colors, lights, and shapes in which we, as viewers, delight. In this strain, Bonaventure says:

> The senses take delight in an object perceived through an abstracted likeness either because of its beauty, as in sight, or because of its sweetness, as in smell and hearing, or because of its wholesomeness, as in taste or touch, if we speak by way of appropriation. (*S*, 71)

Through appropriation, then, the object or species that delights us as beautiful, pleasant, and wholesome suggests that there is a proportion, a correspondence with the Eternal Art. "Now," Bonaventure proclaims, "all enjoyment is based on proportion." The laws of proportion allow the viewer to move from the perception of the outer world into the inner world of the soul (the world of the image of God), and from within the soul upward in the hope of seeing the first Species (God), which contains perfect proportion and is most delightful, most beautiful, and most wholesome and is above us: pure beauty or eternal wisdom.

> Since, therefore, all things are beautiful and in some way pleasurable, and since beauty and pleasure do not exist without proportion, and since proportion exists primarily in numbers, all things must necessarily involve numbers. Thus "number is the foremost exemplar in the mind of the Creator," and in things, the foremost vestige leading to Wisdom. (*S*, 75)

It is divine wisdom that unveils what is beautiful in the natural world, making its "proportion of harmony" delightful to perceive and contemplate, pleasurable to touch, sweet to smell, and inviting to hear. It is wisdom that directs this sensible world to its rightful order, presenting it to the senses through the divine light of the spiritual eye through number as the foremost exemplar in the mind of God and judging it to be an all-embracing and ever-brilliant beauty. Bonaventure insists that the natural world is created by God for the pleasures of each of the five senses. It is created, however, not so much to make us lose ourselves in the midst of sensory delights as to make us see (judge) spiritual beauties.

Therefore we cannot judge with certainty except in view of the Eternal Art which is the form that not only produces all things but also conserves and distinguishes all things, as the being which sustains the form in all things and the rule which directs all things. (*S*, 74)

This, then, is seeing. The eyes capture the whole with its laws of numerical proportion, which in turn progressively direct them from the outside toward the Eternal Art through the form that stands within all things, making them to be what is, and revealing them in harmony with themselves, with other things, and with the Exemplary, or the Creator of all things. Bonaventure writes:

The basis of harmony is the same in large and small objects; neither is it increased by size nor does it change or pass away as things pass away, nor is it altered by motion. It [judgment] abstracts, therefore, from place, time and motion, and consequently is unchangeable, unlimited, endless and is completely spiritual. (*S*, 72)

It is this spiritual form against which and by which numerical proportion (harmony) in the natural world is both perceived through the senses and judged through reason, a proportion that is unchangeable, unlimited, and endless.

Consequently, according to Bonaventure, not to see the form in all things is to be blind. And to see the world with dull eyes is to be indifferent to the laws of numerical proportion and therefore incapable of opening up the five doors of the senses to the beautiful. The beautiful is above all the numerical, the exemplar. As Exemplary, the numerical makes the Eternal Art, the first species known in all bodily and sensible things. In the beautiful, then, the numerical and the spiritual are one, if form truly is that which in all things shines forth brilliantly, delightfully, infallibly, boundlessly, and indivisibly. Sensible form not only points to an invisible, unreachable, incommunicable, and untouchable beauty, but this form also reveals it while at the same time clothing it with a veil of mystery. And the mystery, which allows communion with as well as separation from the Eternal Art, does not shine forth from outside or above things but emanates from within this form. Bonaventure writes:

When by faith the soul believes in Christ as the uncreated Word and Splendor of the Father, it recovers its spiritual hearing and sight: its hearing to receive the words of Christ and its sight to view the splendors of that Light. When it longs in hope to receive the inspired Word, it recovers through desire and affection the spiritual sense of smell. When it embraces in love the Word incarnate, receiving delight from him and passing over into him through ecstatic love, it recovers its senses of taste and touch. (S, 89)

Essentially, then, Bonaventure holds that neither the senses nor reason can climb the ladder of the beautiful without numerical and spiritual proportion. And if the sensible world lacks the splendor of that light, the numerical in its divine Exemplar, the uncreated, inspired, and incarnate Word of God, then the experience of the beautiful remains purely utilitarian, and instead of recovering the spiritual form by which and through which they open themselves up to the beautiful, the senses close themselves up within the laws of numerical proportion in vestiges. In this case, instead of serving as a road to the beautiful, the numerical becomes an unbridgeable gulf between things as they are outwardly (signs, representations, expressive numbers, pictures) and what they are inwardly (true form, true light, true beauty). And so it is that the eyes and the soul must see and break through to the inward reality.

> The eye, concentrating on various differences of color, does not see the very light by which it sees other things; and if it does see this light, it does not advert to it. In the same way, the mind's eye, concentrating on particular and universal being, does not advert to being itself, which is beyond every genus, even though it comes to our minds first and through it we know other things. (*S*, 96)

Bonaventure tells us that in the luminous form of the beautiful, the genus, the being, or the numerical of things is both perceived and judged by and through the mind's eye as a proportion between sensible things and Eternal Art, or being-in-itself. This being-in-itself belongs to the beautiful, makes all things delightful, and is beyond every genus in the sense that it is the numerical without the laws of proportion; it is light without colors, form without shape, one in many, the One without numbers. It is the first principle, the source of all things, and as such, it has neither mode, species, nor order, for it is the negation, the pure nothing, the true darkness, and therefore, it is absolutely beyond the eye's perception, beyond the soul's grasp.

> Thus our mind, accustomed to the darkness of beings and the images of the things of sense, when it glimpses the light of the supreme Being, seems to itself to see nothing. It does not realize that this very darkness is the supreme illumination of our mind . . . just as when the eye sees pure light, it seems to itself to see nothing. (*S*, 96–97)

All this simply means that the eyes move from the perception of the outside to the contemplation of the within of things, and from their within, upward into the realm of supreme being, namely, God's witness or the mind's eye in us. Through the mind's eye we see things as both illumined and unillumined—unillumined in the sense that all creatures have no being in themselves, for their being depends on God's light, which sharpens the eye's perception of things to such a point as to make the senses grasp the beautiful in the vestiges as wholes, as well as making the intellect understand the beginning, the exemplar, and the end of all things. It is the mind's eye that allows the natural world to be seen as revealed through Scripture, purging, illuminating, and perfecting all things since it is God's light as Word incarnate who makes visible the invisible light of the Father by his death. Through his death, Christ restores the numerical and spiritual proportion that reached total disproportionality in original sin and prevented the mind's eye from opening up further the five doors of the senses to the beautiful. This is what Bonaventure means when he says that when the "eye sees pure light, it seems to itself to see nothing." But from the mind's eye, which focuses on things from Scripture, the natural world attains to God himself, the source of all being. In the light of being, everything is seen in numerical and spiritual proportion with the Eternal Art, which is God as exemplar within us, the life of faith, hope, and love, a life that both connects us with and separates us from the Exemplary, the Image, the One, God. For according to Bonaventure, it is not so much "rational consideration" that delights and satisfies the soul as the "affective" experience of the mystery of God in the three theological virtues of faith, hope, and charity, which allow the senses to internalize themselves and the soul to externalize itself further in the contemplation of the One through its hierarchical acts (apprehension, understanding, and judgment). Bonaventure writes:

> This takes place through the three . . . theological virtues and the spiritual senses which have been reformed and the three . . . ecstatic stages and hierarchical acts of the soul, by which our soul enters back into its interior, there to behold God. . . . There, as in a chamber, the soul *sleeps and rests . . .* while the Bridegroom entreats that she be not awakened until she pleases to come forth. (*S*, 91–92)

In speaking of the soul returning within its interior only to go forth again to experience the beautiful, Bonaventure is describing the last stage of the soul's journey when it finally comes to rest, to sleep in the contemplation of God through the Bridegroom Christ. In this way, the soul goes forth out of itself in ecstasy to attain ultimate communion with the Eternal Art where the laws of numerical and spiritual proportion are transformed into God's love, which embraces all things in hierarchical order of beauties, returning them to their primordial beauty where difference is transcended. The soul, thus, goes forth into God's chamber where it is completely at home in the mystical unity of the Trinity. According to Bonaventure:

When, therefore, the soul considers itself, it rises through itself as through a mirror to behold the blessed Trinity of the Father, the Word and Love: three persons, coeternal, coequal and consubstantial. Thus each one dwells in each of the others; nevertheless one is not the other but the three are one in God. (*S*, 84)

There at last the soul rests in the "superluminous darkness of a silence," a darkness in which everything shines forth, and a silence in which everything is delightful since all things are experienced in the similitude of the divine Light, the Eternal Art. The Holy Spirit thus is the Third Person of the Trinity, revealing the beauty of the Eternal Art, a beauty that realizes itself outside (the vestiges), within (the form), and above (the light).

The esthetic of Bonaventure thus leads to an affective experience of delight and vision in the love of the beautiful as it reveals itself outside us, within us, and above us. If, on the one hand, ecstatic love is the highest manifestation of the beautiful, the supreme joy of the "spiritual senses," and if, on the other hand, this manifestation is experienced sensually, then, even the delight of physical objects contains some degree of ecstasy in which the eyes see with the soul and the heart touches with the mind's eye, while the senses are inundated with a joy both sensory and spiritual. The joy is sensory, since the beautiful is experienced by the senses, and spiritual, since the same senses are capable of eternalizing themselves by a proportion or similitude with the beautiful. This similitude is not congruence, however. Rather, it is like the curve of the hyperbola that always retains a distance separating the soul and God. And yet, despite this distance still there is possible the highest communion, the finest sensibility, the most exquisite delight, the most gentle kiss proceeding from the soul's reunion with the triune God.

Thus at the summit of contemplation in what Bonaventure calls prayer, the soul sees the light (image of the Trinity), which perfects it by purifying it. In the act of contemplating God, the soul comprehends itself in the intellectual faculties of understanding, will, and memory. It sees itself as in a mirror; that is, as image of the triune God.

Giotto's Representation of Images

As a narrative of Christ's Incarnation and Redemption, Giotto's images allow the observer to experience a sense of delight, a feeling of lyrical tenderness, a touch of exquisite grace, a smell of the finest fragrance, and, as Bonaventure would say, a sound of an invisible harmony, a sight of an unspeakable silence, and a darkness of complete luminosity. This delight, this harmony, this silence, and this light spring from Giotto's artistic ability to capture the beautiful in things and at the same time elevate the soul to see their image and appreciate the highest image, divine beauty. Giotto achieves this through his use of nature as mirror by which the entire universe (creation) reveals itself as a hierarchy of the material itself (vestiges), the spiritual significance of the material (exemplar, image), and the spiritual itself (Exemplary, Image). Indeed, Giotto's frescoes place the beholder before the entrance of the Eternal Art, before God's Image, the deepest reality itself, and invite the viewer to wander and journey, first horizontally through landscapes of the natural world where things exist corporeally and temporally, and then vertically, in the contemplation of the within (image) of things, which is spiritual and eternal, since it is the image of God as exemplar, and finally to rest in the fragrant and silent garden of the above of things, which is pure beauty, light, image, being, divine delight, eternal goodness.

This is to say that the viewer participates in this meditative poem on the Incarnation and Redemption; that the observer participates in a self-disclosing universe that opens itself up (blossoms) to the mind's eye, which penetrates further and further into the physical world, moving beyond the material reality of nature to the world of God above. This movement to the contemplation of the Eternal Art or Image, to the oneness of things, is made possible through Giotto's transformation of nature into an image where human beings seem to wander in silence and at the same time be awakened to the reality that they are walking through creation, which has a past in the Fall, a future in the coming of Christ. In Giotto's paintings, it is Christ who dissolves the darkness into a luminous path; it is Christ who opens the world of silence to the spiritual word of God the Father, veiling it with a breath of love and a light of mystery, thereby drawing the eye in the direction of God's eye so that humankind may see as God sees—that the universe is harmonious, proportioned, integral, and good.

Giotto sees nature as that real window through which the viewer can contemplate the ultimate, the deepest reality. His paintings are an effort to open the window. In fact, Giotto's art opens the window in the sense that it reveals the connection existing between human beings and God. This is not to say, however, that total union with God is attained when the paintings are contemplated. Rather, Giotto's art still contains a closed physicality that separates the artistic representation from God. Unlike Byzantine art, which identifies exclusively with the spiritual, leaving behind the natural world, Giotto's pictures recover the sensory world, as this world points beyond itself through numerical proportion, which both hides the spiritual (the image) within the laws of immanence and reveals it as the world of transcendence, of the above.

Consequently, unlike Byzantine art, Giotto's paintings express a real tension between the natural and the spiritual, or the Fall and Redemption, which mirrors the tension in human existence. It is this tension which allows and even encourages the viewer's affective participation, which Giotto reveals as both historical and personal and in which the viewer's self becomes luminous as the mirror of God's revelatory Word. Only when Giotto's frescoes are seen against this background can they serve to open the natural window, which in a way is proportioned to and correlated with human experiences. Thus humanity wills either to connect with or to separate from the divine world. In this way, Giotto's images call the viewer to see that humanity is one of the vestiges—that human beings are also exemplars, images of God's incarnate Word and not mere things. Humankind is realized in the tension between sinfulness and redemption, hope and despair, joy and sorrow, peace and anxiety, fear and expectation. Just as chiaroscuro creates a tension between adjacent colors so that the resultant color is neither one nor the other, so Giotto's images place the observer in the tension between birth and corruption, and this in-betweenness of light and darkness, openness and closedness makes it impossible to find oneself. Moved to contemplate the meaning of life in its prototype image, the observer grasps and embraces it as if it were emerging for the first time from the creative abyss, from the dark night, finding it delightful since it arises from the knowledge of God through the love of the Holy Spirit in the crucified Christ.

Giotto's frescoes thus mediate between the possibility that we as observers may enter a fuller, more intimate, and richer life (redemption) on the one hand, or remain closed off (in sin) to the deepest mystery of existence. This means that in the mirror of the frescoes we can come to know ourselves, a knowledge that Bonaventure refers to as "an expressed likeness to the image of God," a knowledge in the likeness of faith, hope, and charity through the incarnation and redemptive works of Christ who opens the depths and heights of the human condition. This, then, is the image, the luminous, beautiful reality that Giotto paints in the walls of the Arena Chapel, a reality that is natural and intrinsically hidden and mysterious, because it cannot be expressed simply as it appears (phenomenon) but must also convey the prototype image: what it is. And what it is (the image and likeness of God) is revealed through the frescoes in the tension they demonstrate and that the viewer seeks to understand as truthful and good.

Indeed, then, Giotto's frescoes illuminate the image of existence in the *Virtues* and *Vices* by the exemplar, the archetypal human image. This image is perfected in Christ (as giver of virtues and remover of vices) who has access to the innermost, mysterious core of creation as God's incarnate Word. As One and Exemplary, and yet as One who is to be understood only in the context of each individual person's and humanity's history of the Fall and Redemption, Christ is the image, the expression of God's love, of God's light. To this end, Giotto's *Virtues* and *Vices* speak allegorically of human beings in their true essence as primal image, an image that has been plunged into the darkness of sin (vices) and restored (virtues) by Christ to the luminous and yet still dark light of God.

For example, the vice *Envy*, and the virtue *Charity* on the walls of the Arena Chapel represent humanity's journey through time, from when it closes itself off within the flames of lust for material reality (phenomenon) as revealed by *Envy*, to the elevation of the within (the soul, the image, the heart) to God in *Charity*. Their juxtaposition on the walls of the Chapel is an image of the Fall and of Redemption. Whereas *Envy* is an external expression of the vanished image, of the darkness by the burning desire for the outside, *Charity* manifests what the soul has attained, how it has attained it, and the fruits of that attainment. *Envy*, represented on the left side of the wall, tightly clutches with her left hand a bag of money while her right hand, clawlike, greedily grabs for what she desires. Focused on that object of desire (the material), her eyes are oblivious to the self-destruction effected by the consuming flames of the passions at her feet (the striving after the sensory, the phenomenal) and the slanderous viper that is literally "backbiting" the woman's eyes as it issues from her mouth. The heaviness of her body, the smothering, mindless wrapping of her head, the rapacious horn protracting from her head, the distorted enlargement of her ear, all these indicate a kind of outer darkness coming from the destruction of the archetypal image that cuts itself off from both communion with other beings and with God, the divine Image.

Charity, on the other hand, indicates the presence of grace. This manifestation of grace is shown in the image by the crown of flowers the woman wears on her head, by the offering of her heart to God with her left hand, by the holding of a basket of fruits with her right hand, and by her intent gaze upon God. Flowers, heart, fruits, and open eyes are an outer representation of the transfigured state of human beings, an actual manifestation of the spiritual world, the world of humanity's inner perfection, and of the unlike radiancy coming from having attained the summit of spiritual ecstasy, of seeing God in the human image of the incarnate Word, Christ-Man. This is why she is oblivious to the sacks of money lying under her feet; she is calling us to go beyond the vestiges (the phenomenal), to see with the mind's eye the prototype image in the redemptive works of Christ, to ascend further to a fuller and more intimate communion (prayer) with God by charity, which crowns the head and fills the heart and the whole body with spiritual fruits (images, the gifts of the Holy Spirit), thereby perfecting earthly fruits (phenomena, cardinal virtues). All is brought here to a supreme image of beauty; in the image or kingdom of God there is no ugliness, for the phenomenal and the human (understanding, will, and memory) have been refined and purified by divine grace, by the Holy Spirit.

Proust's Esthetics: The Icon

The prototype image, in the knowledge of God, human beings, and

Giotto, *Envy.* **Arena Chapel, Padua.** (*Courtesy of the Civic Museum of Padua 3811.*)

Giotto, *Charity***. Arena Chapel, Padua.** (*Courtesy of the Civic Museum of Padua 3819.*)

things, is of great importance for Giotto. Proust, on the other hand, declares that Giotto's representations have no meaning beyond the purely mental construct of the artist. In speaking of *Charity* and *Envy*, Proust claims through his narrator:

> Par une belle invention du peintre elle [la Charité] foule aux pieds les trésors de la terre, mais absolument comme si elle piétinait des raisins pour en extraire le jus ou plutôt comme elle aurait monté sur des sacs pour se hausser; et elle tend à Dieu son coeur enflammé, disons mieux, elle le lui "passe", comme une cuisinière passe un tire-bouchon par le soupirail de son sous-sol à quelqu'un qui le lui demande à la fenêtre du rez-de-chaussée. L'Envie, elle, aurait eu davantage une certaine expression d'envie. Mais dans cette fresque-là encore, le symbole tient tant de place et est représenté comme si réel, le serpent qui siffle aux lèvres de l'Envie est si gros, il lui remplit si complètement sa bouche grande ouverte . . . et que l'attention de l'Envie . . . tout entière concentrée sur l'action de ses lèvres, n'a guère de temps à donner à d'envieuses pensées. (*R*, 81)[5]

Clearly, Giotto's artistic portrayal, the image, is interpreted by Proust as belonging neither to the within of things in their archetypal image nor to their outward expression (phenomena), which, as symbol, should reveal the ultimate meaning: that is, their relation to God, humanity, and all reality. Instead, Giotto's images are "aussi vivants que la servante enceinte, et qu'elle-même ne me semblait pas beaucoup moins allégorique" (*R*, 82). This is so because in their essence images have been transformed into icons; that is, they are no longer an integral part of the vestiges nor of the soul's journey into God; they cease to be a meditative poem by which we as observers come to see ourselves in the image of divine incarnation and redemption. In other words, if symbols manifest any meaning at all now, they must testify to the subjective dimension of existence. Thus, what is a prototype image becomes an icon by which thought, idea, form, and essence are the symbols that ultimately and exclusively express the self in its transfigured, divinized state. So meditation is synonymous with self-divinization; everything is stripped of its participation in divine life, its correspondence to the image, and its relation to the incarnate Word, the Image (Christ-Man). What exists is subjugated to the individual truth of the inner self, the mind's eye, the reserve, the spotless mirror of the artist as creator, the image of the artist's self-projection.

To be sure,

> Ce qu'on prend en présence de l'être aimé n'est qu'un cliché negatif, on le développe plus tard, une fois chez soi, quand on a retrouvé à sa disposition cette chambre noire intérieure dont l'entrée est "condamnée" tant qu'on voit du monde. (*R*, 872)[6]

As the expression of the inner darkroom of the self, of the loved object as merely a photographic negative to be processed, the icon does not manifest the luminous presence of the beloved; instead, what it reveals is a representation that is as true as what is developed within (ideas, thoughts, reserve) the self. Whereas, on the one hand the mind processes these negatives into symbols as remembrance of things past, on the other hand the remembrance also serves as an inexhaustible source from which and on which the self, as artist, constructs numerous figures that correspond neither to the phenomenal nor to their archetypal image. What these figures express, instead, is the self incapable of penetrating beyond itself to behold the light, the prototype image as divine beauty hidden in things. Love as found within the inner darkroom of the self is nothing other than the artist's self-projection, which takes the place of vision, of face-to-face encounter, with the object of love; for Proust's artist enters into the darkroom to stand face to face with the objects he has created in his own likeness. And so, the beauty of the negative is the beauty of the icon, of the imagined symbol of the self whose beauty is visible to the mind's eye, to the eyes of memory of the artist. Of his narrator's entrance into Elstir's studio, Proust writes:

> Et l'atelier d'Elstir m'apparut comme le laboratoire d'une sorte de nouvelle création du monde, où, du chaos que sont toutes choses que nous voyons, il avait tiré, en les peignant sur divers rectangles de toile qui étaient posés dans tous les sens, ici une vague de la mer écrasant avec colère sur le sable son écume lilas, là un jeune homme en coutil blanc accoudé sur le pont d'un bateau. (R, 834)[7]

And, at the summit of creativity, in what Proust calls poetic understanding, the artist reproduces things not according to the preconceived notion of the intellect but in conformity with immediate sensations, impressions. In fact,

> L'effort qu'Elstir faisait pour se dépouiller en présence de la réalité de toutes les notions de son intelligence était d'autant plus admirable que cet homme qui avant de peindre se faisait ignorant, oubliait tout par probité (car ce qu'on sait n'est pas à soi), avait justement une intelligence exceptionnellement cultivée. (R, 840)[8]

Proust's artist thus is the creator, the poet, the primordial figure, precisely because he strips both himself and the objects of contemplation of all conceptual and temporal limitations (habits of thoughts). He is not a man of the past, but he is not a man of the future either. He is of the here and now; he has a transtemporal destiny (self-divinization) that neither escapes nor denies time but does not get entangled in it either: he merely suspends time. He holds that it is in the formless that he sees and in the ignorance that he has attained—by the cessation of all distinction between thought, the object of thought, and the act of contemplation, thinking—that poetic understanding takes place. His art not only excludes the prototype image of what Bonaventure calls the "Light of the Cross" but also all traces of the phenomenal (the habitual creation of the intellect). His inner darkroom signifies the mind's understanding of itself as symbol, precisely because the mind (memory) has become the very soul of the self and of all things; because it is the photographic negative from which all these things are created. In itself, the memory is quiescent, autonomous, and luminous; it gives Proust's artist access to things perceived and from this memory he paints icons from the power of the recreative imagination. In the inner darkroom of the memory, the things that the artist recreates are neither of the phenomenal nor of the divine Incarnation: they are copies, pictures, photographs, portraits, projections of his within, of his self-divinization, of his self-transformation. In other words, uniting with the memory of the inner self, Proust's artist passes through darkness and ignorance with respect to the outer world, since all things have lost their correspondence with the prototype image, and then assumes the likeness of the creator, God, whose creatures make visible the thought, the idea, the symbol. Similarly, Proust's creations reveal his own symbol or reserve.

> Par le souvenir Swann reliait ces parcelles, abolissait les intervalles, coulait comme en or une Odette de bonté et de calme pour laquelle il fit plus tard . . . des sacrifices que l'autre Odette n'eût pas obtenus. . . . Savoir ne permet pas toujours d'empêcher, mais du moins les choses que nous savons, nous les tenons, sinon entre nos mains, du moins dans notre pensée où nous les disposons à notre gré, ce qui nous donne l'illusion d'une sorte de pouvoir sur elles. (*R*, 314–15)[9]

The power of the memory to record photographs, pictures, and copies of things independent of one another, thus eliminating any links, any kind of sequence among the pictures portrayed, makes it possible for the artist to create an "image différente de celles que nous avons l'habitude de voir" yet true to nature. Such an image (symbol) recalls an earlier impression, an ideal moment in which the objects perceived did not yet exist, since they had not been given their poetic beauty, "quelque chose de poétique," by the artist. In order for creative beauty to reveal itself, the sacrifice of real objects must take place so that the perfection of things comes about according to the remembrance and the eyes of the memory of the artist alone. Thus, the redeeming work of the artist as creator, or, more appropriately, the incarnation of the word as metaphor, becomes directly linked to the divinization of things in complete union with the reserve of the artist. Now, if this union has been accomplished in the poetic understanding of the artist, who is the thinking symbol, the remembering symbol, it is necessary that each thing in turn partake of this creation by being a symbol, a projection of the within of the artist. The link with the prototype image is broken, and symbolic realism, based on the incarnation and redemption of the Image (Christ-Man) of God, disappears through the absence of the latter and through losing its link with objective reality.

> Chaque être est détruit quand nous cessons de le voir; puis son apparition suivante est une création nouvelle, différente de celle qui l'a immédiatement précédée, sinon de toutes. . . . Dans la confrontation de notre souvenir à la réalité nouvelle, c'est cela qui marquera notre déception ou notre surprise, nous apparaîtra comme la retouche de la réalité en nous avertissant que nous nous étions mal rappelé. A son tour l'aspect la dernière fois négligé du visage, et, à cause de cela même, le plus saisissant cette fois-ci, le plus réel, le plus rectificatif, deviendra matière à rêverie, à souvenirs. C'est un profil langoureux et rond, une expression douce, rêveuse que nous désirerons revoir. Et alors, de nouveau, la fois suivante, ce qu'il y a de volontaire dans les yeux perçants, dans le nez pointu, dans les lèvres serrées, viendra corriger l'écart entre notre désir et l'objet auquel il a cru correspondre. (R, 917–18)[10]

This correspondence between the real and the remembered, between the lost moment and the new one, between the outer and the within is not accidental. Remembering is not simply looking back at a photographic negative, but constantly recreating things, redeveloping photographs, reentering the inner self so that the outside comes to echo what is within (intellect) of the artist. Poetic understanding, which is more than just remembering, means that the will corrects the within, which mirrors what it is not. That is, reality becomes less and less real and more and more poetic; it has become the projections, dreams, and impressions of the artist. Whereas on the one hand, thought and its expression as icon are still divided by the separation of the without and the within, on the other hand, the sensory and the symbol are really a unity. What bridges this gap is the will.

> Mais en moi, la volonté ne partagea pas un instant cette illusion, la volonté qui est le serviteur persévérant et immuable de nos personnalités successives; cachée dans l'ombre, dédaignée, inlassablement fidèle, travaillant sans cesse, et sans se soucier des variations de notre moi, à ce qu'il ne manque jamais du nécessaire. (R, 870)[11]

In this faithful servant, the will, the revelation in artistic creation is poetic since it expresses the reserve. The reserve has two faces: the one looks out (physical eyes) toward exterior things, the sphere of the senses; the other looks within (eyes of memory), the sphere of the symbolic, of the iconic. In the outer world, reason and understanding (habitual modes of thought) rule; in the inner world, will and memory direct the reserve into that mysterious, unknown, and beautiful world of icons (mirrors of absolute subjective beauty and truth) which have been created thanks to the ignorance of the artist of the prototype image of external reality. The role of Proust's artist, then, is to communicate the internal expression of the reserve outwardly, by a symbolic language created by the artist. External reality (phenomenon), recreated in the inner darkroom (imagination) of the artist, is thus transformed into the symbol, which makes it possible for the same reality to be expressed poetically as a mental construct, as a dream.

> Et comme le rêve d'une femme qui m'aurait aimé était toujours présent à ma pensée, ces étés-là ce rêve fut imprégné de la fraîcheur des eaux courantes; et quelle que fût la femme que j'évoquais, des grappes de fleurs violettes et rougeâtres s'élevaient aussitôt de chaque côté d'elle comme des couleurs complémentaires. Ce n'était pas seulement parce qu'une image dont nous rêvons reste toujours marquée, s'embellit et bénéficie du reflet des couleurs étrangères qui par hasard l'entourent dans notre rêverie; car ces paysages des livres que je lisais n'étaient pas pour moi que des paysages plus vivement représentés à mon imagination que ceux que Combray mettait sous mes yeux, mais qui eussent été analogues. (*R*, 86)[12]

This image (symbol) indicates that the outer world has become a symbolic (sensory) expression of the artist's reserve. It also means that the same image represents whoever and whatever corresponds to the artist's dream in which a particular symbol is invented and stored as remembrance of things past, as ideal photographs, as supreme copies of a transfigured outer world, as disembodied selves, as icons. And, as icons, the figures in *A la recherche du temps perdu* receive the same glorification, the same veneration, the same divinization, since they express the incarnation of the artist's creation, of the word as metaphor as is ascribed by traditional Catholic theology to God as Creator. For the will opens the door to the suprasensible world, the above, in what is the ultimate esthetic expression (the icon) in the sense that this world of the above is now perceived by the senses subjectively, without any intermediaries.

> Et la pensée de Swann se porta pour la première fois dans un élan de pitié et de tendresse vers ce Vinteuil, vers ce frère inconnu et sublime qui lui aussi avait dû tant souffrir; qu'avait pu être sa vie? au fond de quelles douleurs avait-il puisé cette force de dieu, cette puissance illimitée de créer? (*R*, 348)[13]

Conclusion: From Image to Icon

As a contemplative poem, Giotto's frescoes symbolically reveal and conceal the unity and diversity of God's triune action in the world, the divine plan. The frescoes, both individually and collectively, from the *Virtues* and *Vices*, to the *Last Judgment*, point to what is an upward and downward movement of creation in its prototype image. The frescoes, then, are a meditative poem, a contemplation, a prayer, in which Giotto expresses the soul's journey to God. In fact, we have attempted to show that Giotto undertakes to mirror in his frescoes a vision of the world through the contemplation of vestige (phenomenon), exemplar (soul, intellect), and Exemplary (God). The paintings are an effort to unveil the tensional pull between natural and spiritual existence, between the Fall and Redemption.

In their beauty, Giotto's frescoes are images of nature, which make visible the superluminous beauty of the ordering art that by means of numerical and spiritual proportion penetrates creation. The poem the frescoes create expresses the three movements of Bonaventure's song of beauty: the contemplation of the outer, the recognition of the within, and the ascent to the above. If we visit the chapel, we can perceive the beautiful of the outside of things, but we may be closed to their inner beauty unless the mind's eye opens the senses to the prototype image, the spiritual, which shines forth as exemplar and also directs the mind's eye toward God through faith, hope, and charity. In this way, the observer passes from sensory images into spiritual awareness through understanding, and from mental consciousness the senses flow upward into the single image of the Persons of the Holy Trinity where the soul comes to rest in the sight of the most beautiful, divine love, that is, charity. In this esthetic state, according to Bonaventure's *Soul's Journey into God*, the soul delights itself in the absolute harmony of the eternal beauty.

For Proust, on the other hand, Giotto's frescoes, instead of being a meditative poem by conveying symbolically God's incarnate Word through the prototype image, become mental constructs, projections, illusions of the world or of the figures they represent; they become icons where our inner perfection, idealization, self-divinization, thoughts, ideas, and our reserve are transmitted as symbols of remembrance of things past, of an imagined moment, person, or landscape, of memories. In Proust's poetic understanding, Giotto's images come to mean the purely phenomenal and subjective world of the artist (as expressed in the icon). According to Proust, the source that feeds that world is not the grace of the triune image of God but the will of the artist; or, as Proust says:

> . . . ce rôle des croyances, il es vrai que quelque chose en moi le savait, c'était la volonté, mais elle le sait en vain si l'intelligence, la sensibilité continuent à l'ignorer; celles-ci sont de bonne foi quand elles croient que nous avons envie de quitter une maîtresse à laquelle seule notre volonté sait que nous tenons. (*R*, 857)[14]

8
Augustine and Proust on Time

[Florence et Venise] le devinrent encore plus pour moi, quand mon père . . . les fit sortir toutes deux non plus seulement de l'Espace abstrait, mais de ce Temps imaginaire où nous situons non pas un seul voyage à la fois, mais d'autres, simultanés. . . . (R, 392)[1]

What then is time? I know what it is if no one asks me what it is; but if I want to explain it to someone who has asked me, I find that I do not know. (C, 267)

The artistically created icons mentioned in the previous chapter exist only in Proust's memory and function only within the dream world that memory produces. This means that the creative artist is not bound by any sort of temporal limitations and may construct both icons and a supertemporal dream world where the memory creates the divine world of privileged moments. These psychological and subjective aspects of time are by no means a new intellectual endeavor. Although centuries apart, Augustine (354–430) and Proust demonstrate that the relativity of time is apprehended either from introspection on a lost past, as in Proust, or from an unfulfilled future, as in Augustine. For each of them, time is neither theological nor scientific but philosophical and therefore psychological. Time is based on the mind's reflections and its seeking out the reasons for its existence. In their reflections on the whatness of time they reconstruct what Augustine calls "fleeting moments," or what Proust calls "des moments privilégiés" of the human person's life, and consequently a concept of the self emerges. Each of them penetrates reality, thereby enabling us, through a reading of The Confessions and of A la recherche du temps perdu, to see both time and the self in a new way.

Augustine on Time

Essentially, Augustine locates time in creation: the passing away of minutes, the chain of hours, and the sequence of years—the mutability of nature. To Augustine, the clock of time, the changes in time, the order of human history, time as past, present, and future, or time as measure of reality, all exist within this created universe. Hence, God is in creation; but in God time simply is. That is to say that in God time is not clock-time, as in physical reality, or "void-time" (or nothingness) but eternally present: "Nor was ever a time in which there was no time" (*C*, 267). Temporal time, then, is itself a creation of God, who, as Creator, stands outside time. Consequently, God created this universe not in time but with time; created things began to clock away, that is, undergo change. But what is time, Augustine asks? Although he says he does not know, he goes on to point out:

> But in what sense can we say that those two times, the past and the future, exist, when the past no longer is and the future is not yet? Yet if the present were always present and did not go by into the past, it would not be time at all, but eternity. If, therefore, the present (if it is to be time at all) only comes into existence because it is in transition toward the past, how can we say that even the present *is*? For the cause of its being is that it shall cease to be. (*C*, 267–68)

Augustine concludes that there is no real existence of a time past and a future time; for how can we say a long and a short time, yesterday and tomorrow, when the frame of reference is time in transition? Should we not simply say, says Augustine, that time *is*? But then, how can we say that time *is* when the *is* of time has meaning only insofar as it ceases to be? Yet time can be measured. But where is time measured? For Augustine time exists in the mind and can be measured there.

> For these three do exist in the mind, and I do not see them anywhere else: the present time of things past is memory; the present time of things present is sight; the present time of things future is expectation. (*C*, 273)

Time, then, does exist and it is comparatively measured. But eternal or immutable time, or the time that has neither duration nor extension exists now only in the memory of past experiences and the expectation of things to come.

> As things pass by they leave an impression in you; this impression remains after the things have gone into the past, and it is this impression which I measure in the present, not the things which, in their passage, caused the impression. It is this impression which I measure when I measure time. Therefore, either this itself is time or else I do not measure time at all. (*C*, 281)

The impression in the mind of things as they pass by is the compass by which Augustine measures time. And the impression of things is either diminished to a point when it ceases to exist, or it grows through a remembrance of things past to a point when it simply exists in the eternal present of God of which time is a mere impression or image (*C*, 217).

Up to this point it would seem that Augustine has a great deal in common with modern philosophers in asserting that reality depends upon whatever impressions are present in the mind of the individual who is experiencing things as they move. But Augustine precisely defines the relation that exists between the created world on the one hand and the eternal world on the other and suggests that ultimate reality (the world of intelligible and incorruptible forms) that exists beyond time can be attained through the human journey into the mind or soul and, in turn, the soul's journey into the mystery of creation or God himself. That is to say, Augustine's world is not a world of unconnected perceptions, of unconscious and involuntary recollection, of a realized ideal in the impression objects leave on the mind. Instead, it is a world where there exists a deep harmony and continuity between the world of fleeting moments—the world of motion—and the eternal world—the world of intelligible forms—and that this link is made possible but not actualized through calling to mind, or simply *cogitare* (*C*, 222).

Since Augustine writes his *Confessions* "that I shall show not what I was, but what I now am and continue to be" (*C*, 213–14), he explains that what he is is not simply bodily sensations but a thinking being, and as such he is capable of freeing himself from both the mutability of the material world or nature and the restlessness of his life. As a result, he sees the inner self, or the self associated with mind or soul, to be better than the outer self, or the self of the senses. It is better because Augustine finds there an ecstatic delight "that no breeze dispenses," a radiancy "that space cannot contain," and a music "that time cannot carry away." In short, what he finds in the mind is immutability with respect to the sensory world (*C*, 215). There, in the mind, Augustine tells us, time, past and future, is under the power of the memory, which converts both expectation of a future time and remembrance of things past into the sight of an ever present *now* that alone *is*, and in which Augustine finds himself to be what he is.

> Great indeed is the power of memory! It is something terrifying, my God, a profound and infinite multiplicity; and this thing is the mind, and this thing is myself. What then am I, my God? What is my nature? A life various, manifold, and quite immeasurable. (*C*, 227)

In this way Augustine recalls incidents in his life, such as the stealing of the pear, the journey from Carthage to Rome to Milan; he remembers the conversations he had with astrologers, with Ambrose, and with his mother Monica; he recollects the faces of the people he has seen and the objects he has felt, smelled, and touched. He recalls his life as it was, "spilled and scattered among times," and remembers that such a life is and will continue to be as such until he "can flow into" God, where the brilliant light of divine wisdom, "by whom all these things are made both what is past and what is to come," will take him up into the eternal world where God's presence is present: that is, it is no longer an impression but a living reality (*C*, 201).

The Confessions, then, is not so much a recalling, a remembrance of a life "various, manifold and immeasurable," as it is a life's flight into eternity, a life delivered from time. But Augustine has felt the temptations of his boyhood, the spectacles of vanity, the deceptions of life, the sins of pride, lust, avarice, imprudence, intemperance, and injustice. He has experienced the disorder, weariness, tearing apart, emptiness, sorrow, sterility, and cries of his inner self. He has felt the loss of the self in the distractions of the many and is conscious that the "true measure of love" is difficult to achieve. Merely calling to mind his past in no way guarantees him deliverance from time, from the clock of created things as they move toward corruption. His flight into eternity comes only when the will is "set on fire" and carried upward by God's love from which everything moves and in which all things find rest. Hence, to Augustine it is not a question of looking within the self as much as coming to see through the mirror of the soul an image, an impression of God. And God's image is touched, or grasped, or embraced, or darkly seen by Augustine as he meditates on divine Wisdom.

> Terrified insofar as I am unlike it, on fire insofar as I am akin to it. It is Wisdom, Wisdom herself that shines through me, splitting through the cloud in which I am wrapped and which, as I faint away from it, again enfolds me in the thick mist and weight of my punishment. (*C*, 264)

Accordingly, the inner self, like Wisdom, is a trinitarian self: "I am, I know that I am, and I know that I will," and if we understand this, concludes Augustine, we will find an "inseparable life," "one essence," and "one mind." But this does not mean that we have grasped in actuality the immutable, the eternal, and the incorruptible in us; for the immutable exists, knows, and wills eternally, that is, from everlasting to everlasting. In other words, as long as the self is in time, and time has no duration or extension in the mind, there cannot be an absolute and complete identity among thought, essence, and life as there is a perfect and complete identity between Wisdom and the divine Trinity.

But whether because of these three there is in God also a Trinity, or whether all three are in each Person so that each Person has three aspects, or whether both views are correct and in some unimaginable way, in simplicity and in multiplicity, It itself, though unbounded, is within Itself and bound to Itself, by which it exists and is known to itself and is sufficient to itself, unchangeably the Selfsame in the plentiful magnitude of its unity—who can easily grasp this in his mind? (*C*, 323)

The mind, then, is unable to understand God's existence, knowledge, and will because, whereas the mind sees in time and moves in time, God does "not see in time nor move in time nor rest in time" (*C*, 349). Yet the mind can grasp his Presence, which comes from time in the memory of which "these three aspects" present are merely an impression, an image of a triune God in whom "nothing passes by; everything is present" (*C*, 265).

Proust on Time

If, indeed, according to Proust, from a long and distant past nothing subsists, if he writes *A la recherche du temps perdu* in order to bring back "des moments privilégiés," and if it is true that the past is hidden beyond the reach of the intellect, in some material object, then where does time really exist for Proust? "Le temps dont nous disposons chaque jour est élastique; les passions que nous ressentons le dilatent, celles que nous inspirons le rétrécissent, et l'habitude le remplit" (*R*, 612). By conceiving of time as elastic, contracting to a point when it no longer exists and expanding to infinity where it becomes memory (remembrance) or absolute time (in the sense that it is a slice of the continuity of physical time), depending upon what we feel when the impressions are first made, Proust affirms that physical time is not a distinct and separate entity that, because of its separability from the passions may be viewed quantitatively. Besides, even from the point of view of measurable time, Proust tells us, the days are not all equal: "Il y a des jours montueux et malaisés qu'on met un temps infini à gravir et des jours en pente qui se laissent descendre à fond de train en chantant" (*R*, 391).

For Proust, time is not a dimension that changes in its modes, measurability, and meaning as it interacts with space, but it is "les passions que nous ressentons" in space and time that coalesce with, melt into, impregnate, or make sterile our everyday existence without any precise point of reference and without separation from the material world. In this way we are aware in theory that the earth revolves, but in practice we do not perceive its motion, for the ground on which we stand does not seem to move.

So it is with time in our life. In order to make the earth's revolutions perceptible to the senses, Proust must transport us into space; first, he must spin us slowly, then he must gradually accelerate us to reach full speed. Similarly, he must accelerate the beat of time to such a speed that he carries us across time and beyond it in a matter of a few seconds, if not in one instant. It follows that time is a moment, a now symbolizing or representing experiences forever gone.

> Les lieux que nous avons connus n'appartiennent pas qu'au monde de l'espace où nous les situons pour plus de facilité. Ils n'étaient qu'une mince tranche au milieu d'impressions contiguës qui formaient notre vie d'alors; le souvenir d'une certaine image n'est que le regret d'un certain instant; et les maisons, les routes, les avenues, sont fugitives, hélas! comme les années. (R, 427)[2]

And indeed, time is so fugitive, so fleeting that it is nothing else than those contiguous impressions of our memory which bring together many slices of our experiences into an infinite flow, as though the very life we have lived, the very places we have seen, the very people we have touched and loved, the very delights we have experienced were only syllables, merely recorded for our convenience in order for us to make our journey on this earth, an earth that spins as fast as the years, months, hours, and minutes of our lives. In fact, our lives are so inseparable from the world of space that we can experience only continual regret with each successive moment; regret because time as past, present, and future does not exist except in the memory that recreates it. "Certes, ce qui palpite ainsi au fond de moi, ce doit être l'image, le souvenir visuel, qui, lié à cette saveur, tente de la suivre jusqu'à moi" (R, 46). However, even if this image, this past moment, this dead instant, were to reach consciousness, it would preserve nothing of the passions of the past, and therefore it would be mere pain unto death, a prolonged agony, a nothing, or a mere dream of yesterday. What, then, Proust asks himself, is the true relationship between time and memories? He expresses this so beautifully that the entire passage merits full quotation.

> C'est pourquoi la meilleure part de notre mémoire est hors de nous, dans un souffle pluvieux, dans l'odeur de renfermé d'une chambre ou dans l'odeur d'une première flambée, partout où nous retrouvons de nous-même ce que notre intelligence, n'en ayant pas l'emploi, avait dédaigné, la dernière réserve du passé, la meilleure, celle qui, quand toutes nos larmes semblent taries, sait nous faire pleurer encore. Hors de nous? En nous pour mieux dire, mais dérobée à nos propres regards, dans un oubli plus ou moins prolongé. C'est grâce à cet oubli seul que nous pouvons de temps à autre retrouver l'être que nous fûmes, nous placer vis-à-vis des choses comme cet être l'était, souffrir à nouveau, parce que nous ne

sommes plus nous, mais lui, et qu'il aimait ce qui nous est maintenant indifférent. Au grand jour de la mémoire habituelle, les images du passé pâlissent peu à peu, s'effacent, il ne reste plus rien d'elles, nous ne le retrouverons plus. (*R*, 643)[3]

The oblivion and discontinuity of time, the self as sandwiched between the world of space and that of the memory, the inability of the intellect to grasp logically what we are, the desire to love passionately, then love no more, and finally to become indifferent to love, the pain of memories that attempt to recapture the smell, touch, and perfume of moments gone by, the tears that accompany the futility of life—all these give us an image of humanity spinning and dissolving in space. And like the physical world, the world of memory moves according to "les lois de l'habitude," laws that divest life of its immediacy with the world of objects where alone the passions find ecstatic delight.

In this state of prolonged oblivion life finds its radiancy, its true meaning, its essence, its beauty, its transcendence, its grace, its elegance and its extratemporal delights, which are felt in a drop of rain, in the smell of flowers, in the taste of the "petites madeleines," in the sight of Venice, in the kiss of Albertine, in the music of Vinteuil, in the art of Giotto, in the drama of Phèdre, in the meeting of Gilberte, and in the architecture of Elstir, or in those things the intellect rejects. For in this state of prolonged oblivion the passions are experienced inversely, through the regrets, fears, tears, disappointments, failures, and anguish felt, on the one hand, for wishing "d'arrêter, d'immobiliser les moments" before the senses of the visual memory and, on the other hand, for realizing "qu'ils sont de courte durée" (*R*, 449). In this sense, and in this sense alone, moments that have been experienced in the past bring back to us, if we see them through the visual memory, not only their spatial dimensions but their essence, that is, the passions with which we were filled when we first experienced them. And so the taste of "les petites madeleines" filled Proust's narrator "avec une essence précieuse, avec une puissante joie," lifting him up from the contingencies of life into the motionless world of his memory, where, not by mental but by sensory association objects are transformed into something immaterial, something of the same nature as the sensations he felt when he first experienced them and with which, indissolubly, they blend.

Et dès que j'eus reconnu le goût du morceau de madeleine . . . toutes les fleurs de notre jardin et celles du parc de M. Swann, et les nymphéas de la Vivonne, et les bonnes gens du village et leurs petits logis et l'église et tout Combray et ses environs, tout cela qui prend forme et solidité, est sorti, ville et jardins, de ma tasse de thé. (*R*, 47–48)[4]

From this intensity of feelings, from this fullness of passions, Proust in turn believed that the rain, the flowers, the madeleine, Combray, as well as

Venice, Florence, Balbec, Albertine and Gilberte, art, music, literature and sculpture were really real in that they became permanent images in his memory.

Reality, then, is not merely reality, time is not merely time, moments are not merely moments, the self is not merely the self; but they are a cup full of scents, sounds, and real love, the love stripped of its habitual memory, a love illuminated to its finest movement, is art. Through art, Proust tells us, we rediscover, we bring back to consciousness, we remember the forgotten past of other people in the immediate sensations we feel as we contemplate the works of art. In short, through art we relive our own individual lives in "les lois générales" of life itself, which artists perceive and reveal in their works. And these laws of life are that we must love passionately, that we must cease to love, that we must wait for a prolonged suffering before we can begin to love again (if chance allows it), that we must die perhaps without having loved at all. From this point of view, artists' lives resemble their works, which, on a deeper level, reveal the short duration of other people's lives. The artist, then, does not repudiate the past but draws out of it something, an image, an impression, a dot, if you will, that transcends it. And it is the passions alone that bring forth the works and, as the passions contract and expand, so too the artist must move from person to person, from object to object, since they, of necessity, cannot sustain for a long time the intensity of the passions. This process is repeated over and over again. But the repetitions, concludes Proust, convey the ultimate truth that what exists is not the person or the object, but "cette image elle-même, parce que derrière cette image je sentais se cacher la raison pour laquelle elle m'était décochée en plein coeur" (R, 406).

More explicitly, only the artist can uncover, penetrate, bring to light, or unveil the dark abyss of existence by adorning and illuminating it with a life, a soul that points beyond time and space; the artist alone can give meaning to an otherwise meaningless past; the artist alone can give form, substance, solidity, and weight to reality itself; the artist alone can give dimensions to space and time. In short, the artist alone can redeem the prolonged oblivion of time, can taste the tears, can feel the sufferings, can touch the anguish, can hear the cries, can smell the desires, can flavor the vanities of this fading universe of ours. By plunging into the memories of humanity itself, Proust's artist creates, in fear and trembling, in terror, weary, tired, and without hope, a life for himself, a life colored, shaped, and patterned in the depth, width, and height of those lives which, like his own, are of a dustlike existence, although artificially separated by mere intervals of time in the dimension of space. To live, then, is to create, to rediscover the common elements of life at their source, that is, in the passionate moments lost. Of the madeleine incident, Proust writes:

Je pose la tasse et me tourne vers mon esprit. C'est à lui de trouver la vérité. Mais comment? Grave incertitude, toutes les fois que l'esprit se sent dépassé par lui-même; quand lui, le chercheur, est tout ensemble le pays obscur où il doit chercher et où tout son bagage ne lui sera de rien. Chercher? pas seulement: créer. Il est en face de quelque chose qui n'est pas encore et que seul il peut réaliser, puis faire entrer dans sa lumière. (*R*, 45)[5]

Conclusion: Time as Interior Experience, as Vocation

These two thinkers, separated by time and their vision of the world and humanity, share a common ground: what Augustine calls public time is inadequate to an understanding of our inner life, the life of vocation. Both Augustine and Proust reduce space and time to conceptual and perceptual space and time, which are the human person's inner experiential life, or the memory of time. However, this is not merely a case of the difference between objective and subjective time. Instead, time is connected with persons and with change. Therefore, the objective or scientifical measurement of time is just as mysterious or arbitrary as are Augustine's and Proust's concepts of memory in its attempt to grasp time by a calling to mind, or a remembrance of things past.

Accordingly, time deals with the self as that self undergoes change. But for Augustine God is time without change, and time is an image, an impression, a temporal duration of God measured by the memory as objects move. Hence, unlike God, for whom the moment includes all time, for human beings, instead, the moment can be short and long and then go by as though it had never been. In a way, then, even for us the moment is the only real time we have, one that includes past, present, and future. But our moment is finite, whereas God's is eternal. This is what Augustine seeks, and this is what he found in the life of a Christian monk. This life is the life of prayer, silence, contemplation, and the living out of past memories in love.

Proust also gives us time as vocation, as a life lived interiorly. He also seeks the eternal now, the ecstatic moment where the laws of habit, of public time, and of habitual memory do not disturb the precious essence, the all-powerful joy, the bliss, the voluptuous delights, the mystery of the "petites madeleines" as he recalls them in his memories. In remembrance, then, the self no longer changes but is timelessly present to itself and, in a way, contemplates its former self, the self of the past. Hence, through remembrance the moments are stripped of their orderly time, of their spatial dimensions; they become illuminated with a brilliant flash of light, generating permanent moments before the "I" (the artist). Therefore, as an artist, Proust discovers his privileged moments in the sounds and rhythms of music, in the lives of artists he admires, in the places he visits, in the art and architecture he sees, in the passions of the people he loves, in the whispers of nature itself, and in words as means of penetrating the mystery of existence. But this "moi intérieur" of Proust, this "I" of the artist, is not the "I" of Augustine, the Christian man who is awakened and made sensitive to what is by the Word of God in his soul. Yet, Proust reveals his vocation in the confusions, the anguish, the abyss, the tears, the oblivion, the corruptibility that are his life.

Conclusion

This study of the creative silence of Proust discloses to us the purely subjective and phenomenological element of Proust's thought, as well as its objective aspect. It shows us that Proust belongs not only to twentieth-century French culture but that he can take his place with great thinkers such as Augustine and Bonaventure. His call to silence echoes through all ages. It is an invitation to all of us to purge the noisy element of our existence, to hold in abeyance ordinary thought, everyday speech, in order to perceive the "grand réservoir," the "réserve" of things, an image of "l'Esprit éternel." It is a call to see the beautiful and claim it as a subjective terrain, as something deeper than ordinary eyes perceive.

The focal point of this study has been to consider silence in the context of the perception of phenomenal reality, in its relation to artistic expression and in particular to the written word, and finally, in its connection with time. Thereby the philosophical content of *A la recherche du temps perdu* is revealed. Such a focus does indeed have to consider the search for truth and beauty: truth and beauty encounter each other in silence, and they emerge out of this silence as expressions of thought. Silence is thought expressing itself through signs. And signs grasp life in its nascent form, in its archaic past, in its everlasting Origin.

Proust enters the silence of things, their inexhaustible beauty, their deepest secrets, their hidden forms, and draws from this silence immaterial parts that protect it from everyday experience, which would cover it with noise. In Proust's novel, Bergotte's words, Vinteuil's little phrase, Elstir's paintings, which allow no memory of the phenomenal world to intrude upon the inner world of silence where the poetry to be written, the music to be composed, the painting to be done, and the love to be experienced, reveal themselves and prevail over the madeleine, over the Ponte Vecchio of Florence, over the narrator's love for Albertine, over the church at Balbec, which depend on memory and, therefore, still refer to a phenomenal explanation, to habitual thought connected to the flow of social noises. This is the meaning of created silence; namely, those privileged moments in which the "médiocre contenu" of the everyday world is purged only to be replaced by a world of dreams, appearances, phantoms, the transmutation of material reality; the noise of the world of phenomena is expelled and is replaced by the silence of artistic forms.

This transmutation begins with an actual perception of phenomenal things and finally places the perceiver in a state of intoxication, hallucination, and continuous ecstasy. This is not a mystical ecstasy but a purely mental state in which reality is totally transfigured or metamorphosed in the mind. Thought and silence go together. Thought would make its way down to the darkest region, to the void, to the abyss, if silence were not there to prevent it from taking with it the mysterious splendor, the light, the great reservoir of things. It is silence that gives phenomenal things their evaporation zone so that they rise above the opaque world and become part of an illumined universe. This illumined universe is the inner darkroom of humanity's own "sol mental," which opens on the side of infinite thought. In thought, memory is forced to restore the past in order that the mind may see the unity of time in the embracing gaze of silence. In thought, time past is time regained; the waking life is the sleeping night; timeless existence is an actual reality, a real silence stretching over the pure landscape in the garden of Combray, the park of Swann, the water lilies of the Vivonne, the woods of Boulogne.

Upon reading Proust, we perceive nature as an urn of silence, full of tears, mystery, and splendor. Nature begins to speak as soon as it has been purified by tears of longing; it remains silent as long as it is incarnate in phenomenal forms; it openly speaks to the "dormeur éveillé" while it remains silent and closed to the ordinary person. The silence found in this urn is symphonic: its sound is carried by the creative breath of the dreamer over the evaporation zone where thought beholds beauty or the ideal form, separating light from darkness, transcendental realities from material realities. The world of beauty is the twilight of silence, the dawn of the world revealing itself, the appearances of phenomenal forms, and the perpetual recreation of images or birth of time itself. This world of beauty is the world of dreams. The dreamlike atmosphere of the phenomenal spreads its tints and tones over the "zone d'air pur," producing a harmonious spectacle in the likes of a Giorgione, a Watteau, or a Redon and revealing the transparent and luminous essence of a sleeping world, a world itself without form. Sleep is of short duration; beauty gives to sleep "le fil des heures, l'ordre des années et des mondes" that enable it to create a divine world, a world savored by artistic forms that are sweet and fragrant and cease to be only when sleep ends.

Deeply submerged in the world of sleep, light, beauty, and love, Proust's "dormeur éveillé" becomes marked with the characteristics and properties of the gods in that the mysterious splendor of beauty shines forth in him by means of his incarnation as divine artist. Standing on the spiritual border, this "dormeur éveillé" bears within himself the creative word, the revealing silence. This "dormeur éveillé" loses himself in the sleep of remembrance; he longs to clothe himself in the luminous garment of rebirth without removing sensory and mental garments. Whenever the sleep ends, this "dormeur éveillé" is reduced to tears, tears that flow from the infinite distance between the dread of oblivion and the regret for lost privileged moments where the self that is subject to death is temporarily absorbed into a blissful experience. Like two resonating musical notes, the sound of these tears echoes eternally across the universe in the chords of silence, separate, yet melting into one harmony. And when this music pierces the soul of this "dormeur éveillé," he hears the silence of his own solitude, his own emptiness, his own barrenness. This silence consumes him in his yearning to touch and savor the sweet fragrance of love, since love and oblivion encounter each other in this silence. The love that this "dormeur éveillé" seeks on this earth can only be consummated in death. While death spreads its silence across the opaque landscape of the phenomenal world, love is a ray of light, a pure tone, a mysterious splendor, arising from the ultimate silence, death. And death is carried within the beauty that this "dormeur éveillé" experiences within himself as he dreams in the night. In the night, all is mystery to the sensory eyes, all is splendor to the mind and to the memory, because all is seen from the world of "le profond sommeil," the world of eternity.

This, then, is the world of sleep, the world of dreams. The whole universe is nothing but its rays. When the phenomenal world in its darkest moment reveals itself as we gaze at death, we see our own solitude, with no one to illumine our path but the immaterial parts that offer us the hope of salvation from this death. Artistic forms are Proust's only world; they allow him contact with the beautiful, while at the same time they separate him from the ugliness and death of the exterior world, the world of the social self. The outside world is ugly because it is buried under layers of habit, preventin the symphony of silence from ringing out. We learn from Proust that nothing less than the created silence is beautiful; and, at the same time, the only true beauty is the beauty of the metaphor, which is thought listening to itself in the distilled air of the Idea. Thought impregnates phenomenal forms with the germs of eternal ideas, unique forms or exemplars, which reveal themselves in the silent world of remembrance. Remembrance is not the absence of speech; it is metaphors replacing thought. Through metaphors, thought cuts itself off from habitual speech for the sake of attaining inner silence, for the sake of realizing artistic creation.

Unlike ordinary, philosophical, and scientific language, this inner silence is poetic speech. In poetic discourse, the self stands face to face with the privileged moments, through which it becomes one with "l'Esprit éternel." The poetic word conceals the essence of the Idea, while at the same time disclosing its mystery. The mystery of the poetic word does not dwell within the Idea, Thought, or Being; rather, its place is in the creative thought. The poet's search for the idea, the form, the essence, is a search for that absolute moment of self-intoxication or hallucination, when the self experiences itself as separated from all phenomenal ties, freed from all time. This experience of the absolute, this voluptuous enjoyment of immaterial parts, this creative longing to touch the abyss, is something that the poet can neither attain nor endure because time intrudes upon the creative silence and limits it. Then there are no longer dreams, but only the passage of time, the flow against time, the stream of remembered yesterdays, "l'obscurité du silence" where *A la recherche du temps perdu* silently achieves its privileged moment, its esthetic splendor, its mysterious unity, its angle of vision in the deepest layer of the reader's memory.

> Et comme l'art recompose exactement la vie, autour des vérités qu'on a atteintes en soi-même flottera toujours une atmosphère de poésie, la douceur d'un mystère qui n'est que le vestige de la pénombre que nous avons dû traverser, l'indication, marquée exactement comme par un altimètre, de la profondeur d'une oeuvre. (*R*, 3:898)[1]

Notes

Chapter 1. *A la recherche du temps perdu* as Creative Word

1. In a language that we know, we have substituted for the opacity of sounds the transparency of ideas.

2. So it is with all great writers: the beauty of their sentences is as unforeseeable as is that of a woman whom we have never seen; it is creative, because it is applied to an external object which they have thought of . . . and to which they have not yet given expression.

3. After all, the old forms of speech must also in their time have been . . . images difficult to follow, when the listener was not yet cognisant of the universe which they depicted. But for a long time it has been taken to be the real universe, and is instinctively relied upon.

4. At certain points in the conversation . . . it was a long time before I discovered an exact correspondence with the parts of his books in which his form became so poetic and so musical. At those points he could see in what he was saying a plastic beauty independent of whatever his sentences might mean, and as human speech reflects the human soul, though without expressing it as does literary style, Bergotte appeared almost to be talking nonsense, intoning certain words and, if he were pursuing, beneath them, a single image, stringing them together uninterruptedly on one continuous note, with a wearisome monotony.

5. And so . . . it was because Bergotte applied that thought with precision to the reality which pleased him that his language had in it something down-to-earth, something over-nourishing. . . . Moreover the quality, always rare and new, of what he wrote was expressed in his conversation by so subtle a manner of approaching a question, ignoring every aspect of it that was already familiar, that he appeared to be seizing hold of an unimportant detail, to be off the point, to be indulging in paradox, so that his ideas seemed as often as not to be confused, for each of us sees clarity only in those ideas which have the same degree of confusion as his own.

6. Besides, as all novelty depends upon the prior elimination of the stereotyped attitude to which we had grown accustomed, and which seemed to us to be reality itself, any new form of conversation . . . must always appear complicated and exhausting. It is based on figures of speech with which we are not familiar, the speaker appears to us to be talking entirely in metaphors; and this wearies us, and gives us the impression of a want of truth.

7. And it is true that there was in Bergotte's style a kind of harmony similar to that for which the ancients used to praise certain of their orators in terms which we now find hard to understand, accustomed as we are to our own modern tongues in which effects of that kind are not sought.

8. Above all, he [Bergotte] was a man who in his heart of hearts only really

loved certain images and . . . composing and painting them in words. . . . And if he had had to plead before a tribunal, he would inevitably have chosen his words not for the effect that they might have on the judge but with an eye to certain images which the judge would certainly never have perceived.

9. . . . the words that he [Bergotte] was now uttering were quite intelligible to me, and gave me a fresh reason for taking an interest in Berma's acting. I tried to picture her again in my mind. . . . But in order for these thoughts to enhance for me the beauty of Berma's gesture, Bergotte would have had to put them into my head before the performance. Then, while that attitude of the actress actually existed in flesh and blood before my eyes, at that moment when the thing that is happening still has the plenitude of reality, I might have tried to extract from it the idea of archaic sculpture. But all that I retained of Berma in that scene was a memory which was no longer susceptible of modification; as meagre as an image devoid of those deep layers of the present in which one can delve and genuinely discover something new, an image on which one cannot retrospectively impose an interpretation that is not subject to verification and objective sanction.

10. Sitting alone, I continued to fashion remarks such as might have pleased or amused the Swanns, and . . . putting to myself fictitious questions so chosen that my brilliant epigrams served simply as apt repartee. Though conducted in silence, this exercise was nonetheless a conversation and not a meditation, my solitude a mental social round in which it was not I myself but imaginary interlocuters who controlled my choice of words. . . .

11. Philosophy distinguishes often between free and necessary acts. Perhaps there is none to the necessity of which we are more completely subjected than that which . . . brings back . . . a memory until then levelled down with all the rest by the oppressive force of bemusement and makes it spring to the surface because unknown to us it contained more than any of the others a charm of which we do not become aware until the following day. And perhaps, too, there is no act so free, for it is still unprompted by habit, by that sort of mental obsession which . . . encourages the invariable reappearance of the image of one particular person.

12. We imagine always when we speak that it is our own ears, our own mind, that are listening. . . . The truth which one puts into one's words does not carve out a direct path for itself, is not irresistibly self-evident. A considerable time must elapse before a truth of the same order can take shape in them.

13. And so I would read, or rather sing his sentences in my mind, with rather more *dolce*, rather more *lento* than he himself had perhaps intended, and his simplest phrase would strike my ears with something peculiarly gentle and loving in its intonation. More than anything else I cherished his philosophy, and had pledged myself to it in lifelong devotion.

14. So that, if there were no such thing as habit, life must appear delightful to those of us who are continually under the threat of death—that is to say, to all mankind. Then, if our imagination is set going by the desire for what we cannot possess, its flight is not limited by a reality perceived in these casual encounters in which the charms of the passing stranger are generally in direct ratio to the swiftness of our passage.

15. Then a whole promontory of the inaccessible world emerges from the twilight of dream and enters our life, our life in which, like the sleeper awakened, we actually see the people of whom we had dreamed with such ardent longing that we had come to believe that we should never see them save in our dreams.

16. But happiness can never be achieved. If we succeed in overcoming the force of circumstances, nature at once shifts the battle-ground, placing it within

ourselves, and effects a gradual change in our hearts until they desire something other than what they are about to possess.

17. Suddenly I fell asleep, plunged into that deep slumber in which vistas are opened to us of a return to childhood, the recapture of past years, and forgotten feelings, of disincarnation, the transmigration of souls, the evoking of the dead, the illusions of madness, retrogression towards the most elementary of the natural kingdoms . . . all those mysteries which we imagine ourselves not to know and into which we are in reality initiated almost every night, as into the other great mystery of extinction and resurrection.

18. In a language that we know, we have substituted for the opacity of sounds the transparency of ideas. But a language which we do not know is a fortress sealed, within whose walls the one we love is free to play us false, while we, standing outside, desperately keyed up in our impotence, can see, can prevent nothing.

19. If it is true that the sea was once upon a time our native element, in which we must plunge our blood to recover our strength, it is the same with the oblivion, the mental nothingness of sleep; we seem then to absent ourselves for a few hours from time, but the forces which have gathered in that interval without being expended measure it by their quantity as accurately as the pendulum of the clock or the crumbling hillocks of the hourglass. Moreover, one does not emerge more easily from such a sleep than from a prolonged spell of wakefulness, so strongly does everything tend to persist; and if it is true that certain narcotics make us sleep, to have slept for a long time is an even more potent narcotic, after which we have great difficulty in making ourselves wake up.

20. I could not . . . lay down the novel of his [Bergotte]. . . . Then I observed the rare, almost archaic expressions he liked to employ at certain moments, in which a hidden stream of harmony, an inner prelude, would heighten his style; and it was at such points as these, too, that he would begin to speak of the "vain dream of life," of the "inexhaustible torrent of fair forms," of the "sterile and exquisite torture of understanding and loving," of the "moving effigies which ennoble for all time the charming and venerable fronts of our cathedrals," that he would express a whole system of philosophy, new to me, by the use of marvellous images that one felt must be the inspiration for the harp-song which then arose and to which they provided a sublime accompaniment. . . . And so, realising that the universe contained innumerable elements which my feeble senses would be powerless to discern did he not bring them within my reach, I longed to have some opinion, some metaphor of his, upon everything in the world. . . .

Chapter 2. Proust and Merleau-Ponty on Perception

1. When I saw an external object, my consciousness that I was seeing it would remain between me and it, surrounding it with a thin spiritual border that prevented me from ever touching its substance directly; for it would somehow evaporate before I could make contact with it, just as an incandescent body that is brought into proximity with something wet never actually touches its moisture, since it is always preceded by a zone of evaporation.

2. All inner perception is inadequate because I am not an object that can be perceived, because I make my reality and find myself in the act. . . . It is through my relation to 'things' that I know myself; inner perception follows afterwards, and

would not be possible had I not already made contact with my doubt in its very object.

3. Last night I had been nothing more than an empty vessel, weightless, and . . . [I] had been unable to refrain from moving about and talking, no longer had any stability, any centre of gravity; I had been set in motion and it seemed that I might have continued on my dreary course until I reached the moon. But if, while I slept, my eyes had not seen the time, my body had nevertheless contrived to calculate it, had measured the hours not on a dial superficially decorated with figures, but by the steadily growing weight of all my replenished forces which, like a powerful clock, it had allowed, notch by notch, to descend from my brain into the rest of my body where they now accumulated as far as the top of my knees the unimpaired abundance of their store.

4. A "real" person . . . is in a great measure perceptible only through our senses, that is to say, remains opaque, presents a dead weight which our sensibilities have not the strength to lift. If some misfortune comes to him, it is only in one small section of the complete idea we have of him that we are capable of feeling any emotion; indeed it is only in one small section of the complete idea he has of himself that he is capable of feeling any emotion either. The novelist's happy discovery was to think of substituting for those opaque sections, impenetrable to the human soul, their equivalent in immaterial sections, things, that is, which one's soul can assimilate.

5. And once the novelist has brought us to this state, in which, as in all purely mental states, every emotion is multiplied ten-fold, into which his book comes to disturb us as might a dream, but a dream more lucid and more abiding than those which come to us in sleep, why then, for the space of an hour he sets free within us all the joys and sorrows in the world, a few of which only we should have to spend years of our actual life in getting to know, and the most intense of which would never be revealed to us because the slow course of their development prevents us from perceiving.

6. For even if we have the sensation of being always enveloped in, surrounded by our own soul, still it does not seem a fixed and immovable prison; rather do we seem to be borne away with it, and perpetually struggling to transcend it, to break out into the world, with a perpetual discouragement as we hear endlessly all around us that unvarying sound which is not an echo from without, but the resonance of a vibration from within. We try to discover in things, which become precious to us on that account, the reflection of what our soul has projected on to them. . . .

7. In vain did I compress the whole landscape into my field of vision, draining it with an exhaustive gaze which sought to extract from it a female creature. . . . I would stare interminably at the trunk of a distant tree, from behind which she would emerge and come to me; I scanned the horizon, which remained as deserted as before; night was falling; it was without hope now that I concentrated my attention, as though to draw up from it the creatures which it must conceal, upon that sterile soil, that stale, exhausted earth . . . I ceased to think of those desires which came to me on my walks, but were never realised, as being shared by others, or as having any existence outside myself. They seemed to me now no more than the purely subjective, impotent, illusory creations of my temperament. They no longer had any connection with nature, with the world of real things, which from then onwards lost all its charm and significance, and meant no more to my life than a purely conventional framework. . . .

8. Suddenly I stood still, unable to move, as happens when we are faced with a vision that appeals not to our eyes only but requires a deeper kind of perception

and takes possession of the whole of our being. A little girl with fair, reddish hair, who appeared to be returning from a walk, and held a trowel in her hand, was looking at us, raising towards us a face powdered with pinkish freckles. . . . I gazed at her, at first with that gaze which is not merely the messenger of the eyes, but at whose window all the senses assemble and lean out, petrified and anxious, a gaze eager to reach, touch, capture, bear off in triumph the body at which it is aimed, and the soul with the body; then (so frightened was I lest at any moment my grandfather and my father, catching sight of the girl, might tear me away from her by telling me to run on in front of them) with another, an unconsciously imploring look, whose object was to force her to pay attention to me, to see, to know me.

9. Alas! in the freshest flower it is possible to discern those just perceptible signs which to the instructed mind already betray what will, by the desiccation or fructification of the flesh that is to-day in bloom, be the ultimate form, immutable and already predestined, of the autumnal seed. . . . I knew that . . . there dwelt beneath the rosy inflorescence of Albertine, Rosemonde, Andrée, unknown to themselves, held in reserve until the occasion should arise, a coarse nose, a protruding jaw, a paunch which would create a sensation when it appeared, but which was actually in the wings, ready to "come on," unforeseen, inevitable . . . emerging suddenly in answer to the call of circumstances from a nature anterior to the individual himself, through which he thinks, lives, evolves, gains strength or dies, without ever being able to distinguish that nature from the particular motives he mistakes for it. . . . For we grasp only the secondary ideas, without detecting the primary cause . . . that inevitably produced them, and which we manifest when the time comes.

10. And since, at the same time, we wish to continue to think of [the young girl], the mind prefers to imagine [her] in the future tense, to continue to bring about the circumstances which may make [her] recur—which, while giving us no clue as to the real nature . . . saves us the trouble of recreating [her] within ourselves and allows us to hope that we may receive [her] afresh from without.

11. . . . and my body, the side upon which I was lying, faithful guardians of a past which my mind should never have forgotten, brought back before my eyes the glimmering flame of the night-light in its urn-shaped bowl of Bohemian glass that hung by chains from the ceiling, and the chimney-piece of Siena marble in my bedroom at Combray, in my grandparents' house, in those far distant days which at this moment I imagined to be in the present without being able to picture them exactly, and which would become plainer in a little while when I was properly awake.

12. Certainly I was now well awake; my body had veered round for the last time and the good angel of certainty had made all the surrounding objects stand still around me. . . . But for all that I now knew that I was not in any of the houses of which the ignorance of the waking moment had, in a flash, if not presented me with a distinct picture, at least persuaded me of the possible presence, my memory had been set in motion; as a rule I did not attempt to go to sleep again at once, but used to spend the greater part of the night recalling our life in the old days at Combray with my great-aunt, at Balbec, Paris, Doncières, Venice, and the rest; remembering again all the places and people I had known, what I had actually seen of them, and what others had told me.

13. We have the experience of an I not in the sense of an absolute subjectivity, but indivisibly demolished and remade by the course of time. The unity of either the subject or the object is not a real unity, but a presumptive unity on the horizon of experience.

14. To say that I have a visual field is to say that by reason of my position I have access to and an opening upon a system of beings, visible beings, that these are at the disposal of my gaze in virtue of a kind of primordial contract and through a gift of nature, with no effort made on my part; from which it follows that vision is prepersonal. And it follows at the same time that it is always limited, that around what I am looking at a given moment is spread a horizon of things which are not seen, or which are even invisible. Vision is *a thought subordinated to a certain field*, and this is what is called a *sense*.

15. In every focusing movement my body unites present, past and future, it secretes time, or rather it becomes that location in nature where, for the first time, events, instead of pushing each other into the realm of being, project round the present a double horizon of past and future and acquire a historical orientation.

16. Perception is always in the mode of the impersonal 'One'. It is not a personal act enabling me to give a fresh significance to my life. The person who, in sensory exploration, gives a past to the present and directs it towards a future, is not myself as an autonomous subject, but myself in so far as I have a body and am able to 'look'. Rather than being a genuine history, perception ratifies and renews in us a 'prehistory'.

17. The constitution of a spatial level is simply one means of constituting an integrated world: my body is geared to the world when my perception presents me with a spectacle as varied and as clearly articulated as possible, and when my motor intentions, as they unfold, receive the responses they expect from the world. This maximum sharpness of perception and action points clearly to a perceptual *ground*, a basis of my life, a general setting in which my body can co-exist with the world.

18. When we say that thought is spontaneous, this does not mean that it coincides with itself; on the contrary it means that it outruns itself, and speech is precisely that act through which it immortalizes itself as truth.

19. For each object . . . there is an optimum distance from which it requires to be seen. . . . This is obtained through a certain balance between the inner and outer horizon. . . . The distance from me to the object is not a size which increases or decreases, but a tension which fluctuates around a norm.

20. We have relearned to feel our body; we have found underneath the objective and detached knowledge of the body that other knowledge which we have of it in virtue of its always being with us and of the fact that we are our body. In the same way we shall need to reawaken our experience of the world as it appears to us in so far as we are in the world through our body, and in so far as we perceive the world with our body.

21. All thought of something is at the same time self-consciousness, failing which it could have no object. At the root of all our reflections, we find, then, a being which immediately recognizes itself, because it is its knowledge both of itself and of all things, and which knows its own existence, not by observation and as a given fact, nor by inference from any idea of itself, but through direct contact with that existence. Self-consciousness is the very being of mind in action.

22. Since . . . I have no evidence of my past other than this present testimony and yet have the idea of a past, I have no reason to set over the unreflective, as an unknowable, against the reflection which I bring to bear on it. But my confidence in reflection amounts in the last resort to my accepting and acting on the fact of temporality, and the fact of the world as the invariable framework of all illusion and all disillusion: I know myself only in so far as I am inherent in time and in the world, that is, I know myself only in my ambiguity.

23. My set of experiences is presented as a concordant whole, and the synthesis

takes place not in so far as they all express a certain invariant, and in the identity of the object, but in that they are all collected together, by the last of their number, in the ipseity of the thing. The ipseity is, of course, never *reached*: each aspect of the thing which falls to our perception is still only an invitation to perceive beyond it, still only a momentary halt in the perceptual process.

Chapter 3. Proust and Claudel on Music and Silence

1. The little phrase appeared, dancing, pastoral, interpolated, episodic, belonging to another world.

2. Ah, do not disturb the silence, let me wait for this perfume which, I know, will come again!

3. But ever since, more than a year before, discovering to him many of the riches of his own soul, the love of music had, for a time at least, been born in him, Swann had regarded musical *motifs* as actual ideas, of another world, of another order, ideas veiled in shadow, unknown, impenetrable to the human mind, but none-the-less perfectly distinct from one another, unequal among themselves in value and significance.

4. And then suddenly, having reached a certain point from which he [Swann] was preparing to follow it, after a momentary pause, abruptly it changed direction, and in a fresh movement, more rapid, fragile, melancholy, incessant, sweet, it bore him off with it towards new vistas. Then it vanished. He hoped, with a passionate longing, that he might find it again, a third time. And reappear it did, though without speaking to him more clearly, bringing him, indeed, a pleasure less profound. But when he returned home he felt the need of it: he was like a man into whose life a woman he has seen for a moment passing by has brought the image of a new beauty which deepens his own sensibility, although he does not even know her name or whether he will ever see her again.

5. . . . Swann found in himself, in the memory of the phrase that he had heard, in certain other sonatas which he had made people play to him . . . the presence of one of those invisible realities in which he had ceased to believe and to which, as though the music had had upon the moral barrenness from which he was suffering a sort of recreative influence, he was conscious once again of the desire and almost the strength to consecrate his life.

6. Perhaps it is not-being that is the true state, and all our dream of life is inexistent; but, if so, we feel that these phrases of music, these conceptions which exist in relation to our dream, must be nothing either. We shall perish, but we have as hostages these divine captives who will follow and share our fate. And death in their company is somehow less bitter, less inglorious, perhaps even less probable.

7. The little phrase continued to be associated in Swann's mind with his love for Odette . . . [which] did not correspond to anything outside itself . . . [This thirst for an unknown delight] was awakened in him by the little phrase, but without bringing him any precise gratification to assuage it. With the result that those parts of Swann's soul in which the little phrase had obliterated all concern for material interests . . . were left vacant by it, blank pages on which he was at liberty to inscribe the name of Odette.

8. Not that the heart, too, is not bound in time, when separation is complete, to feel the analgesic effect of habit; but until then it will continue to suffer. And our

dread of a future in which we must forego the sight of faces and the sound of voices which we love and from which today we derive our dearest joy, this dread, far from being dissipated, is intensified, if to the pain of such a privation we feel that there will be added what seems to us now in anticipation more painful still: not to feel it as a pain at all—to remain indifferent; for then our old self would have changed. . . .

9. He would make Odette play it over to him again and again, ten, twenty times on end, insisting that, as she did so, she must never stop kissing him. Every kiss provokes another. Ah, in those earliest days of love how naturally the kisses spring into life!

10. . . . the idea that [Odette] was none-the-less in the room with him still, by the piano, at that very moment, ready to be kissed and enjoyed, the idea of her material existence would sweep over him [Swann] with so violent an intoxication that, with eyes starting from his head and jaws tensed as though to devour her, he would fling himself upon this Botticelli maiden and kiss and bite her cheeks. . . . And, noticing as he drove home that the moon had now changed its position relatively to his own and was almost touching the horizon, feeling that his love, too, was obedient to these immutable natural laws, he asked himself whether this period upon which he had entered would last much longer, whether presently his mind's eye would cease to behold that beloved face save as occupying a distant and diminished position, and on the verge of ceasing to shed on him the radiance of its charm.

11. How beautiful the dialogue which Swann now heard between piano and violin, at the beginning of the last passage! The suppression of human speech, so far from letting fancy reign there uncontrolled . . . had eliminated it altogether; never was spoken language so inexorably determined, never had it known questions so pertinent, such irrefutable replies. At first the piano complained alone, like a bird deserted by its mate; the violin heard and answered it, as from a neighbouring tree. It was as at the beginning of the world, as if there were as yet only the two of them on the earth, or rather in this world closed to all the rest, so fashioned by the logic of its creator that in it there should never be any but themselves: the world of this sonata. Was it a bird, was it the soul, as yet not fully formed, of the little phrase, was it a fairy—that being invisibly lamenting, whose plaint the piano heard and tenderly repeated?

12. The ineffable utterance of one solitary man, absent, perhaps dead (Swann did not know whether Vinteuil was still alive), breathed out above the rites of those hierophants, sufficed to arrest the attention of three hundred minds, and made of that platform on which a soul was thus called into being one of the noblest altars on which a supernatural ceremony could be performed.

13. For a long time I used to go to bed early. Sometimes, when I had put out my candle, my eyes would close so quickly that I had not even time to say to myself: "I am falling asleep." And half an hour later the thought that it was time to go to sleep would awaken me; I would make as if to put away the book which I imagined was still in my hands, and to blow out the light; I had gone on thinking, while I was asleep, about what I had just been reading, but these thoughts had taken a rather peculiar turn; it seemed to me that I myself was the immediate subject of my book. . . . Then it would begin to seem unintelligible, as the thoughts of a former existence must be to a reincarnated spirit; the subject of my book would separate itself from me, leaving me free to apply myself to it or not; and at the same time my sight would return and I would be astonished to find myself in a state of darkness, pleasant and restful enough for my eyes, but even more, perhaps, for my mind, to which it appeared incomprehensible, without a cause, something dark indeed.

14. The soul makes use of the same word that has been directed to it in order to respond; it is congenital to that same question that has been directed to it. It declares itself passionately to God who alone exists. . . . Under the exigency of its lover, suddenly the soul is snatched from this darkness. . . . From this darkness which is its proper element, the soul makes itself the instrument of its confession. This darkness provides it with nourishment, form, and organ.

15. In order to know Being, it is our being that we must place with him in a relation anterior to the dawn. . . . The new vision is but the unfolding of this glorious night of faith in us.

16. This sonorous touch is the foretaste and pledging of a prolonged and detailed economy which, henceforth, seems realizable to the extent that our inner disposition *does not impede the music*. There is, then, in the divine sound, deep within ourselves, at the same time an impregnation of our intelligence and the shaking of our will.

17. Ah, this evening is mine! ah, this dark night is mine! . . .

   Ah, I am drunk! ah, I am possessed by the god! I hear a voice in me and the measure accelerating, the movement of joy. . . . What do all men matter to me now! Not for them am I made, but to be
Carried away by that sacred measure! . . .
   What do some of them matter? Only that rhythm. Whether they follow me or not? What does it matter whether they understand me or not?

18. How long yet in this darkness? you do see that I am almost drowning! The darkness is my dwelling place.
   Darkness of the intelligence! darkness of sound!
   Darkness of the privation of God! Active darkness which leaps on you like a panther. . . .
   O God, how long yet? this solitary watch and the endurance of this darkness which you did not make?

19. . . . a cry in the depth of night!
I hear my ancient sister arising from the darkness, climbing once again towards me,
   The nocturnal spouse who once again comes towards me speechless,
   Once again towards me with her heart, like a meal which one shares in the darkness,
   Her heart like a suffering bread, like a vessel full of tears.

20. . . . and I am the cause between your arms, and I am Ysé, your soul! . . .
   And I hear your voice deep within me like a cry which cannot be endured. . . .
   Let there be nothing else but you and me, and in you only me, and in me only the possession of you, and rage, and compassion, and to destroy you and to be no longer impeded . . . .
   Ah, it is not happiness I bring you, but death, and mine with it.
   But what does it matter to me if I make you die,
   And myself, and everything, provided that at that price, which is you and me,
   Surrendered, thrown down, torn, lacerated, consumed,
   I feel your soul, for a moment which is all eternity, touching,
   Taking,
   Mine as lime seizes the sand, burning and hissing!

21. It is the soul that receives the soul, and everything in you becomes clear.
   There, then, at the threshold of my home, the Word is like an eternal little girl!

Open the door! and the Wisdom of God is before you like a tower of glory,
like a crowned queen! . . .

Do not touch me! do not try to take my hand.

22.   Let me be among men like a featureless person, and my
Word on them be soundless like one sowing silence, sowing darkness, sow-
ing churches,
Sowing God's measure.

23.   Because, on the one hand, all of nature is vain without me; it is I who give
it its meaning; everything in me becomes
Eternal, in the notion that I have of it; it is I who consecrate and sacrifice
it.

Water washes the body as well as the soul; my bread becomes for me the
very substance of God.

Chapter 4. Proust and Braque: Form and Reality

1. . . . I could no longer look at Mme Elstir without a feeling of pleasure, and
her body began to lose its heaviness, for I filled it with an idea, the idea that she was
an immaterial creature, a portrait by Elstir. . . . One feels strongly, when seeing
side by side ten portraits of different people painted by Elstir, that they are, first
and foremost, Elstirs.

2. Since I had seen such things depicted in water-colours by Elstir, I sought to
find again in reality, I cherished as though for their poetic beauty . . . I tried to find
beauty there where I had never imagined before that it could exist, in the most
ordinary things, in the profundities of "still life."

3. All that artificial harmony which a woman has succeeded in imposing upon
her features . . . that harmony the keen eye of the great painter instantly destroys,
substituting for it a rearrangement of the woman's features such as will satisfy a
certain pictorial ideal of femininity which he carries in his head.

4. We do not receive wisdom, we must discover it for ourselves, after a journey
through the wilderness which no one else can make for us, which no one can spare
us, for our wisdom is the point of view from which we come at last to regard the
world.

5. But the rare moments in which we see nature as she is, poetically, were those
from which Elstir's work was created. One of the metaphors that occurred most
frequently in the seascapes which surrounded him here was precisely that which,
comparing land with sea, suppressed all demarcation between them. It was this
comparison . . . which gave it that multiform and powerful unity. . . .

6. The fact that such objects can exist, beautiful quite apart from the painter's
interpretation of them, satisfies a sort of innate materialism in us, against which our
reason contends, and acts as a counterpoise to the abstractions of aesthetic theory.

7. Probably what is wanting, the first time, is not comprehension but memory.
For our memory, relatively to the complexity of the impressions which it has to face
while we are listening, is infinitesimal, as brief as the memory of a man who in his
sleep thinks of a thousand things and at once forgets them, or as that of a man in his
second childhood who cannot recall a minute afterwards what one has just said to
him.

8. Nature . . . like the metamorphosis of a nymph, has arrested us in an accustomed movement. Similarly, our intonation embodies our philosophy of life, what

a person invariably says to himself about things. No doubt these characteristics did not belong only to these girls. They were those of their parents. The individual is steeped in something more general than himself. By this reckoning, our parents furnish us not only with those habitual gestures which are the outlines of our face and voice, but also with certain mannerisms of speech, certain favourite expressions, which, almost as unconscious as our intonation, almost as profound, indicate likewise a definite point of view towards life. It is true that in the case of girls there are certain of these expressions which their parents do not hand on to them until they have reached a certain age, as a rule not before they are women. They are kept in reserve.

9. I looked at the three trees; I could see them plainly, but my mind felt that they were concealing something which it could not grasp. . . . Were they not rather to be numbered among those dream landscapes, always the same, at least for me in whom their unfamiliar aspect was but the objectivation in my sleeping mind of the effort I made while awake either to penetrate the mystery . . . or to try to put mystery back into a place which I had longed to know and which, from the day on which I had come to know it, had seemed to me to be wholly superficial, like Balbec?

10. [I] felt perfectly happy, for, with the help of all the sketches and studies that surrounded me, I foresaw the possibility of raising myself to a poetical understanding, rich in delights, of manifold forms which I had not hitherto isolated from the total spectacle of reality.

11. Was I to suppose, then, that they came from years already so remote in my life that the landscape which surrounded them had been entirely obliterated from my memory? . . . Or again, were they concealing no hidden thought, and was it simply visual fatigue that made me see double in time as one sometimes sees double in space? I could not tell. And meanwhile they were coming towards me; perhaps some fabulous apparition, a ring of witches or of Norns who would propound their oracles to me. I chose rather to believe that they were phantoms of the past, dear companions of my childhood, vanished friends who were invoking our common memories.

12. Since I had seen such things depicted in water-colours by Elstir, I sought to find again in reality, I cherished as though for their poetic beauty, the broken gestures of the knives lying across one another, the swollen convexity of a discarded napkin into which the sun introduced a patch of yellow velvet, the half-empty glass which thus showed to greater advantage the noble sweep of its curved sides and, in the heart of its translucent crystal, clear as frozen daylight . . . the displacement of solid objects, the transmutation of liquids by the effect of light and shade, the shifting colours of the plums which passed from green to blue and from blue to golden yellow in the half-plundered dish, the chairs, like a group of old ladies, that came twice daily to take their places round the white cloth spread on the table as on an altar at which were celebrated the rites of the palate, and where in the hollows of the oyster-shells a few drops of lustral water had remained as in tiny holy water stoups of stone; I tried to find beauty there where I had never imagined before that it could exist, in the most ordinary things, in the profundities of "still life."

Chapter 5. Proust and Gabriel Marcel on the Mystery

1. So Swann was not mistaken in believing that the phrase of the sonata really

did exist. Human as it was from this point of view, it yet belonged to an order of supernatural beings whom we have never seen. . . . This was what Vinteuil had done with the little phrase.

2. Therefore, we have now to ask ourselves what this urgent inner need for transcendence exactly consists of. I think we must first of all try to map it out in relation to life as it is concretely lived, and not to outline its shape in the rarefied air of pure thought.

3. Like the fires caught and fixed by a great colourist from the impermanence of the atmosphere and the sun, so that they should enter and adorn a human dwelling, they invited me, those chrysanthemums . . . to taste with a greedy rapture during that "tea-time" hour the all-too-fleeting pleasures of November, whose intimate and mysterious splendour they set ablaze all around me.

4. My desire had sought so avidly to learn the meaning of eyes which now knew and smiled at me, but which, that first day, had crossed mine like rays from another universe. . . . I would gaze at those lovely forms, dark and fair, so dissimilar in type, scattered around me on the grass, without emptying them, perhaps, of all the mediocre content with which my everyday experience had filled them, and yet (without expressly recalling their celestial origin) as if, like young Hercules or Tele-machus, I had been playing amid a band of nymphs.

5. I found Albertine in bed. . . . The sight of Albertine's bare throat, of those flushed cheeks, had so intoxicated me (that is to say had so shifted the reality of the world for me away from nature into the torrent of my sensations which I could scarcely contain), that it had destroyed the equilibrium between the immense and indestructible life which circulated in my being and the life of the universe, so puny in comparison. . . . I bent over Albertine to kiss her. Death might have struck me down in that moment and it would have seemed to me a trivial, or rather an im-possible thing, for life was not outside me but in me. . . . How could it have been possible; how could the world have lasted longer than myself, since I was not lost in its vastness, since it was the world that was enclosed in me, in me whom it fell far short of filling, in me who, feeling that there was room to store so many other treasures, flung sky and sea and cliffs contemptuously into a corner.

6. . . . a colour more precious, more moving than their own, and, whether sparkling beneath the water-lilies in the afternoon in a kaleidoscope of silent, watchful and mobile contentment, or glowing, towards evening, like some distant haven, with the roseate dreaminess of the setting sun, ceaselessly changing yet remaining always in harmony, around the less mutable colours of the flowers them-selves, with all that is most profound, most evanescent, most mysterious—all that is infinite—in the passing hour, it seemed to have made them blossom in the sky itself.

7. For my intelligence must be one—and perhaps indeed there exists but a single intelligence of which everyone is a co-tenant, an intelligence towards which each of us from out of his own separate body turns his eyes, as in a theatre where, if everyone has his own separate seat, there is on the other hand but a single stage.

8. "And see you this, my boy, there comes in all our lives a time, towards which you still have far to go, when the weary eyes can endure but one kind of light, the light which a fine evening like this prepares for us in the stillroom of darkness, when the ears can listen to no music save what the moonlight breathes through the flute of silence."

9. It was the steeple of Saint-Hilaire that shaped and crowned and consecrated every occupation, every hour of the day, every view in the town. . . . It was always to the steeple that one must return, always the steeple that dominated everything else, summoning the houses from an unexpected pinnacle, raised before me like the

Finger of God, whose body might have been concealed below among the crowd of humans without fear of my confusing it with them.

10. Sweet Sunday afternoons beneath the chestnut-tree in the garden at Combray, carefully purged by me of every commonplace incident of my personal existence, which I had replaced with a life of strange adventures and aspirations in a land watered with living streams, you still recall that life to me when I think of you, and you embody it in effect by virtue of having gradually encircled and enclosed it . . . in the crystalline succession, slowly changing and dappled with foliage, of your silent, sonorous, fragrant, limpid hours.

11. . . . Swann felt its [the little phrase] presence like that of a protective goddess, a confidante of his love, who, in order to be able to come to him through the crowd and to draw him aside to speak to him, had disguised herself in this sweeping cloak of sound. And as she passed, light, soothing, murmurous as the perfume of a flower, telling him what she had to say, every word of which he closely scanned, regretful to see them fly away so fast . . . the harmonious, fleeting form. He felt that he was no longer in exile and alone since she, who addressed herself to him, was whispering to him of Odette.

12. And then, even my own life was entirely hidden from me by a new scene. . . . The turn in which I was now playing a part was in the manner of an Oriental fairy-tale; I retained no knowledge of my past or of myself, on account of the extreme proximity of this interposed scenery. . . . Suddenly I awoke and discovered that, thanks to a long sleep, I had not heard a note of the concert.

13. The Christian idea of an indwelling of Christ in the man who is completely faithful to Him, an idea which corresponds exactly in the religious order to the position which I am trying to define on the philosophical plane, involves a categorical rejection of this purely imaginary way of picturing it.

14. Therefore, we have now to ask ourselves what this urgent inner need for transcendence exactly consists of. I think we must first of all try to map it out in relation to life as it is concretely lived, and not to outline its shape in the high voidor "pure thought"; for my method of advance does invariably consist, as the reader will have noticed already, in working my way up from life to thought and then down from thought to life again, so that I may try to throw more light upon life.

15. '. . . the appresentating being should be placed in the middle of a light that will allow something to appear to that being, to be made manifest to it. This "something" must span or traverse a domain open to our encounter.'

16. I mean that if we were to do something that cannot be done, and sweep the idea of this structure away, the idea of truth would at the same time lose its meaning.

17. It is at this point that we have to bring in the idea of the body not as an object but as a subject. It is in-so-far as I enter into some kind of relationship (though relationship is not an adequate term for what I have in mind) with the body, some kind of relationship which resists being made wholly objective to the mind, that I can properly assert that I am identical with my body; one should notice, also, that, like the term 'relationship', the term 'identity' is inadequate to our meaning here, for it is a term fully applicable only in a world of things or more precisely of mental abstractions from things, a world which our incarnate condition inevitably transcends.

18. . . . because I cannot even be certain that I may not make myself unworthy of the gift, so unworthy that I should be condemned to losing it, did not grace come to my assistance: and finally *with wonder*, because this gift brings as its companion the light, because this gift *is light*.

19. . . . That He *is* the symphony in its profound and intelligible unity; a unity in

which we can hope to be included only by degrees, through individual trials, the sum total which, though it cannot be foreseen by each of us, is inseparable from his own vocation.

20. The spirit of truth is nothing if it is not a light which is seeking for the light; intelligibility is nothing if it is not at once a coming together and the nuptial joy which is inseparable from this coming together. The more I tend to raise myself towards this Uncreated Light, without which I am left in the dark—which would mean that I have no being at all—the more I in some way advance in faith.

21. The fact is that in a general way it is almost impossible for us to think of union except in relation to what is akin to us, in which case we integrate ourselves into a whole whose elements are homogeneous. In the case of prayer such a union cannot be thought of. Here the mystery lies in that I have to merge in something which infinitely transcends me, and at first it seems impossible to conceive such a thing.

22. The effect of Incarnation is in fact to spread radiance, and it is just for that reason that today there can still be witnesses of Christ, whose evidence has a value that is not only exemplary but strictly apologetic.

23. The being I love is exposed to all the vicissitudes to which things are liable, and there is no doubt that it is in-so-far as he participates in the nature of things that he himself is subject to destruction. But here we must proceed with great caution: the whole question—and it is certainly an extremely obscure one—turns upon knowing whether this destruction can overtakethat by which this being is truly a being. Now, it is this mysterious quality which is aimed at in my love.

24. Salvation is nothing if it does not deliver us from death. . . . The truth is rather that there is not and cannot be any salvation in a world whose very structure makes it liable to death. . . . If we really look deeply into the matter, we shall be obliged to ask whether death is not in some way the price to be paid for sin, though we should not take that literally nor apply it within the framework of individual existence. . . . Each one of us is involved at all events in countless structures in which a spirit of good faith cannot fail to perceive the presence of sin.

25. We must fully realize that this being whom I love is not only a *Thou*; in the first place he is an object which comes within my view, and towards whom I can effect all the operations whose possibility is included in my condition of physical agent. He is a *that*, and it is precisely to that extent that he is a thing; insofar, on the other hand, as he is a *Thou*, he is freed from the nature of things, and nothing that I can say about things can concern him, can concern the *Thou*.

Chapter 6. Proust's Esthetics and Renaissance Art

1. The words "Florentine painting" were invaluable to Swann. They enabled him, like a title, to introduce the image of Odette into a world of dreams and fancies which, until then, she had been debarred from entering, and where she assumed a new and nobler form.

2. Sometimes, too, as Eve was created from a rib of Adam, a woman was born during my sleep. . . . Conceived from the pleasure I was on the point of consummating, she it was, I imagined, who offered me that pleasure. My body, conscious that its own warmth was permeating hers, strove to become one with her, and I would awake.

3. Perhaps it is not-being that is the true state, and all our dream of life is inexistent; but, if so, we feel that these phrases of music, these conceptions which

exist in relation to our dream, must be nothing either. We shall perish, but we have as hostages these divine captives who will follow and share our fate. And death in their company is somehow less bitter, less inglorious, perhaps even less probable.

4. But as soon as I had finished reading the letter, I thought of it, it became an object of reverie, it too became *cosa mentale*, and I loved it so much already that every few minutes I had to re-read it and kiss it. Then at last I was conscious of my happiness.

5. . . . I never ceased to believe that they corresponded to a reality independent of myself, and they made me conscious of as glorious a hope as could have been cherished by a Christian in the primitive age of faith on the eve of his entry into Paradise. . . . And for all that the motive force of my exaltation was a longing for aesthetic enjoyments, the guide-books ministered even more to it than books on aesthetics, and, more again than the guide-books, the railway time-tables.

6. In a work such as Vinteuil's sonata the beauties that one discovers soonest are also those of which one tires most quickly, and for the same reason, no doubt— namely, that they are less different from what one already knows. But when those first impressions have receded, there remains for our enjoyment some passage whose structure, too new and strange to offer anything but confusion to our mind, had made it indistinguishable and so preserved intact; and this, which we had passed every day without knowing it, which had held itself in reserve for us, which by the sheer power of its beauty had become invisible and remained unknown, this comes to us last of all. But we shall also relinquish it last. And we shall love it longer than the rest because we have taken longer to get to love it.

7. What such an ideal inspired in Elstir was indeed a cult so solemn, so ex- acting, that it never allowed him to be satisfied with what he had achieved; it was the most intimate part of himself; and so he had never been able to look at it with detachment, to extract emotion from it, until the day on which he encountered it, realised outside himself, in the body of a woman . . . who had in due course become Mme Elstir and in whom he had been able (as is possible only with something that is not oneself) to find it meritorious, moving, divine. How restful, moreover, to be able to place his lips upon that ideal Beauty which hitherto he had been obliged so laboriously to extract from within himself, and which now, mysteriously incarnate, offered itself to him in a series of communions, filled with saving grace.

8. That Albertine was scarcely more than a silhouette, all that had been super- imposed upon her being of my own invention, to such an extent when we love does the contribution that we ourselves make outweigh—even in terms of quantity alone—those that come to us from the beloved object. And this is true of loves that have been realized in actuality.

9. Since my first sight of Albertine I had thought about her endlessly, I had carried on with what I called by her name an interminable inner dialogue in which I made her question and answer, think and act, and in the infinite series of imaginary Albertines who followed one after the other in my fancy hour by hour, the real Albertine . . . appears, out of a long series of performances, in the few first alone.

10. My eyes alighted upon her skin; and my lips, at a pinch, might have believed that they had followed my eyes. But it was not only to her body that I should have liked to attain; it was also the person that lived inside it, and with which there is but one form of contact, namely to attract its attention, but one sort of penetration, to awaken an idea in it.

11. But just as it would not have sufficed that my lips should find pleasure in hers without giving pleasure to them too, so I could have wished that the idea of me which entered this being and took hold in it should bring me not merely her atten- tion but her admiration, her desire, and should compel her to keep me in her memory until the day when I should be able to meet her again.

12. But . . . in the state of exaltation in which I was, Albertine's round face, lit by an inner flame as by a night-light, stood out in such relief that, imitating the rotation of a glowing sphere, it seemed to me to be turning, like those Michelangelo figures which are being swept away in a stationary and vertiginous whirlwind.

13. And the pleasure which the music gave him [Swann], which was shortly to create in him a real need, was in fact akin at such moments to the pleasure which he would have derived from experimenting with perfumes, from entering into contact with a world for which we men were not made . . . because it eludes our understanding, to which we may attain by way of one sense only . . . hearing alone. And since he sought in the little phrase for a meaning to which his intelligence could not descend, with what a strange frenzy of intoxication did he strip bare his innermost soul of the whole armour of reason and make it pass unattended through the dark filter of sound!

14. When he [Swann] had sat for a long time gazing at the Botticelli, he would think of his own living Botticelli, who seemed even lovelier still, and as he drew towards him the photograph of Zipporah he would imagine that he was holding Odette against his heart.

15. He [Swann] no longer based his estimate of the merit of Odette's face on the doubtful quality of her cheeks and the purely fleshly softness which he supposed would greet his lips there should he ever hazard a kiss, but regarded it rather as a skein of beautiful, delicate lines which his eyes unravelled, following their curves and convolutions, relating the rhythm of the neck to the effusion of the hair and the droop of the eyelids, as though in a portrait of her in which her type was made clearly intelligible.

16. I put down the cup and examine my own mind. It alone can discover the truth. But how? What an abyss of uncertainty, whenever the mind feels overtaken by itself; when it, the seeker, is at the same time the dark region through which it must go seeking and where all its equipment will avail it nothing. Seek? More than that: create. It is face to face with something which does not yet exist, to which it alone can give reality and substance, which it alone can bring into the light of day.

17. There must have been a strong element of reality in those Virtues and Vices of Padua, since they appeared to me to be as alive as the pregnant servant-girl, while she herself seemed scarcely less allegorical than they. And, quite possibly, this lack (or seeming lack) of participation by a person's soul in the virtue of which he or she is the agent has, apart from its aesthetic meaning, a reality which, if not strictly psychological, may at least be called physiognomical.

18. And so it was not with the pleasure which otherwise I should doubtless have felt that I suddenly discerned at my feet . . . the marine goddesses for whom Elstir had lain in wait and whom he had surprised there, beneath a dark glaze as lovely as Leonardo would have painted, the marvelous Shadows, sheltering furtively, nimble and silent, ready at the first glimmer of light to slip behind the stone. . . .

19. I looked at the three trees; I could see them plainly, but my mind felt that they were concealing something which it could not grasp, as when an object is placed out of our reach, so that our fingers, stretched out at arm's-length, can only touch for a moment its outer surface, without managing to take hold of anything. . . . That pleasure, the object of which I could only dimly feel, which I must create for myself, I experienced only on rare occasions . . . and that in attaching myself to the reality of that pleasure alone could I at length begin to lead a true life. I put my hand for a moment across my eyes, so as to be able to shut them without Mme de Villeparisi's noticing. I sat there thinking of nothing, then with my thoughts collected . . . I sprang further forward in the direction of the trees, or

rather in that inner direction at the end of which I could see them inside myself. I felt again behind them the same object, known to me and yet vague, which I could not bring nearer. And yet all three of them, as the carriage moved on, I could see coming towards me. . . . In their simple and passionate gesticulation I could discern the helpless anguish of a beloved person who has lost the power of speech, and feels that he will never be able to say to us what he wishes to say and we can never guess.

Chapter 7. Bonaventure and Proust: From Image to Icon

1. Since my first sight of Albertine I had thought about her endlessly, I had carried on with what I called by her name an interminable inner dialogue in which I made her question and answer, think and act, and in the infinite series of imaginary Albertine . . . the real Albertine . . . appears . . . in the few first alone. That Albertine was scarcely more than a silhouette, all that had been superimposed upon her being of my own invention. . . .

2. But I was able to discern from these that the charm of each of them lay in a sort of metamorphosis of the objects represented, analogous to what in poetry we call metaphor, and that, if God the Father had created things by naming them, it was by taking away their names or giving them other names that Elstir created them anew.

3. Once again I fashioned such a being, utilising for the purpose the name Simonet and the memory of the harmony that had reigned between the young bodies which I had seen deployed on the beach in a sportive procession worthy of Greek art or of Giotto.

4. For just as the figure of this girl had been enlarged by the additional symbol which she carried before her, without appearing to understand its meaning, with no awareness in her facial expression of its beauty and spiritual significance . . . [the image] which is portrayed in the Arena Chapel beneath the lable "Caritas" . . . embodies that virtue, for it seems impossible that any thought of charity can ever have found expression in her vulgar and energetic face.

5. By a fine stroke of the painter's invention she [Charity] is trampling all the treasures of the earth beneath her feet, but exactly as if she were treading grapes in a wine-press to extract their juice, or rather as if she had climbed on to a heap of sacks to raise herself higher; and she is holding out her flaming heart to God, or shall we say "handing" it to him, exactly as a cook might hand up a corkscrew through the skylight of her basement kitchen to someone who has called down for it from the ground-floor window. The "Invidia," again, should have had some look of envy on her face. But in this fresco, too, the symbol occupies so large a place and is represented with such realism, the serpent hissing between the lips of Envy is so huge, and so completely fills her wide-opened mouth . . . and her attention . . . is so utterly concentrated on the activity of her lips as to leave little time to spare for envious thoughts.

6. What we take, in the presence of the beloved object, is merely a negative, which we develop later, when we are back at home, and have once again found at our disposal that inner darkroom the entrance to which is barred to us so long as we are with other people.

7. And Elstir's studio appeared to me like the laboratory of a sort of new creation of the world in which, from the chaos that is everything we see, he had ex-

tracted, by painting them on various rectangles of canvas that were placed at all angles, here a sea-wave angrily crashing its lilac foam on to the sand, there a young man in white linen leaning on the rail of a ship.

8. The effort made by Elstir to strip himself, when face to face with reality, of every intellectual notion, was all the more admirable in that this man who made himself deliberately ignorant before sitting down to paint, forgot everything that he knew in his honesty of purpose (for what one knows does not belong to oneself), had in fact an exceptionally cultivated mind.

9. By the process of memory, Swann joined the fragments together, abolished the intervals between them, cast, as in molten gold, the image of an Odette compact of kindness and tranquillity, for whom . . . he was later to make sacrifices which the other Odette would never have won from him. . . . To know a thing does not always enable us to prevent it, but at least the things we know we do hold, if not in our hands, at any rate in our minds, where we can dispose of them as we choose, and this gives us the illusion of a sort of power over them.

10. Every person is destroyed when we cease to see him; after which his next appearance is a new creation, different from that which immediately preceded it, if not from them all. . . . In confronting our memory with the new reality it is this that will mark the extent of our disappointment or surprise, will appear to us like a revised version of the reality by notifying us that we had not remembered correctly. In its turn, the facial aspect neglected the time before, and for that very reason the most striking this time, the most real, the most corrective, will become a matter for day-dreams and memories. It is a languorous and rounded profile, a gentle, dreamy expression which we shall now desire to see again. And then once more, next time, such resolution, such strength of character as there may be in the piercing eyes, the pointed nose, the tight lips, will come to correct the discrepancy between our desire and the object to which it has supposed itself to correspond.

11. But, inside, my will did not for a moment share this illusion, that will which is the persevering and unalterable servant of our successive personalities; hidden away in the shadow, despised, downtrodden, untiringly faithful, toiling incessantly, and with no thought for the variability of the self, its master, to ensure that that master may never lack what he requires.

12. And since there was always lurking in my mind the dream of a woman who would enrich me with her love, that dream in those two summers was quickened with the fresh coolness of running water; and whoever she might be, the woman whose image I called to mind, flowers, purple and red, would at once spring up on either side of her like complementary colours. This was not only because an image of which we dream remains forever stamped, is adorned and enriched, by the association of colours not its own which may happen to surround it in our mental picture; for the landscapes in the books I read were to me not merely landscapes more vividly portrayed in my imagination than any which Combray could spread before my eyes but otherwise of the same kind.

13. And Swann's thoughts were borne for the first time on a wave of pity and tenderness towards Vinteuil, towards that unknown, exalted brother who must also have suffered so greatly. What could his life have been? From the depths of what well of sorrow could he have drawn that god-like strength, that unlimited power of creation?

14. It is true that something in me was aware of this role that beliefs play: namely, my will; but its knowledge is vain if one's intelligence and one's sensibility continue in ignorance; these last are sincere when they believe that we are anxious to forsake a mistress to whom our will alone knows that we are still attached.

Chapter 8. Augustine and Proust on Time

1. [Florence and Venice] became even more real to me when my father . . . made them both emerge, no longer only from the abstraction of Space, but from that imaginary Time in which we place not one journey at a time but others simultaneously. . . .

2. The places we have known do not belong only to the world of space on which we map them for our own convenience. None of them was ever more than a thin slice, held between the contiguous impressions that composed our life at that time; the memory of a particular image is but regret for a particular moment; and houses, roads, avenues are as fugitive, alas, as the years.

3. That is why the better part of our memories exists outside us, in a blatter of rain, in the smell of an unaired room or of the first crackling brushwood fire in a cold grate: wherever, in short, we happen upon what our mind, having no use for it, had rejected, the last treasure that the past has in store, the richest, that which, when all our flow of tears seems to have dried at the source, can make us weep again. Outside us? Within us, rather, but hidden from our eyes in an oblivion more or less prolonged. It is thanks to this oblivion alone that we can from time to time recover the person that we were, place ourselves in relation to things as he was placed, suffer anew because we are no longer ourselves but he, and because he loved what now leaves us indifferent. In the broad daylight of our habitual memory the images of the past turn gradually pale and fade out of sight, nothing remains of them, we shall never recapture it.

4. And as soon as I had recognised the taste of the piece of madeleine . . . all the flowers in our garden and in M. Swann's park, and the water-lilies on the Vivonne and the good folk of the village and their little dwellings and the parish church and the whole of Combray and its surroundings, taking shape and solidity, sprang into being, town and gardens alike, from my cup of tea.

5. I put down the cup and examine my own mind. It alone can discover the truth. But how? What an abyss of uncertainty, whenever the mind feels overtaken by itself; when it, the seeker, is at the same time the dark region through which it must go seeking and where all its equipment will avail it nothing. Seek? More than that: create. It is face to face with something which does not yet exist, to which it alone can give reality and substance, which it alone can bring into the light of day.

Conclusion

1. And as art exactly reconstitutes life, around the truths to which we have attained inside ourselves there will always float an atmosphere of poetry, the soft charm of a mystery which is merely a vestige of the shadow which we had to traverse, the indication, as precise as the making of an altimeter, of the depth of a work.

Select Bibliography

General Studies

Albérès, René M. *L'aventure intellectuelle du XXe siècle: panorama des littératures européennes 1900–1959*. Paris: Albin Michel, 1959.

Alston, William P. *Philosophy of Language*. Englewood Cliffs, N.J.: Prentice-Hall, 1964.

Antoine, Gérald. *Vis-à-vis: ou le double regard critique*. Paris: Presses Universitaires de France, 1982.

Barr, Alfred H., Jr. *Cubism and Abstract Art*. New York: Museum of Modern Art, 1936.

Beardsley, Monroe. *Aesthetics from Classical Greece to the Present*. New York: Macmillan, 1966.

Benda, Julien. *La France byzantine*. Paris: Union Générale d'Editions, 1970.

Bersani, Léo. *Marcel Proust: The Fictions of Life and of Art*. New York: Oxford University Press, 1965.

Block, Haskell M. *Nouvelles tendances en littérature comparée*. Paris: Nizet, 1970.

Blunt, Anthony. *Artistic Theory in Italy, 1450–1600*. Oxford: Clarendon Press, 1940.

Bosanquet, Bernard. *Three Lectures on Aesthetic*. London: Allen and Unwin, 1934.

Bridges, Robert S. *The Testament of Beauty*. New York: Oxford University Press, 1930.

Burch, George Bosworth. *Early Medieval Philosophy*. New York: King's Crown Press, 1951.

Burgos, Jean. *Pour une poétique de l'imaginaire*. Paris: Seuil, 1982.

Cagnon, Maurice. *Ethique et esthétique dans la littérature française du XXe siècle*. Saratoga, Calif.: Anma Libri, 1978.

Chiari, Joseph. *The Aesthetics of Modernism*. London: Vision, 1970.

———. *Art and Knowledge*. New York: Gordian, 1977.

———. *Twentieth-Century French Thought: From Bergson to Levi-Strauss*. New York: Gordian, 1975.

Chipp, Herschel. *Theories of Modern Art*. Berkeley and Los Angeles: University of California Press, 1969.

Cohn, Robert G. *A Critical Work i. Modes of Art*. Saratoga, Calif.: Anma Libri, 1975.

Cole, Bruce. *Giotto and Florentine Painting, 1280–1375*. New York: Harper and Row, 1976.

Cooper, Douglas. *The Cubist Epoch*. New York: Phaidon, 1971.

Corstius, Jan Brandt. *Introduction to the Comparative Study of Literature*. New York: Random House, 1968.

Dauenhauer, Bernard P. *Silence: The Phenomenon and its Ontological Significance*. Bloomington: Indiana University Press, 1980.

De Bruyne, Edgar. *The Esthetics of the Middle Ages*. Translated by Eileen B. Hennessy. New York: Ungar, 1969.

Derrida, Jacques. *De la grammatologie*. Paris: Minuit, 1967.

———. *L'écriture et la différence*. Paris: Seuil, 1970.

Descombes, Vincent. *Modern French Philosophy*. Translated by L. Scott-Fox and J. M. Harding. New York: Cambridge University Press, 1980.

Dujardin, Edouard. *Le monologue intérieur*. Paris: Messein, 1931.

Eco, Umberto. *Art and Beauty in the Middle Ages*. Translated by Hugh Bredin. New Haven, Conn.: Yale University Press, 1986.

Ellis, John. *The Theory of Literary Criticism*. Berkeley and Los Angeles: University of California Press, 1974.

Fleming, John. *From Bonaventure to Bellini*. Princeton, N.J.: Princeton University Press, 1982.

Focillon, Henri. *La vie des formes*. Paris: Alcan, 1947.

Friedlaender, Walter. *Caravaggio Studies*. Princeton, N.J.: Princeton University Press, 1955.

Friedman, Melvin. *Stream of Consciousness: A Study in Literary Method*. New Haven, Conn.: Yale University Press, 1955.

Fry, Edward. *Cubism*. New York: McGraw-Hill, 1966.

Genette, Gérard. *Narrative Discourse: An Essay in Method*. Translated by Jane E. Lewin. Ithaca, N.Y.: Cornell University Press, 1980.

Gilson, Étienne. *The Arts of the Beautiful*. New York: Scribner, 1965.

———. *Painting and Reality*. New York: Pantheon, 1957.

———. *The Philosopher and Theology*. Translated by Cécile Gilson. New York: Random House, 1962.

———. *The Christian Philosophy of St. Augustine*. Translated by L. E. Lynch. New York: Random House, 1960.

———. *Elements of Christian Philosophy*. Garden City, N.Y.: Doubleday, 1960.

———. *The Philosophy of St. Bonaventure*. Translated by D. I. Trethowan and F. J. Sheed. Paterson, N.J.: St. Anthony Guild Press, 1965.

Gleizes, Albert, and Jean Metzinger. *Du cubisme*. Paris: Figuière, 1912.

Golding, John. *Cubism: A History and an Analysis, 1907–14*. London: Faber and Faber, 1959.

Goldwater, Robert. *Primitivism in Modern Art*. Cambridge: Harvard University Press, 1986.

Gombrich, Ernst H. *Art and Illusion*. New York: Pantheon, 1960.

Greimas, A. J. *Sémantique structurale*. Paris: Larousse, 1966.

Hatzfeld, Helmut. *Literature through Art: A New Approach to French Literature*. New York: Oxford University Press, 1952.

Hautecoeur, Louis. *Littérature et peinture en France du XVIIe au XXe siècle*. Paris: Colin, 1942.

Hersch, Jeanne. *L'Être et la forme*. Neuchâtel: Editions de la Baconnière, 1946.

Huyghe, René. *La relève de l'imaginaire*. Paris: Flammarion, 1976.

Jervolino, D. *Il Cogito e l'ermeneutica. La questione del soggetto in Ricoeur*. Naples: Generoso Procaccini Editore, 1984.

Johansen, Sven. *Le symbolisme: étude sur le style des symbolistes français*. Copenhagen: Einar Munksgaard, 1945.

Kandinsky, Wassily. *Concerning the Spiritual in Art, and Painting in Particular*. New York: Wittenborn and Schultz, 1947.

Kierkegaard, Soren. *Fear and Trembling, and The Sickness Unto Death*. Translated by W. Lowrie. Garden City, N.Y.: Doubleday, 1954.

Klemm, D. E. *The Hermeneutical Theory of Paul Ricoeur. A Constructive Analysis*. Lewisburg, Penn.: Bucknell University Press, 1983.

Kolenda, Konstantin. *Philosophy in Literature: Metaphysical Darkness and Ethical Light*. Totowa, N.J.: Barnes and Noble, 1982.

Langer, Susanne. *Feeling and Form: A Theory of Art*. New York: Scribner, 1953.

———. *Problem of Art*. New York: Scribner, 1957.

Lemaitre, Henri. *L'aventure littéraire du XXe siècle, première époque: 1890–1930. Deuxième époque: 1920–1960*. Paris: Pierre Bordas et Fils, 1984.

Louth, Andrew. *Discerning the Mystery: An Essay on the Nature of Theology*. Oxford: Oxford University Press, 1983.

Magnani, Giovanni. *Filosofia della religione*. Rome: Università Gregoriana, 1982.

Male, Émile. *Chartres*. Translated by Sarah Wilson. New York: Harper and Row, 1983.

———. *Religious Art: From the Twelfth to the Eighteenth Century*. New York: Pantheon, 1949.

———. *Art et artistes du moyen âge*. Paris: Colin, 1927.

Malraux, André. *Les voix du silence*. Paris: Gallimard, 1951.

Margolis, Joseph. *Art and Philosophy*. Atlantic Highlands, N.J.: Humanities Press, 1980.

Maritain, Jacques. *Art et scolastique*. Paris: Rouart, 1935.

———. *Creative Intuition in Art and Poetry*. New York: Pantheon, 1953.

Maurois, André. *De Proust à Camus*. Paris: Librairie Académique Perrin, 1965.

Mazzeo, Anthony J. *Renaissance and Seventeenth-Century Studies*. New York: Columbia University Press, 1964.

Mendilow, A. A. *Time and the Novel*. New York: Humanities Press, 1952.

Moir, Alfred. *The Italian Followers of Caravaggio*. Cambridge: Harvard University Press, 1967.

Ortega y Gasset, José. *The Dehumanization of Art*. Translated by Willard R. Trask. Garden City, N.Y.: Doubleday, 1956.

Ouspensky, Leonid, and Vladimir Lossky. *The Meaning of Icons*. Translated by G. E. H. Palmer and E. Kadloubousky. New York: St. Vladimir's Seminary Press, 1982.

Panofsky, Erwin. *Studies in Iconology: Humanistic Themes in the Art of the Renaissance*. New York: Harper and Row, 1967.

———. *Renaissance et Renascences in Western Art*. Stockholm: Almqvist and Wiksell, 1960.

————. *Idea: A Concept in Art Theory.* Translated by J. Peake. Columbia: University of South Carolina Press, 1968.

Pater, Walter. *The Renaissance: Studies in Art and Poetry.* Edited by D. L. Hill. Berkeley and Los Angeles: University of California Press, 1980.

Picon, Gaëtan. *Introduction à une esthétique de la littérature.* Paris: Gallimard, 1953.

Poulet, Georges. *Études sur le temps humain.* Paris: Plon, 1953.

————. *Mesure de l'instant.* Paris: Plon, 1968.

Reagan, C. E. *Studies in the Philosophy of Paul Ricoeur.* Edited by C. E. Reagan. Athens: Ohio University Press, 1979.

Rewald, John. *The History of Impressionism.* New York: Museum of Modern Art, 1961.

Ricoeur, Paul. *History and Truth.* Translated by C. Kelbley. Evanston, Ill.: Northwestern University Press, 1965.

————. *La metaphore vive.* Paris: Seuil, 1975.

————. *Time and Narrative.* 2 vols. Translated by Kathleen McLaughlin and David Pellauer. Chicago: University of Chicago Press, 1984–86.

————. *The Conflict of Interpretations: Essays in Hermeneutics.* Edited by D. Ihde. Evanston, Ill.: Northwestern University Press, 1974.

Rivière, Jacques. *Études.* 9éd. Paris: Gallimard, 1925.

Rorty, Richard. *Philosophy and the Mirror of Nature.* Princeton, N.J.: Princeton University Press, 1979.

Rosenblum, Robert. *Cubism and Twentieth-Century Art.* New York: Abrams, 1976.

Rousset, Jean. *Forme et signification.* Paris: Corti, 1962.

Sartre, Jean-Paul. *Les mots.* Paris: Gallimard, 1964.

————. *L'imaginaire: psychologie phénoménologique de l'imagination.* Paris: Gallimard, 1948.

Smart, Alastair. *The Assisi Problem and the Art of Giotto.* Oxford: Oxford University Press, 1971.

Sokolowski, Robert. *Presence and Absence: A Philosophical Investigation of Language and Being.* Bloomington: Indiana University Press, 1978.

Spiegelberg, Herbert. *The Phenomenological Movement.* 2 vols. The Hague: Nijhoff, 1960.

Stokes, Adrian. *Colour and Form.* London: Faber and Faber, 1950.

Stubblebine, James H. *Giotto: The Arena Chapel Frescoes.* Edited by J. H. Stubblebine. New York: Norton and Co., 1969.

Terdiman, Richard. *The Dialectics of Isolation.* New Haven, Conn.: Yale University Press, 1976.

Theau, Jean. *La philosophie française dans la première moitié du XXe siècle.* Ottawa: Editions de l'Université d'Ottawa, 1977.

Todorov, Tzvetan. *Littérature et signification.* Paris: Larousse, 1967.

Trilling, Lionel. *The Opposing Self: Nine Essays in Criticism.* New York: Viking Press, 1955.

Ullmann, Stephen. *The Image in the Modern French Novel.* Cambridge: Cambridge University Press, 1960.

Venturi, Lionello. *History of Art Criticism.* Translated by C. Marriott. New York: E. P. Dutton, 1936.

Vigée, Claude. *Revolte et louanges: essais sur la poésie moderne.* Paris: Librairie José Corti, 1962.

Wellek, René. *Concepts of Criticism.* New Haven, Conn.: Yale University Press, 1963.

Wind, Edgar. *Pagan Mysteries in the Renaissance.* London: Faber and Faber, 1958.

Wölfflin, Heinrich. *Principles of Art History.* New York: Dover, 1950.

Zaehner, R. C. *Mysticism, Sacred and Profane.* Oxford: Clarendon Press, 1957.

Augustine Studies

Balthasar, Hans Urs von. *The Glory of the Lord.* Edited by J. Riches. Translated by A. Louth, F. McDonagh, and B. McNeil. San Francisco: St. Ignatius Press, 1984, p. 95.

Bertram, Martin A. "Augustine on Time, with Reference to Kant." *The Journal of Value Inquiry* 20 (1986): 223–34.

Bochet, Isabelle. *Saint Augustin et le désir de Dieu.* Paris: Études Augustiniennes, 1982.

Bourke, Vernon J. *Wisdom from St. Augustine.* Houston, Tex.: University of St. Thomas, 1984.

Caranfa, Angelo. "Augustine and Proust on Time." *History of European Ideas* 7 (1986): 161–74.

Cullmann, Oscar. *Christ and Time.* Translated by F. Filson. Philadelphia: Westminster Press, 1964.

Gilson, Étienne. *The Christian Philosophy of Saint Augustine.* Translated by L. E. Lynch. New York: Random House, 1960.

Gross, Charlotte. "Twelfth-Century Concepts of Time: Three Reinterpretations of Augustine's Doctrine of Creation *Simul.*" *Journal of the History of Philosophy* 23 (July 1985): 325–38.

Guitton, J. *Le temps et l'éternité chez Plotin et saint Augustine.* Paris: Vrin, 1959.

Jordan, Robert. "Time and Contingency in St. Augustine." *The Review of Metaphysics* 8 (1954–55): 394–417.

Markus, R. A. "Augustine, St." *The Encyclopedia of Philosophy.* Edited by P. Edwards. New York: Macmillan, 1967, vol. 1, p. 204.

Mundle, C. W. K. "Time, Consciousness of." *The Encyclopedia of Philosophy.* Vol. 8, p. 136.

Pelikan, Jaroslav. *The Mystery of Continuity.* Charlottesville, Va.: University Press of Virginia, 1986.

Smart, J. J. C. "Time." *The Encyclopedia of Philosophy.* Vol. 8, p. 126.

Teske, Roland J. "The World-Soul and Time in St. Augustine." *Augustinian Studies* 14 (1983): 75–92.

Bonaventure Studies

Balthasar, Hans Urs von. *The Glory of the Lord*. Edited by J. Riches. Translated by A. Louth, F. McDonagh and B. McNeil. San Francisco: St. Ignatius Press, 1984, p. 260.

Bettoni, Efrem. *Saint Bonaventure*. Translated by A. Gambatese. Westport, Conn.: Greenwood Press, 1981.

Bowman, Leonard J. "A View of St. Bonaventure's Symbolic Theology." *Proceedings of the American Catholic Philosophical Association* 48 (1974): 25–32.

Cousins, Ewert. "Franciscan Meditation: The Mind's Journey into God." *Journal of Dharma* 38 (April 1977): 137–51.

Dreyer, Elizabeth. "Affectus in St. Bonaventure's Theology." *Franciscan Studies* 42 (1982): 5–20.

Gilson, Étienne. *The Philosophy of St. Bonaventure*. Translated by D. I. Trethowan and F. J. Sheed. Paterson, N.J.: St. Anthony Guild Press, 1965.

Mathias, Thomas R. "Bonaventurian Ways to God through Reason." *Franciscan Studies* 36 (1976): 192–232; 37 (1977): 153–206.

Musurillo, Herbert. "Bonaventure's *The Soul's Journey to God*." *Thought* 46 (Spring 1971): 105–18.

Ost, David E. "Bonaventure: The Aesthetic Synthesis." *Franciscan Studies* 36 (1976): 233–47.

Quinn, John F. *The Historical Constitution of St. Bonaventure's Philosophy*. Toronto: Pontifical Institute of Mediaeval Studies, 1973.

Reynolds, Philip L. "Threefold Existence and Illumination in Saint Bonaventure." *Franciscan Studies* 42 (1982): 190–215.

Shahan, Robert W., and F. J. Kovach, ed. *Bonaventure and Aquinas: Enduring Philosophers*. Norman, Okla.: University of Oklahoma Press, 1976.

Spargo, Emma J. M. *The Category of the Aesthetic in the Philosophy of Saint Bonaventure*. New York: The Franciscan Institute of St. Bonaventure, 1953.

Braque Studies

Apollonio, U., and A. Martin. *Georges Braque*. Paris: Hachette, 1966.

Brion, Marcel. *Georges Braque*. New York: Abrams, 1976.

Brunet, Christian. *Braque et l'espace: langage et peinture*. Paris: Klincksieck, 1971.

Cafritz, Robert. *Georges Braque*. Washington, D.C.: The Phillips Collection, 1982.

Cassou, Jean. *Braque*. Paris: Flammarion, 1956.

Chipp, Herschel. *Georges Braque: The Late Paintings, 1940–1963*. Washington, D.C.: The Phillips Collection, 1982.

Cogniat, Raymond. *Georges Braque*. New York: Abrams, 1976.

Cooper, Douglas. *Braque: Paintings, 1909–1947*. London: Lindsay Drummond, 1948.

———. *Braque: The Great Years*. Chicago: The Art Institute of Chicago, 1972.

Damase, Jacques. *Georges Braque*. London: Blandford, 1963.

Elgar, Frank. *Braque, 1906–1920*. Paris: Hazan, 1958.

Fumet, Stanislas. *Braque*. Paris: Maeght, 1965.

Gieure, Maurice. *Georges Braque*. Paris: Tisné, 1956.

Grenier, Jean. *Braque: peintures, 1909–1948*. Paris: Editions du Chêne, 1948.

Heron, Patrick. *Braque*. London: Faber and Faber, 1958.

Leymarie, Jean. *Braque*. Translated by J. Emmons. Geneva: Skira, 1961.

Mullins, Edwin B. *Braque*. London: Thames and Hudson, 1968.

Russell, John. *Georges Braque*. London: Phaidon, 1959.

Vallier, Dora. *Braque, la peinture et nous*. Basel: Phoebus, 1962.

Valsecchi, M., and M. Carra. *L'opera completa di Braque, 1908–1929; dalla composizione cubista al recupero dell'oggetto*. Milan: Rizzoli, 1971.

Vinca, L. *Georges Braque*. Florence: Sansoni, 1969.

Claudel Studies

Caranfa, Angelo. *Claudel: Beauty and Grace*. Lewisberg, Penn.: Bucknell University Press. 1989.

Lioure, Michel. *L'esthétique de Paul Claudel*. Paris: Colin, 1971.

Plourde, Michel. *Paul Claudel: une musique du silence*. Montreal: Presses de l'Université de Montréal, 1970.

Tonquédec, Joseph de. *L'oeuvre de Paul Claudel*. 3éd. Paris: G. Beauchesne, 1927.

Gabriel Marcel Studies

Belay, Marcel. *La mort dans le théâtre de Gabriel Marcel*. Paris: Vrin, 1980.

Facco, Maria L. *Metafisica e diaristica in Gabriel Marcel*. Genoa: Università di Genova, 1983.

Gallagher, Kenneth T. *The Philosophy of Gabriel Marcel*. New York: Fordham University Press, 1975.

Gillman, Neil. *Gabriel Marcel on Religious Knowledge*. Washington, D.C.: University Press of America, 1980.

Gozzoli, Mauro. *L'uomo in cammino verso . . . L'attesa e la speranza in Gabriel Marcel*. Rome: Abete, 1979.

Ngimbi, Nseka. *Tragique et intersubjectivité dans la philosophie de Gabriel Marcel*. Mayidi: Grand Séminaire de Mayidi, 1981.

Merleau-Ponty Studies

Heidsieck, François. *L'ontologie de Merleau-Ponty*. Paris: Presses Universitaires de France, 1971.

Hyppolite, Jean. *Sens et existence dans la philosophie de Maurice Merleau-Ponty*. Oxford: Clarendon Press, 1963.

Langan, Thomas. *Merleau-Ponty's Critique of Reason*. New Haven, Conn.: Yale University Press, 1966.

Mallin, Samuel B. *Merleau-Ponty's Philosophy*. New Haven, Conn.: Yale University Press, 1979.

Merleau-Ponty, M. *The Visible and the Invisible*. Edited by Claude Lefort. Translated by A. Lingis. Evanston, Ill.: Northwestern University Press, 1968.

———. *Phénoménologie de la perception*. Paris: Gallimard, 1945.

———. *Signs*. Translated by Richard C. McCleary. Evanston, Ill.: Northwestern University Press, 1964.

———. *The Prose of the World*. Edited by Claude Lefort. Translated by J. O'Neill. Evanston, Ill.: Northwestern University Press, 1973.

Proust Studies

Albaret, Céleste. *Monsieur Proust*. Edited by G. Belmont. Paris: Robert Laffont, 1973.

Autret, Jean. *L'influence de Ruskin sur la vie, les idées et l'oeuvre de Marcel Proust*. Geneva: Droz, 1955.

Bardèche, Maurice. *Marcel Proust, romancier*. 2 vols. Paris: Sept Couleurs, 1971.

Beckett, Samuel. *Proust*. New York: Grove Press, 1957.

Bedriomo, Émile. *Proust, Wagner et la coïncidence des arts*. Paris: Editions Jean-Michel Place, 1984.

Bell, William Stewart. *Proust's Nocturnal Muse*. New York: Columbia University Press, 1962.

Benedetti, Carla. *La soggettività nel racconto. Proust e Svevo*. Napels: Liguori Editori, 1984.

Benoist-Mechin, Jacques. *La musique et l'immortalité dans l'oeuvre de Marcel Proust*. Paris: S. Kra, ca. 1926.

Bersani, Jacques, ed. *Les critiques de notre temps et Proust*. Paris: Garnier, 1971.

Bonnet, Henri. *Le progrès spirituel dans l'oeuvre de Marcel Proust*. 2 vols. Paris: Vrin, 1946–49.

———. *Marcel Proust de 1907 à 1914*. Paris: Nizet, 1971.

Brée, Germaine. *Du temps perdu au temps retrouvé: introduction à l'oeuvre de Marcel Proust*. Paris: Les Belles Lettres, 1950.

———. *The World of Marcel Proust*. London: Chatto and Windus, 1967.

Bucknall, Barbara J. *The Religion of Art in Proust*. Urbana: University of Illinois Press, 1969.

Buisine, Alain. *Proust et ses lettres*. Lille: Presses Universitaires de Lille, 1983.

Butor, Michel. *Les oeuvres d'art imaginaires chez Proust*. London: Athlone Press, 1964.

Cattaui, Georges. *Proust et ses métamorphoses*. Paris: Nizet, 1972.

Chantal, René de. *Marcel Proust, critique littéraire*. 2 vols. Montreal: Presses de l'Université de Montréal, 1967.

Chernowitz, Maurice Eugene. *Proust and Painting*. New York: International University Press, 1945.

Cocking, John M. *Proust: Collected Essays on the Writer and His Art*. Cambridge: Cambridge University Press, 1982.

———. "Proust and Painting." In *French 19th Century Painting and Literature*. Edited by Ulrich Finke. New York: Harper & Row, 1972, p. 305.

Daniel, Georges. *Temps et mystification dans "A la recherche du temps perdu."* Paris: Nizet, 1963.

Deleuze, Gilles. *Marcel Proust et les signes*. Paris: Presses Universitaires de France, 1964.

Ellison, David R. *The Reading of Proust*. Baltimore, Md.: Johns Hopkins University Press, 1984.

Fiser, Émeric. *L'esthétique de Marcel Proust*. Paris: Redier, 1933.

Girard, René. *Proust: A Collection of Critical Essays*. Edited by R. Girard. Englewood Cliffs, N.J.: Prentice-Hall, 1962.

Graham, Victor E. *The Imagery of Proust*. Oxford: Basil Blackwell, 1966.

Grandsaigne, Jean de. *L'espace Combraysien: monde de l'enfance et structure sociale dans l'oeuvre de Proust*. Paris: Minard, 1981.

Green, Frederick Charles. *The Mind of Proust: A Detailed Interpretation of "A la recherche du temps perdu."* Cambridge: Cambridge University Press, 1949.

Henry, Anne. *Marcel Proust: théories pour une esthétique*. Paris: Klincksieck, 1981.

Hewitt, James R. *Marcel Proust*. New York: Ungar, 1975.

Hier, Florence. *La musique dans l'oeuvre de Marcel Proust*. New York: Columbia University Press, 1933.

Hindus, Milton. *The Proustian Vision*. New York: Columbia University Press, 1954.

———. *A Reader's Guide to Marcel Proust*. London: Thames and Hudson, 1962.

Jaloux, Edmont. *Avec Marcel Proust*. Paris: La Palatine, 1953.

Kadi, Simone. *La peinture chez Proust et Baudelaire*. Paris: La Pensée Universalle, 1973.

Kneller, John William. "The Musical Structure of Proust's 'Un Amour de Swann.'" *Yale French Studies* 2, no. 2 (1949): 55–62.

Kolb, Philip. "Proust et Ruskin: nouvelles perspectives." *Cahiers de l'Association Internationale des Études Françaises* 12 (June 1960): 259–73.

Martin-Deslias, Nöel. *Idéalisme de Marcel Proust*. Paris: Nagel, 1952.

Mauriac, Claude. *Proust par lui-même*. Paris: Seuil, 1957.

Mauriac, François. *Du côté de chez Proust*. Paris: Table Rond, 1947.

Maurois, André. *A la recherche de Marcel Proust*. Paris: Hachette, 1949.

———. *Le côté de Chelsea*. Paris: Gallimard, 1932.

Megay, Joyce N. *Bergson et Proust*. Paris: Vrin, 1976.

Mein, Margaret. *A Foretaste of Proust: A Study of Proust and His Precursors.* New York: Atheneum, 1974.

Milly, Jean. *La phrase de Proust.* Paris: Larousse, 1975.

Monnin-Hornung, Juliette. *Proust et la peinture.* Geneva: Droz, 1951.

Moss, Howard. *The Magic Lantern of Marcel Proust.* London: Faber and Faber, 1963.

Mouton, Jean. *Proust.* Bruges: Desclée De Brouwer, 1968.

Muller, Marcel. *Préfiguration et structure romanesque dans "A la recherche du temps perdu."* Lexington, Ky.: French Forum, 1979.

Nattiez, Jean-Jacques. *Proust musicien.* Paris: Christian Bourgois, 1984.

Painter, George Duncan. *Marcel Proust: A Biography.* 2 vols. London: Chatto and Windus, 1959–65.

Pierre-Quint, Léon. *Marcel Proust, sa vie, son oeuvre.* Paris: Sagittaire, 1925.

Piroué, Georges. *La musique dans la vie, l'oeuvre et l'esthétique de Proust.* Paris: Denoël, 1960.

Pluchart-Simon, Bernard. *Proust: l'amour comme vérité humaine et romanesque.* Paris: Larousse, 1975.

Richard, Jean-Pierre. *Proust et le monde sensible.* Paris: Seuil, 1974.

Sansom, William. *Proust and His World.* New York: Scribner, 1973.

Shattuck, Roger. *Proust.* London: Fontana, 1974.

————. *Proust's Binoculars: A Study of Memory, Time and Recognition in "A la recherche du temps perdu."* New York: Random House, 1963.

Stambolian, George. *Marcel Proust and the Creative Encounter.* Chicago: University of Chicago Press, 1972.

Strauss, Walter A. *Proust and Literature.* Cambridge: Harvard University Press, 1957.

Trahard, Pierre. *L'art de Marcel Proust.* Paris: Dervy, 1953.

Vial, André. *Proust: structures d'une conscience et naissance d'une esthétique.* Paris: Julliard, 1963.

Index